CARD *Talk*

Winning Communication Games

Revised Printing

William Donohue

Michigan State University

Kendall Hunt
publishing company

To Denise for all her love and support!

Kendall Hunt
publishing company

www.kendallhunt.com
Send all inquiries to:
4050 Westmark Drive
Dubuque, IA 52004-1840

Table of Contents

Making effective decisions is a function of collecting information, using it
to create a thorough understanding of the problem, developing options to
address the problems, then selecting and implementing the best options.
Success in activating this process in a group hinges on your ability to play the
right talk cards at the right time.

Leadership is all about creating cards capable of providing vision and direction
to groups and organizations. Topics and styles on these cards must expand to
meet the challenges.

Change is difficult for most people in most organizations. Following the
diffusion process by playing the right card, using the right media at the right
time is the key to successful change.

Focusing on how the media educate people, this chapter addresses the media
card. How do the media structure their cards to indirectly and directly
educate their audiences?

Entertainment is designed to stimulate emotions to help people escape. Thus,
topics and styles of entertainment messages must be structured to get the
audience excited and panting for more.

The art of public speaking is about connecting with people to make sure that
your ideas are understood clearly and persuasively.

Introduction

Texas Hold-em

Maybe you've seen it on TV—Texas Hold-em. This is high-stakes poker card game consisting of two cards being dealt face down to each player and then five community cards being placed by the dealer – a series of three ("the flop") then two additional single cards ("the turn" and "the river"), with players having the option to check, bet, or fold after each deal (i.e. betting may occur prior to the flop, "on the flop," "on the turn," and "on the river").

Four people sit facing one another under low-hanging shaded light concentrating on each other's every move. One bearded, middle-aged man wears a cowboy hat pulled low over his eyes. He studies the two cards in his hand very intensely and scowls. Is it a bad hand or an act designed to manipulate the others' perceptions of his hand?

Across from him sits a 20-something man—baseball cap on backward. He takes one look at his hand, makes no expression, and carefully lays down his cards. Is he portraying confidence, youthful cockiness or just being cautious? To his right is a sharply-dressed woman who casually looks over her cards, then begins intently studying each of the other players for clues about how this game will play out.

Opposite her sits a very trim, older gentleman, well polished and professional looking. He rearranges his two cards and signals to the dealer that he is ready to play—he wants the flop. Suddenly, the dealer complies by turning over three cards. Each player looks at the other. It's the cowboy's turn to bet. He lays down $20,000 in chips to open the betting—he's in.

Poker is all about the betting and what the betting communicates. If you eagerly throw in a large amount of money, you are signaling to the others that either you have a good hand or you're bluffing. Then it's baseball boy's turn to bet. He must decide if the cowboy is bluffing or has good cards. After he bets, then the foxy lady must bet. She has to interpret the other bets in relation to her cards. When the sharp gentleman bets, he must look at the whole table and all the players' habits and approaches to place his wager.

And this is just the first round of betting on the flop. This process is repeated with the turn card and the river card until a winner is declared. It's a very stressful game because it's about more than just the cards; it's about studying one another and paying close attention to the verbal and nonverbal communication.

Communication Hold-em

Talk Cards. Communication is like a card game that resembles Texas Hold-em. Instead of card games with playing cards we play Talk Games with Talk Cards. To understand this analogy, let's focus first on Talk Cards. Whenever we craft a message by talking, writing, calling, or texting someone, we frame that message from the role we're playing in relation to the other person. I might be talking to a student as a professor or sometimes as a friend. I can talk to my wife as her husband or her business partner since we are in business together. When I craft a message playing the husband role, I am in essence playing my Husband Card. I select a certain topic from that card to discuss depending on what I want to accomplish, then I add a style or tone to the message that helps get my point across. I play many roles in my life and each one demands a different card. I have a Friend Card, a Professor Card, a Colleague Card, and so on.

Talk Games. Now, what are Talk Card Games? A Talk Game is a message exchange between people associated with a specific goal. For example, if I want to calm down my wife after a rough day I might start asking her questions about her day to help her debrief the troublesome events. She then responds with thoughts about her day. The goal of this exchange becomes the name of the Talk Card Game we want to play. I call this particular game the Chill Game. When she reciprocates and plays her Wife Card and debriefs her day and calms down, we are playing a Talk Card Game. As we move through our day we play many games with all kinds of people. The key is playing them well and winning these games.

Winning Talk Games. In playing Texas Hold-em, the goal is to win the game by taking the pot of money. Only one can win while the others all lose. Most talk games, like the Chill Game, are different. Most Talk Games are cooperative events in which both people want to win by achieving their goals. I want to calm down my wife after a tough day and she wants to be calmed down as well. If the exchange is successful, we both win the game together. Of course there are games in which people try to gain an advantage over one another as in poker card games. These games are typical in negotiated business dealings or in interpersonal conflict. One might win and accomplish her goals while the other loses. But, in general, most Talk Games are cooperative events in which both are trying to help one another win by accomplishing their goals.

To review briefly, a Talk Card is the package of messages that are communicated in playing a specific role. To play any role competently the communicator needs to have a strong list of messages ready to go that others believe effectively reflects that role. So, in essence, I can't be a good husband unless I can "talk" like a good husband. A Talk Game reflects the goal the messages are designed to accomplish. Winning means both parties accomplishing their goals.

The Strategic Advantage

The complexity of playing Talk Games becomes apparent when people are playing different games than they think they are playing. A guy might be playing the game of "Casual Conversation" with a Facebook friend, but she might think that he's playing the game of "Stalking a Girl." In fact, sometimes when people send a Facebook message they have to label their game and indicate clearly that they are not stalking. For instance, I recently saw in an example from urbandictionary.com in which a guy sent the following message to a female friend to label his intent: "No stalk, but I noticed you changed your quotes on your profile."

The point is that if we view the process of communication as a Card Game, we can **think more strategically** about our moves, and whether we are making the right moves to be effective. I conduct research on physician-patient communication. When doctors communicate with patients they play their Doctor Card. The game they play is Diagnosis and Treatment. Playing the game well involves learning as much as possible from their patients about their health issues and then teaching them about proper health care while also maybe persuading them to change their habits. When playing their Patient Card, the patients try to be understood and possibly learn to address their health issues. They might also try to deceive the doctor into prescribing some desired medication. The strategy for the doctor is getting the right information to craft the right diagnosis to prescribe the right treatment plan for the patient. If the game is not played well, the patient's life is at risk.

This scenario captures the goal of this book. I want to encourage you to think about communication more strategically. What Talk Cards do you have, what games can you play successfully? How can you more easily connect with others to win those games? We will move through some very critical communication contexts to understand how games are played in those contexts. Winning most of your communication games, whether in public speaking or just chatting with a friend, is the goal of this book and the course.

The Organization of This Book

The cards we use to play games are generally divided into two decks—Personal and Professional. The Personal Deck typically consists of cards we develop first within our families and friends and we use them most often when we communicate. They are usually our default cards. The second deck of cards we play relates more to our professional duties. Of course, these cards overlap a great deal and we create card hands that mix cards from these two decks all the time. But it helps strategically to think about these two decks and how to play our cards to be most effective.

The first eight chapters of this book focus on a variety of topics that are most relevant in developing your Personal Deck of cards. We begin in Chapter 1 talking about how card games work and move through to the issue of interpersonal conflict in Chapter 8. Then the book moves to discussing skills you will need in developing your Professional Deck of cards. Chapter 9 focuses on networks and organizations through to Chapter 15, which deals with giving professional presentations. In other words being an effective communicator means improving your ability to interact with others both personally and professionally.

To better understand how important it is to develop both card decks, consider this example. A student who has worked with the same group of friends for a couple years and suddenly gets promoted to be their immediate supervisor faces a real challenge. For years she developed and played her Friend Card with these folks to reinforce their friendship. But now she's their boss. When meeting with those friends as their supervisor, does she play her Friend Card and talk to them like she has for many years? Her job requires her to create a Supervisor Card so she can discuss work topics with these individuals that are necessary for getting things done. After all, she can't be a supervisor unless she learns to talk like a supervisor.

She must learn to build a new deck of Professional Cards, one of which is called the Supervisor Card and learn how and when to play it depending on the Talk Game being played at any given moment. She will also need other Professional Cards in that deck when she starts to step out into various professional situations such as conferences and meetings. Learning to be a professional means learning to talk like a professional.

In fact, the main challenge for achieving personal and professional success is developing a full deck of Talk Cards for each role and learning how to use them to play Talk Games. Whether the games are personal associated with being a good friend, sister, or wife, or whether they are professional and involve learning to talk like an employee or boss, research results are clear: Success and card choice are synonymous. If you don't have the card, you can't play the role.

The goal of this book is help people overcome these challenges. Everyone needs to think about and evaluate their Talk Card deck, create more and better cards to adapt effectively to different situations, and learn how to play talk games successfully. Using the "Card" metaphor is important because it provides a much simpler path toward communication growth than simply listing skills and hoping people improve.

We will begin by focusing on gender games and how characteristics of language influence the way those games are played. Then we will move from interpersonal through group and organizational communication issues to mass media contexts and finally to giving speeches.

Chapter 1
Talk Cards and Talk Games

Introduction

In the introduction, I described the three important components of the Card Talk idea.

- **A Talk Card** is the package of messages that are communicated in playing a specific role. To play any role competently the communicator needs to have a strong list of messages ready to go that others believe effectively reflects that role. So in essence, I can't be a good husband unless I can "talk" like a good husband.

- **A Talk Game** reflects the goal the messages are designed to accomplish. Winning means both parties accomplishing their goals.

- **A Card Deck** is the set of cards that we have available to play a card game at any given moment. We have both a Personal Deck and a Professional Deck of cards and we must develop both decks well to succeed as communicators.

To understand better about how and why we play card games, let's turn first to some examples of card games that show how they work in practice.

The Scheduling Game. Imagine the student supervisor who is new on the job and has not really developed a Supervisor Card yet. One of her first duties is to create a work schedule of student employees and enforce that schedule to make sure all hours are covered. She must talk with each student and figure out when each can work. Imagine that one of her employees, who happens to be a really good friend comes in to get some special time off to attend a wedding. This person makes the request using her Friend Card. Yet the supervisor cannot

relent. She must play her Supervisor Card and refuse the request. This is a tough lesson in learning to be a supervisor: She will be making some unpopular decisions and possibly losing friends along the way.

The Parenting Plan Game. I conduct a lot of research in the area of divorce mediation. In this context a neutral third party sits down with divorcing parents and tries to help them create a parenting plan for their children after the divorce is final. This facilitator must have an effective Mediator Card to deal with the parties who will alternatively play their Husband and Wife Cards and their Mom and Dad Cards. Typically, the mediator's goal is to encourage parties to play their Mom and Dad Cards so they can focus on the task of building a parenting plan. If they play their Husband and Wife Cards repeatedly, they move away from playing a Parenting Plan Game and more toward a Marital Argument Game, which the mediator would like to avoid.

The Patient Care Plan Game. A third game of interest that I referenced briefly in the Introduction focuses on how physicians play their Doctor Cards to create an effective treatment plan for their patients. The challenge is that doctors must play the game so that patients open up and provide accurate information about their feelings, their history with the health issue, their family, and even their job pressures. All of this information is vital if the physician is able to win the game by creating a plan that will help the patient get better.

Let's use these three games to illustrate some key principles about Talk Cards, Talk Games and Card Decks. We will begin by diving more deeply into the concept of Talk Cards.

Talk Cards

We know from the Introduction that a **Talk Card is the package of messages that are communicated in playing a specific role**. To perform any personal or professional role well the communicator needs to have a strong list of messages ready to go that others believe effectively reflects that role. The message "package" consists of two elements: **content** and **style**. The **content** part is the idea or topic you want the other communicator to understand or to do: Go here, play there, I want this, I care about that. The **style** part deals with how friendly, how formal, and how powerful you want to appear in presenting that topic or idea. Style gives emphasis and fills in meaning about the topic. They work together in the message package.

Card Style. We mix and match three elements in formulating our style. The first is **liking**. We include words, gestures, eye movements, and other facial expressions to show how much we like or dislike someone. Showing extreme liking might involve smiling, getting physically close to someone, or even touching. Showing extreme dislike might start with a scowl and an angry tone. When divorcing parties in mediation play the Marital Argument Game they often show this extreme dislike for one another that the mediator must redirect to keep the focus on the Parenting Plan Game.

The second style element is **formality**. A really formal message is one that includes big words, proper grammar, and long sentences. Of course, a more informal style might include shorter words, slang, sentence fragments, and perhaps an exaggerated accent. People are often very informal when they want to show a lot of liking. When they are angry, sometimes they are also very informal and use profanity, for example. But, they might also use very formal language it is typical of someone being scolded.

The third style form is **power**. Messages always include information about the speaker's status or power in the relationship. Big-power messages might include threats or other reminders of someone's role to indicate their ability and willingness to enforce their will. When the divorcing male plays his Husband Card he might try to intimidate his ex-wife by yelling or using threatening language as a means of increasing his power to impose a solution on the parenting plan.

One way of exercising power that some people use is shoving a card in another person's face. That means really playing that role in a forceful manner. For example, the student supervisor might need to do that if the student she's talking to refuses to play her Employee Card and continues to play his Friend Card to get time off to attend the wedding. The supervisor might have to say, "Look, here's the hours you're going to work because you have the lowest seniority. I don't have any choice!"

An analysis of the supervisor's message reveals low liking, low formality, and high power. This is a typical profile for a message of this kind. She could have said, "I appreciate your concern but I must insist on scheduling you at this time." This message shows medium liking, high formality, and medium power. It certainly contains a different style than the previous "Look" message.

Relational Messages. As it turns out, our topic and style selections send very specific relational messages. Maybe it's the relationship we have in place and maybe it's the relationship we want to have in place. The full Supervisor Card references an employer-employee relationship. The Friend Card reinforces the relationship between the two primarily as friends and not co-workers.

Establishing the employer-employee relationship by using the Supervisor Card is a big challenge. When her friend asked for time off to attend her cousin's wedding the supervisor was probably caught off guard. She thought her friend/employee was coming in to play the Casual Conversation Game and suddenly she changed it to the Scheduling Game and asked for time off. Now the new supervisor has to access her Supervisor Card and talk about the policy that says no special time off is allowed. Pulling out that topic has relational consequences. As indicated above, the supervisor has to discuss the topic with the relational goal of not alienating her friend. That's difficult to do. As she becomes more skilled at her job and develops her Supervisor Card, she will be much more comfortable playing the Scheduling Game and other Business Meeting Games.

This raises the point about the size of our cards. A card is large if we have command of many topics and many different styles in displaying those topics. Once the supervisor learns to develop her Supervisor card she will know how to shift back and forth easily between her Friend Card and her Supervisor Card when talking with her employee-friends with whom she has worked with for some time. In fact, learning a job means developing the cards associated with those jobs.

Personal and Professional Decks. As the supervisor example illustrates, card decks are generally divided into two categories—Personal and Professional. The Personal Cards are typically the ones we develop first within our families and friends and we use them most often when we communicate. In contrast Professional Cards focus on job-related duties.

You can probably empathize with the student supervisor who has to learn the hard way how to develop her Supervisor Card. Not only must she explain policies to people, she has to learn how to train new employees, talk to customers, resolve customer complaints, and deal with her boss, the owner of the establishment. These are all topics she is expected to be able to discuss and she must make the right style choices with each one to be effective. For example, when a customer comes in and plays the Customer Complaint Game with her, she has to know how to a) present herself as a competent problem solver, b) send positive relational messages to avoid alienating the customer, and c) creatively solve the problem to keep the customer happy.

Physicians have these same challenges. When talking with a patient the physician must often switch between Personal and Professional Cards. The physician might play a Friend Card with a patient she has known a long time by sharing personal information about her family. That kind of conversation sets a relaxed, friendly tone to the interaction so when the physician switches to the Doctor Card, she can more easily interview her friend about her health concerns.

Card Play Is Reciprocal

This Physician-Patient Card Game illustrates an important point about card play. When someone plays a card, he or she is **asking the other person to play a card** that typically matches or goes along with the card the person is playing. In other words, **card play is always reciprocal**. For example, when playing the Doctor Card, the physician is asking the patient to play a Patient Card and carefully listen to the physician's instructions. Typically when playing their Patient Cards, people might get nervous and not listen well or feel comfortable asking questions. That's when the physician is wise to switch to a Friend Card which then asks the patient to also switch to a Friend Card and start opening up more as a friend. When people talk casually they reveal a lot of important information to the physician that might impact a good treatment plan.

When the student supervisor's friend came in to ask for time off, she was playing her Friend Card, which essentially asked the supervisor to play her Friend Card in return. But, the supervisor had to play her Supervisor Card in response to do her job and deny the friend's request. The denial could certainly be friendly, and the supervisor could show a little of her Friend Card. But, she had to reject her friend's request to only play her Friend Card and give her the time off.

The key point is this: don't just think about the card you should play. Think also about the card you are asking the other person to play. Is it the right card for you to accomplish your goals?

Talk Game Goals

Types of Goals. What drives us to play talk games? Every time we form a message to communicate we work to accomplish three goals. The first goal is related to our **identity,** or how we define ourselves. These are called **self-presentation goals.** Each person wants to be perceived in a particular way to be accepted and respected by the other person and/or his or her group. Or the person might want to show that he or she is not a part of that group. But, whenever we exchange information in whatever medium, we have self-presentation goals. We will talk more about these self-presentation goals in Chapter 3 which focuses on self-concept and identity needs.

The second kind of goal we pursue is **relational.** Each person inserts information in their messages designed to pull the other closer or push the other further away. Pulling closer is accomplished by using a friendlier, informal style of communication. We work to establish relationships that enable us to accomplish our primary message goals. The first judgment people generally make toward an individual is how "friendly" the person looks or acts.

The third aim of every message is the goal that most communicators focus on most directly—our **achievement** goals. This goal relates to the task that we want our messages to accomplish—some job that must be accomplished. I want to give you some information, persuade you to change your mind, or entertain you with a story. The achievement goal is generally the label we use to describe the purpose of a message. For example, someone might want to tell you about their new job, or persuade you to get a cup of coffee with that person. These are achievement goals and they are often the main motivator for communicating with one another.

However, messages can be motivated primarily by self-presentation or relational purposes. For example, for the newly-appointed supervisor whose employee/ friend comes in asking for time off probably wants to play her Friend Card to her newly-designated supervisor. She wants to present herself as a competent employee (presentation goal), reestablish her friendship (relational goal), and get release time for the wedding (achievement goal). These goals work together for the employee. By playing her Friend Card she emphasizes the relationship, which should afford special privileges. She also shows that she's a good employee by asking for time off rather than just calling in sick.

What's really interesting about this request is how it illustrates the way these three motivations combine to play a communication game. To achieve her goal of getting time off, the employee/friend will want to emphasize the Friend Card while playing the Employee Card, again to get special consideration. Using the Friend Card, she accesses a topic from the card that she and her new boss have probably talked about when they were friends. Pulling a familiar topic from the Friend Card indicates that she wants to play the Casual Conversation Game first to set up the request. So, she might say, "Hey, did you hear my cousin is getting married? I think you guys met. She's really cool." After a few exchanges, the employee/friend might begin to show her Employee Card and say, "By the way, I would really like to go to her wedding so I need some time off."

Winning Card Games. How should the new student supervisor handle the request to "win" the game? Recall that winning means that each person accomplishes his or her goals in the conversation. The supervisor can only win if she is successful in accomplishing her **achievement goal** (getting the employee to work), **relational goal** (keeping the friendship), and **presentation goal** (being a competent employee). On the other hand, her friend probably has the same relational and presentation goals but a different achievement goal (get time off). The best the supervisor can hope for in this exchange is to accomplish her own achievement and presentation goals, but she might sacrifice her relational goal of keeping the friendship. She'll have to play her Supervisor Card in such a way to minimize that, if possible.

These games are difficult to play so that all players achieve their goals. In this context, "winning" a card game means that both parties play the cards in their hands to accomplish their self-presentation, relational, and achievement goals. We "lose" a game if, after the cards are played, one or both parties fails to achieve their goals. For example, the supervisor would lose if she has to say no to her friend in a way that really angers her. She can only win by playing the Supervisor Card carefully while playing some of her Friend Card as well by gently saying no and explaining the policy in a friendly way.

As this example illustrates, Talk Card Games start by one person showing a specific card, the other person seeing the card, and then either reciprocating or not reciprocating with the same card. As this process evolves people get a sense of what they're doing—they define the activity. This activity then becomes "the game." This example also illustrates that games can change quickly. What started as a Casual Conversation Game quickly turned into a Scheduling Meeting Game. And, just as in conventional card games, leading with the wrong card can end in disaster. It was unfortunate that the friend/employee played her Friend Card to try to use her friendship to get a favor from her new boss. Leading with that card may have cost her a friendship just to get a day off.

In many circumstances, misreading cards, and by extension misreading proposed games can have severe consequences. In the Parenting Plan Game, the mediator's goal is to read the couple's cards and figure out if they are playing the Husband and Wife Cards or their Mom and Dad Cards. Then, when they are showing the right cards, are they playing a game that will result in winning the game, which is creating a parenting plan for the children? A key skill in effective communication is reading the other's cards. That awareness is essential in then playing a game that will result in achieving the goals and winning the game.

Card Development

Style Switching. As you recall the underlying motivation to create cards is to satisfy our self-presentation, relationship, and achievement goals. Striving to accomplish these goals when faced with very diverse communication settings creates a need to be able to switch quickly from one style to another and thus develop bigger cards. My senior roommate in college was an African -American guy who was very adept at switching styles (friendliness, formality, and power). When Ron played his Friend Card with me he had learned to speak using a typical Standard English accent. However, when his African -American friends entered the room, Ron immediately adopted their more urban accent when playing his Friend Card with them. That accent is important in establishing friendliness, informality, and equal power. It honors the culture and establishes a connection.

We talked about this switching extensively. He felt that is was very important to switch styles to show solidarity and respect for his African-American friends. He felt that his ability to hang out with them hinged on using that style in their presence. Similarly, he felt that using the more Standard English style was important when hanging out with his White friends.

Actually, we all learn to make subtle shifts in their style to satisfy their needs. High school students will often use the word "like" every fourth or fifth word in communicating with one another. Including this word shows solidarity with friends. When these students speak to older folks they often avoid this word to play more of an Adult Card. Women will play their Female Card by introducing subjects and styles that appeal to their female friends when exchanging social topics. Men display similar quirks in their speech to appeal to their buddies when they play their Man Cards.

Card Origins. As people mature and spend more time outside their families, they learn to expand their cards because they have to fit into more groups. Their identity becomes more complex as they age. Kids go to school and must create both Friend and Student Cards. As friend and family groups expand, they put more cards into their deck as a way of fitting in. By the time we mature into adults, we require a fairly elaborate set of cards to be effective in relating to our increasingly diverse world.

The Ron story illustrates where cards originate. We know what cards we have from two sources. First, we play cards and see how people react to us. If they respond to the cards we play and we achieve our goals, then we know we can hold and play those cards. If they don't respond well, then we probably realize that we don't have or can't play those cards well. I am constantly reminded that I don't have a Youth Card when I can't participate in conversations about new bands, video games, or current fashions. I don't care much about those issues so my cards are small or even non-existent. This is especially difficult for people trying to go back to school and learn a new craft after being laid off. They have to learn to communicate in a whole new fashion for that new career. Many people get comfortable playing the same cards over and over again and never find new ones to play.

Second, we learn about our cards when people reflect on our personalities. They might comment on the style with which we play our cards, for example. "That Sara is a really sensitive," means that she prefers to play her Friend Card frequently by taking time to listen to people she really cares about. Or, "That Bill is a good dad," means that, to that person, Bill's Dad Card really impresses the casual observer.

Card Deck. Your card deck consists of all the cards you have available for any and all communication situations. It's very broad. An easy way to think about your deck is to look in your closet. What sets of clothes do you have for which situations? If you're typical you have various outfits for different situations. You have dressup clothes for formal occasions, business clothes for your job, casual clothes for going to class or hanging out. You can think of these clothes as part of your Card Talk Deck. For example, when you put on your business clothes for your job and you also play your Job Talk Card at work. When you help customers or talk to the boss in your work clothes you present the whole business package to these people. You might even have jewelry or other accessories to complete your deck.

Research generally supports the idea of having as many cards in our deck as possible to manage the broad range of communication challenges we face in life. By virtue of my diverse life experiences, I have been in many situations and learned to build a big deck. And I work with people who are pleased to tell me about my cards and how they're working. So I have many opportunities to learn about my cards.

Imagine what the doctor's card deck must look like. Personally she will need to create a Mom, Wife, Friend, and Daughter Cards. Professionally she will need to create Doctor, Colleague, and Employee Cards in working at the hospital. If you also have a diverse set of life experiences and jump in and out of different situations, then you probably hold many different personal and professional cards. And, you often switch very quickly between these cards as you switch between different card games. One minute the game is Casual Conversation and then next minute it's a Family Chores Game discussing who does what around the house.

Card Tricks. What about card tricks? A card trick involves playing a card or initiating a Card Talk game with the specific intention of hiding true self-presentation, relational, or achievement goals. People do this all the time when they want to fake interest or attention. For self-presentation purposes, I might want to play a card I am asked to play, and I go along, but I really don't want to play that card. These are innocent little diversions that are common in conversation.

This was the challenge that the student supervisor faced when her friend asked for time off. Her friend came in and immediately played her Friend Card and initiated a Casual Conversation Game. Then, she switched immediately and played the Scheduling Game. The switch was a bit of a trick because the Casual Conversation Game was simply a cover for the real achievement goal of getting time off. When both parties show the same or compatible cards over several exchanges and both parties believe they are playing the same game, they have achieved **synchrony**.

When it becomes clear that they are not playing the same game, it is called **dissynchrony**. In extreme circumstances individuals can trick others into believing they are playing one game when in reality they are playing something else. If the mediator allows either divorcing party to play a Husband or Wife Card while the other is trying to play a Mom or Dad Card then dissynchrony might emerge. The party changing the card works to change the game to accomplish different goals other than creating a parenting plan. The mediator must constantly watch for this trap and redirect it when necessary.

Winning for both the mediator and the parents depends largely on achieving synchrony by: a) reading one's own and the others' cards correctly, b) determining if parties are playing the same game, and c) knowing how to expand the rules of the game to widen synchrony opportunities. While we have covered "a" and "b," we have not focused on game rules and how they work. Let's take a look at rules and how to play with them.

Talk Game Rules

What are Game Rules? Each talk game is organized by a set of rules required to play it properly. Of course, the rules that apply to the game depend on how communicators define the game. Once that tacit understanding has occurred, then we recall the rules necessary to complete that activity successfully. But when parties have different definitions of the game, either intentionally or unintentionally, then there are two or more sets of rules. The question is, what are game rules and how do they work?

Card Talk rules regulate the topics and styles that are acceptable in playing the game. If the game has a formal definition, like the Patient Care Plan Game, then the rules are clearer, but also more constraining. When doctors interview patients the purpose of the talk is to understand the issues and create a patient care plan to improve the health status of the patient. In a rigid situation like this, a relatively few number of topics are acceptable to discuss while others are out-of-bounds. It would be appropriate to talk about medically relevant issues but inappropriate to talk about the relative success of various sports teams.

Styles are also constrained in Card Talk. In casual conversation, use of bad grammar or mildly profane language signals a very informal situation. But in a job interview, if a candidate uses this style combination, it suggests that the candidate does not know how to communicate properly in formal situations. The interviewer might even say, "We don't use that kind of language here."

Bending the Rules. Rules are constraining because the person might be prevented from using a style that is more effective in that situation. For example, the doctor might notice that the patient seems overly nervous playing the Patient Care Plan Game. The doctor might decide to break out of the formal interview mode just to put the patient more at ease. So the doctor might play a Friend Card and talk about family issues with the patient.

People bend game rules all the time. Mediators are constantly on guard for parents that try to bend the rules during a mediation session to try and gain an advantage. One of the important rules that mediators try to enforce is the "no interruption" rule. That is a power style move aimed at establishing dominance in conversation. To avoid that show of dominance mediators like to establish the rule that when one person is talking, that person is allowed to complete his or her thought. But instead of overtly interrupting, the husband might make a noise or roll his eyes or doing some other disruptive act that isn't "technically" interrupting. Since many divorced people are not cooperative, the mediator is constantly watching for these rule violations.

Modeling the Card Talk Elements

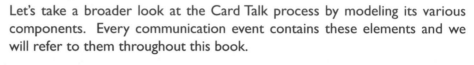

Let's take a broader look at the Card Talk process by modeling its various components. Every communication event contains these elements and we will refer to them throughout this book.

Sources and Receivers. Every communication event includes at least one source and one receiver. The process of communication is different than simply sending information to unknown receivers. That process is simply information dissemination. The process of communication is a higher bar. It means that a source wants to impact a receiver in some way—changing attitudes, beliefs, values, or behaviors in some way. When the source has impacted the receiver even minimally, then we can say that communication has occurred. A source who has a self-presentation goal of looking "cool" and walks into a room with a "hot" outfit and gets the desired reaction of people staring, is communicating. The source had a goal, the clothes and outfit was the message, and receivers were impacted.

Messages. Every communication event involves a message. It might be verbal, written or nonverbal in nature. Using the language for this book, the message shows the talk card that the person is playing, and probably the game, as well. This means that messages are complex. What is the person trying to say, what card or cards are they playing, what game is happening, and what are their goals? Many factors impact these conclusions and we'll talk about those in the model as well. But it's important to note that the receiver's first job is to figure out what the source is communicating and then what it means, and then what should be done (if anything) about it. The source's main job is to send messages, or play cards and games that are most likely to impact the receiver in the intended way. The wrong messages at the wrong times, as we have seen, will not connect with receivers or are taken the wrong way.

The Channels. The channel is the method you use to communicate whether it's face-to-face, electronic, postal mail, or others. If you were a television star, you could say "hi" to your mom using television. Channels are either broad, or narrow. Broad channels carry a lot of information, whereas narrow channels carry much less information. A channel is broad if it involves most of your five senses and narrow if it involves only one sense. Most people control their channels strategically depending on what card they want to play. If the card requires maximum impact, then a face-to-face channel might be best. If self-presentation or relational issues are not critical, then a text might be fine. The key is matching the message with the channel. If you try to send a message through a channel the other person does not use, or if you select a channel that inappropriately fits the message, your communication will most likely fail.

Noise. Noise consists of anything that distracts from, or competes with the intended messages. For example, a patient might have a nervous twitch or be looking around the room while the doctor is trying to conduct an interview. Anything that distracts from playing the intended game is noise. You can think of noise as a ratio—the **Signal-to-Noise ratio.** The Signal is the message sent to accomplish intended self-presentation, relational or achievement goals. It is the numerator or top part of the ratio. Noise is the denominator or bottom part of the ratio. The goal in communicating a message is to have a very strong signal and minimal noise. Playing a card that sends a clear message with little interference is likely to get through much better than a confusing message or a weak message that cannot be heard above the clutter.

Culture. Every message given from every card contains information about the sender's cultural orientations. As we shall see in a later chapter, culture is represented by an individual's values and behaviors. As individuals play their cards, they might use a specific accent or wear a particular outfit to satisfy self-presentation goals that will be viewed positively by their peers. The cards that people select and the style with which they choose to play the cards always reflect their cultural orientations. People want to be categorized into some group to receive acceptance by that group and they will display their cultural orientations accordingly. If I want to be viewed as a member of the hip-hop culture, what cards would I need to have in my deck, what styles would I use to discuss certain topics, what would I have to wear, and what accent would I need to use to present myself as a member of that culture? Gender membership asks the same questions. To be seen as male or female, what cards should I hold, how should I play them and in which settings? We will talk more about culture and gender later in the book.

Contexts. Every time you play a card, you adjust to the context. You read the situation and figure out what game people are playing, what card you've been asked to play, and what the rules are for playing that card to accomplish your goals. What are the elements you analyze? You look at the relationship between yourself and the other party to determine what kind of style to use in covering the topic you play on your card. You scan for the amount of noise in the situation and adjust your card playing accordingly. If there's too much noise, you keep your play shorter—or wait for a different situation. It is important to note that while you are playing cards you are also creating the context as you go. Any given game builds momentum and the rules for playing become clearer as the context becomes clearer.

Impacts. We have talked extensively about the impact of playing cards. The most visible impact of playing a card is reciprocation. Did the other person play the same card you played? Did this exchange satisfy your self-presentation, relational and achievement goals? We tend to look first for evidence of these intended impacts. However, we should also scan the environment for unintended impacts. For example, I might play a card to accomplish the self-presentation goal of being viewed as an authority on a subject. But the audience might not respond as intended. I had a colleague who was perceived by many female students as very attractive. Even though he played his Professor Card during lecture, it was obvious that some of the female students were not responding to that card. The point here is that, controlling communication means having a CLEAR idea about what goals you want to accomplish with your communication. Many people fail because they do not really know what impact they want their communications to achieve.

Lessons Learned

Here are some key lessons from this chapter that should help you both understand Talk Card Games and play them more effectively:

- **Understand what cards you have in your deck.** A talk card is the package of messages that are communicated in playing a specific role. To play any role competently the communicator needs to have a strong list of messages ready to go that others believe effectively reflects that role. It is also important to have the right cards in a deck to be able to switch games quickly and effectively.

- **Understand the cards you are asking the other person to play.** Remember, whenever you play a card, you are also asking the other person to play a card as well. Is the card you are asking the other play going to help win your Talk Card Games?

- **Understand the game you are playing at all times.** By looking at the other's card and how he/she is playing it, you can guess the game the other is playing. If it's a game you like you can continue to play. But people pull card tricks and switch games. It is difficult to win if you don't understand the game.

- **Understand the rules for playing that game.** Once the game becomes clear, a set of rules is established for how to play the game properly. When you play the games long enough you understand the rules and then how to bend them to give you a better chance of winning.

- **Try to win the game for both parties.** Ideally, communication is played as a cooperative event. The more you can approach communication with that goal the more you can select cards and play games that will help everyone accomplish their goals. Sometimes that's not always possible, but we should work hard to do so.

- **Try to minimize noise in the communication process.** Concentrate on organizing the communication process so there is very little noise or interference in getting the message across. The signal strength should be strong and noise minimized.

It is difficult to be a winner consistently if you don't have good cards and don't know the rules for playing the game. This book will walk you through a number of situations that present difficult challenges to most people in their daily lives. Hopefully, you will walk away from this course playing with a full communications deck and winning more games.

Chapter 2
Language Card Games

Introduction

Have you ever met someone who was expected to be able to display a specific ethnic style because of his or her skin color or appearance, yet could not use that style? I have talked with many students facing this challenge. They want to connect with other students who look like them physically, but the students won't readily accept them because they sound different—the accent, slang, and other elements of style just are not available. Some students report that it takes a long time to become accepted by others who do not share an ethnolinguistic heritage.

Language, in its broadest sense, is the tool we use to build our Talk Cards. The question is how does language work? Let's begin answering this question by talking about three interesting card games that illustrate key functions of language.

The Ethnic Proof Game. President Obama gives many speeches every day. For the most part he uses standard English for his speeches without much linguistic variation that would hint at any particular kind of ethnicity. Yet he is America's first African American president. So, which ethnic card is he playing when he speaks? Is it a Euro-American Card, an African American Card, or some other card? In a story that ran in a South Carolina newspaper, *The State*, during the 2008 presidential election, the Reverend Jesse Jackson sharply criticized Barak Obama for "acting like he's white." In a follow-up *Washington Post* (February 16, 2007) columnist Marjorie Valbrun expressed concern that others had accused Mr. Obama of not being "black enough." She argued that this accusation is very narrow-minded. While the Rev. Jackson later apologized for his remarks, it suggests that some folks are expected to show proof of their ethnicity by showing an Ethnic Card.

The Small Talk Game. Later in this chapter we will have some fun about gender differences in communication. In fact, we have a gender quiz to see if you understand gender biases in communication. One of the most difficult communication tasks for men is to engage in the Small Talk Game. This game consists of simple topics about the events of the day with no particular goal in mind; it's all about sharing. Men don't play this game well because they are biased to believe that messages are reserved for accomplishing some specific goal like solving a problem or contributing an idea. When women share small talk men often check out and don't pay attention. In fact, many women will ask, "Are you listening to me?"

The Factory Talk Game. I remember meeting my roommates in college for the first time. Since I worked at a car factory that summer before coming to school I learned to swear a lot. About every third or fourth word was the "F" word. It might be characteristic of how men talk to each other. I am sure women use this word a great deal as well. In the factory we would even split up words and put the "F" word in the middle. On my first day in college I had just come from the factory floor the night before so I was still in factory talk mode. After using that same intense language during my first encounter with my roommates, one of them quickly remarked, "You sure swear a lot!" I had played my Factory Friend Card, a standard part of which included the "F" word because swearing in the factory was how you acknowledged friends. So, I backed off from that point on and formulated a Roommate Card that did not include those words.

The Characteristics of Language

Each of these situations involves some element of being misunderstood. I am sure you've encountered this frustrating problem. You thought you said something, but the other person responded to the card you played in a manner you did not anticipate. Sometimes this happens when you try to be funny. Maybe you played a Friend Card by telling a new friend a joke that you told to one of your old friends in a different situation. But, the new friend didn't understand or appreciate the joke as you had intended.

One of the main reasons this kind of misunderstanding occurs is that we mistakenly assume that language holds some objective meaning. It's not objective at all. Rather, the meaning we derive from language is personal and subjective, or more precisely, negotiated between communicators. In essence we continuously "build" the meaning and significance of any given card exchange. Understanding this idea that the meaning of cards is co-created derives from what we know about the characteristics of language. This understanding is easier when you come to realize that language is symbolic, abstract, arbitrary, and conventional.

Language Is Symbolic. Language is a system of symbols that we string together to create some kind of picture in one another's heads. A symbol stands for something else like an object, person, idea, or place. We can think of symbols as maps. Maps provide a visual representation of some territory to help us find out way. Words function in the same way. For example, when the Rev. Jackson characterized President Obama as "acting like he's white," he was trying to provide people with a map to navigate or understand his perceptions about then-candidate Obama. In every message each word has a meaning, but when all the words are strung together in a sequence they creating a symbolic map to help the other navigate the speaker's thoughts about the topic.

Do your words always help the other navigate your thoughts as precisely as you intend? Most everyone has had the experience of raising a topic that ends up triggering an unintended emotional reaction. Afterward we wonder if we should have created a different map to the ideas bouncing around in our head. Humanity has gone to great lengths to build all kinds of symbolic maps from cave drawings to biblical scrolls to the Declaration of Independence. Each of their creators intended to create a map that presented some important ideas.

Language Is Abstract. As a symbol system, language uses letters and words to represent ideas in our heads or things in the physical world, like baseball, hotdogs, apple pie and Chevrolet. These **referents** work to name the ideas or thoughts we have about the external world. They're what we use to build our maps for people when we play our cards. Referents essentially tag our psychological or emotional thoughts and feelings when we infuse our topics with various style elements. To communicate my interest in fitting in at the summer factory job, I would go over to the guys and say in a casual way, "How the F is everybody?" Each of these style elements chosen to communicate liking from the tone of voice to the inclusion of the "F" word is a referent. It puts a behavioral tag on the speaker's emotions as the message seeks to build a map to help the listener explore the speaker's psychological world.

Language is **abstract** because it refers to things we can't see or point to. Abstractness is a very useful characteristic of language. What would happen if we couldn't refer to "love," for example? Of course, when you play the Love Game with your Boyfriend or Girlfriend Card, you need to express your love in many abstract ways. The abstractness of language allows you to express these concepts even though they have no referent you can touch, not in the way I can touch a computer, the machine on which I am currently typing.

Another valuable reason language is abstract is that symbols can refer to any number of specific referents in a whole class of items. For example, the symbol B-O-O-K can refer both to the novel I just purchased and to any novel of any size, in any location. This aspect of abstraction is often the source of many misunderstandings. When a woman is playing her Girlfriend Card and playing the Small Talk Game with her boyfriend, men often interpret that game as something other than it is. They might hear it as a Need Advice Game and interrupt the small talk just to "solve" her problems. Sometimes the woman will say, "I'm just talking—no need to respond." But, there might need to be some talk about clarifying the game because for the man it might be too abstract.

Language Is Arbitrary. Because language is symbolic, it is necessarily arbitrary, but that makes it really flexible. The symbols that we conventionally assign to objects, people or ideas are just given to us by tradition without any objective rule for its assignment. My coffee cup could have easily been called C-H-A-I-R rather than C-U-P. The French word for cup is T-A-S-S-E. Which is correct? All symbols are "correct" if everyone agrees that the symbols represent the objects. After all, the symbols are chosen arbitrarily to represent their respective objects, feelings, ideas, etc.

This flexibility is valuable because people are free to name things or emotions as they wish and make up new labels if they don't like the old ones. If the new label catches on, that's great and it becomes a better term than the old one. A tweet used to refer to a bird's sound, but now it also refers to a Twitter post. Of course, the down side of this flexibility is that there is no necessary connection between a symbol and its referent and thus no "objective" way of making sure that symbols mean one thing only. Some people have tried to develop a universal language with objective meaning. But all attempts have failed. By using the term "white" in his characterization of then candidate Obama, Reverend Jackson was using a term that could mean anything to anyone. It was an abstract term to refer to some very nebulous cultural concept. The key point, once again, is to insure that when communicating an idea that the listener understands it in the way it was intended to be understood. Feedback is the check for that.

Language Is Conventional. Remember that symbol referents are given to us because of the history of language. It is just through convention that certain symbols refer to certain things or ideas. A convention or norm is a pattern of behavior which we implicitly agree to follow. In the case of language, we "agree" to call a referent by a given name. For example, let's refer to the act of talking for 10 minutes in front of a group of students in a class as S-P-E-A-K-I-N-G. We certainly could call it D-O-I-N-K-I-N-G, but we don't. These conventions can change dramatically over time. As one example the word "gay" used to refer to a lively, happy, exciting event. Now it refers most commonly to sexual orientation.

The problem with convention is that when non-American immigrants acquire a second language, they typically learn only the formal English conventions back home. They don't learn slang, or **idiomatic communication,** until they spend some time with native speakers. Slang is the unique language that friends, groups, or even societies create which has meanings unique to those groups. It's just fun to make up new words for old ideas or objects. We used slang all the time in the factory and made up words constantly. We used to call anyone who was not a native English speaker as a "honyak." I am not sure what that referred to but it was a made up word. Of course, when you play a card using slang it is important to know that the other person is likely to understand the referent for the unique symbols attached to the slang. Otherwise, misunderstandings are again likely to occur.

The takeaway from this discussion is since language is symbolic, it is necessarily abstract, arbitrary and conventional. That makes it fun to play with, but also frustrating to deal with. Choose your language wisely when you play your cards. Pick terms and styles that make sense to the person or people you're playing with.

Elements of Language

These characteristics of language provide the overall framework for creating our Talk Cards. Now let's descend from these abstract, tall trees for a moment and get closer to the ground. Let's explore the specific elements of language that form the building blocks of the messages we assemble on our cards.

Phonetics. One of the first elements of our language that becomes apparent to others when we play a Talk Card is phonetics or the sounds we produce when speaking. The English language consists of 26 letters, but about 44 sounds. For example, five of the six vowels can be either short or long. The letter "a" can be pronounced as a short sound as in the word "cat," or in its long sound as in the word "cane." Standard and non-standard English uses different sounds and they are important to use in proving one's ethnic identity, for example.

Semantics. A second key element of language that impacts how we play our cards is semantics and refers to the **meaning** of a specific sound or word. This is a very important issue for how topics and styles are combined to form a message when a card is played because it relates to the issue of understanding. In fact, there is a field called **General Semantics** that is devoted to repairing or preventing misunderstandings by discovering how words distort or complicate meanings.

The key in crafting a message from any card is making sure that the meaning of each word has the intended impact on the receiver. Will that person interpret the words you use in the way you want them to be interpreted? The first step in building confidence that you will be heard as intended is learning as much as possible about the receiver's message filters. What are filters that impact meaning? Upon hearing or reading messages receivers evaluate them from their subjective positions. They apply their **attitudes** (like or dislike the message), **values** (this is a good or bad message), **beliefs** (this is a true or false message), and **knowledge levels** (here's what I know about this message) to the job of understanding. More knowledge about receivers means you can tailor a message that is more likely to be interpreted accurately by them.

Think for a moment how difficult this is for some men to understand women. Much has been written about this topic and we'll explore it a bit more later in the chapter. But understanding each other's message filters is difficult particularly when someone is from another cultural orientation.

Complicating this already difficult task is that meaning is broken down into very small units. The smallest semantic unit of language is called a **morpheme**. Morphemes are units of meaning that can either stand alone or are attached to words to increase their meaning. For example, prefixes and suffixes change the meaning of a word. The word "call" can be changed by adding -ed. The word "called" now means that the calling occurred in the past. The prefix dis- changes the meaning of a word by negating it. "Dissatisfied" means that satisfaction did not occur. How many morphemes are in the word "unbeatable?" The first is "un-" a bound morpheme (bound to the meaning of the word beat), "beat," which is a free, stand-alone morpheme, and "able," which is a bound morpheme and a suffix. So, there are three.

Such subtle features of language as morphemes are typically taken for granted. We use them all the time when we play with verb tense or even when we make a nonverbal gesture when saying a word. If I wink at my friend while making an insulting comment about his outfit, maybe I want to tell him that I am joking or teasing him about the outfit. The wink is a morpheme but adds a great deal to the semantic meaning of the comment and transforms it from an insult to a joke.

Syntax. A third element of language is syntax or how we assemble morphemes into strings that most often form sentences. Syntax is the process of chunking language into meaningful clumps. We use punctuation for that chunking job. For example, what if you saw a sign outside of an exposed swimming pool that read: "**Private. No swimming allowed.**" This sign is chunked into two sentences—a declarative sentence indicating that the pool is private and a directive sentence telling people not to swim in the pool.

Now, let's alter the syntax by simply changing the punctuation. What if you saw this sign outside the pool: "**Private? No. Swimming allowed!**" The syntax has been changed to produce three sentences—a question, an answer, and a declaration. Now the sign is transformed from a warning to an invitation simply by changing the syntax through the punctuation.

Pragmatics. The final element of language is pragmatics, which focuses on the work we want the messages to perform. We often think about pragmatics in terms of achievement goals. In writing this book I want to play my Professor Card to inform you about some key communication ideas. If you play your Student Card and dutifully absorb this riveting information, then the message is viewed pragmatically as a lecture. In other words, it's the label we apply to the message that defines its pragmatic quality.

Standard and Non-standard Card Talk

One the first judgments people make when listening to a card being played is whether or not it is standard or non-standard English. Is the speaker presenting standard or non-standard phonetic, phonemic, syntactic, and pragmatic elements of language when playing a card? The Ethnic Proof Game is a good example of how these judgments can impact perceptions of others. In his admonition that candidate Obama was "not black enough," was the Rev. Jackson really saying that Obama did not use enough non-standard speech to validate his black ethnicity? Standard English, like the kind of language you might hear in a news report on TV is crisply enunciated, does not include slang, and is delivered in carefully modulated tones. Standard English is so labeled because it is the social gauge for achieving "perfect" language use. Non-standard English typically involves other dialects of English. For example, in the United States, we can distinguish southern English, east coast English, midwestern English,

Latino English, and Ebonics. These dialects are language systems in their own right, but are governed by syntactic, semantic, and phonemic rules that differ in identifiable ways from standard English.

It is important not to confuse standard vs. non-standard English with clear communication. In many communities speaking standard English would be very confusing and would hinder understanding. And, vice-versa is also the case—Non-standard English can also introduce a great deal of noise into the system. The important point is the extent to which the language facilitates connection and understanding, not the form the language takes.

Yet, as we know from the Ethnic Proof Game, people attribute a great deal of significance to the language forms that people use. For many groups labeling one kind of language as the standard of perfection sets up an inevitable comparison. The implication here is that those who speak the non-standard version of a language may be labeled as non-standard people. This is precisely what happens in social interaction. Research shows that people feel greater trust for others who speak similarly to themselves. Therefore, it is a natural and perhaps unconscious response, to mistrust or even dislike those who speak differently.

The goal of playing a non-standard card to others who use the same dialect is self-presentation. The dialect is a key element in demonstrating membership in that language community. The problem emerges when people across these language communities. When language is different it can result in negative judgments or racism, sexism, and class distinctions in our culture. On the other hand, playing a card displaying non-standard language adds to the cultural diversity of any given communication experience.

Theories of Language

Scholars of language have developed several useful theories to explain how we decide what language to use in playing cards. For example, a theory called: **Coordinated Management of Meaning** describes how communicators interpret messages when we play various cards. The theory says that:

1. Over time, as people exchange messages, they develop norms about what talk is acceptable or unacceptable when a card is played.

2. These norms evolve into Card Talk rules about what messages mean (constitutive rules), and which Card Talk topics and styles are acceptable (regulative rules).

3. People use these rules to coordinate their talk or synchronize their interaction.

Does this theory sound familiar? It describes the process laid out in the last chapter about how card games develop rules. The smart card player understands the rules and then works to negotiate them to present topics and styles that are needed in any given situation to win the talk game. The student supervisor example is relevant here. That student needed to negotiate with the employee about what cards needed to be played to deal with the special time off request. The supervisor needed to play her Supervisor Card while also acknowledging the Friend Card. Negotiating these rules to regulate the conversation and turn it from a Casual Conversation Game into a Job Talk Game is tricky but important to understand.

Another important theory is called **Symbolic Interactionism**. This theory explains the role of language in how we come to know or define ourselves. The theory says that:

1. In the process of learning our native language, we also learn our culture's values and morals through the special meanings that our parents and teachers assign to symbols.

2. As we use language we see how others react to us and develop a sense of ourselves as others see us. In other words, we use others as a "mirror" to see what we look like as we're communicating.

3. We rely on significant others in our lives to give us the most important feedback that we take to heart in defining ourselves in particular ways.

As we play cards and see how others play in response to us we begin to understand who we are—we establish an identity or self-concept. The key is that we rely on significant others such as parents, friends or coaches to establish that self-awareness. Next time you are around someone who really influences you, notice how you pay more attention to the cards that person plays in response to yours. You especially value that person's feedback.

A third theory of language that bears discussion is **Communication Accommodation Theory.** This theory explores the issues of synchrony and dissynchrony discussed on the last chapter, and why people are more or less motivated to converge their communications. Accommodation means matching or synchronizing with one another's conversational partners in speed, tone, volume, pitch, rhythm, use of profanity, formal or informal language. The theory says that:

1. When we play the same cards and discuss the same topics with similar styles we are **converging**. We are **diverging** when we intentionally play different cards or select different topics to accomplish some goal. And, we are **maintaining** when we keep our own style just because we can't shift our communication for whatever reason.

2. The more we rely on our own language community for our identity, norms and values, the more we tend to **diverge** or **maintain**, particularly with "outsiders," since diverging emphasizes our identity to outsiders.

3. People tend to diverge from "outsiders" more when they perceive that their language community is under attack as a show of strength or solidarity with the community.

4. When we are less dependent on our own language group for our identity, or when we see our conversational partner more as an individual (than as a representative of some outside group) we are more likely to converge with that person to establish common ground.

These accommodation concepts were definitely in play in the Factory Talk Game. By changing my language to swear a great deal when I played my Friend Card, I was used to converging into my own factory language group. Since I did this all summer it was difficult for me to break out of this when I went to college. It took a while to make the full switch to converge to the College Talk.

The final theory of language that in many ways encompasses the other four theories about language is called **Code Switching Theory**. We know from the Coordinated Management of Meaning Theory that as we interact with someone we coordinate our talk and over time build constitutive and regulative rules that govern which topics and styles are acceptable or unacceptable in any given situation. These rules ultimately create a "look" and "feel" to the language we are creating called a "code." The basic features of the theory are:

1. Codes develop over time in language communities (like my summer job) and situationally, as in telling a joke in the factory.

2. When we want to change goals while communicating, we might switch the code (diverging according to **Communication Accommodation Theory**). For example, while lecturing on an important topic as I play my Professor Card, I might switch the code and play a Friend Card to reengage listeners in the topic. After all, too much "professor talk" can be very boring as most students know.

3. Skillful code-switchers reach their communication goals more often because their ability to code-switch makes them more flexible. They have a greater range of communication strategies to employ across social situations.

4. Code-switching should not be confused with insincerity. Rather, it should be seen as evidence that we know how to adapt to our listeners' needs. We know when to converge and when to diverge, and when to maintain. We have greater control over the messages and the impact of our messages.

Gender and Language

Are you aware of any language differences between men and women? Research tells us that there are male and female language codes—or typical ways that men and women use language. We can call them Male and Female Cards. Let's see if you can distinguish between Girl and Boy Cards. Here are two Facebook wall postings: Can you tell which was written by a teen boy and which from a teen girl?

1. "Seriously, countdown to p's and c's!? We can even skip our birthday haha, and it can be March madness/spring training tomorrow, i'd be more than fine."

2. "Hey. I'm good. Working a lot and hopping around different TV shows. Its fun. Just looking for that break. Its good to hear from you and I hope the job search goes well."

These are two of my students, both older teens. Break down the code. Notice there are grammatical errors in these two postings because that's what you get on Facebook walls. So which one is male and which one is female? If you look at the first entry, the topics include p's and c's (whatever those are), birthdays, March Madness, and baseball spring training. Now look at the style elements on display in the first posting. Look at the use of the words, "seriously" to begin, and "haha" in the middle. These communicate high liking and informality, and low power. Are boys or girls more likely to use this language?

Contrast the first posting with the second. Notice that this positing begins with the expression, "Hey. I'm good." Would a boy or girl more likely to say that? What about the topics? In the second posting, the person is talking about hopping around different TV shows. Is that more male or female?

The first posting is from a young teen-aged female and the second from a young male. The point is that every person carries a gender card to tell others how they would like their gender to be displayed. If we could see the parties, they would give us even more clues as to their gender. If you look at Facebook, can you notice any differences between the way females display pictures from males? Is the dress any different, are there more people in the photos—what are they doing in the photos?

Of course, in many homes there is very little differentiation between male and female talk. Perhaps a female might come from a home with all boys, or from a home promoting little or no gender differences. Perhaps you know people who cannot play their Gender Cards. They can't "talk like a girl," or "talk like a guy." While you may know people who don't hold Boy and Girl Cards, most people carry a Gender Card and play it on a regular basis.

To see how much you know about Gender Cards complete this quiz. Below are a number of findings from various sources about gender communication trends. Indicate whether you believe that the trends are true or false.

Gender Communication Knowledge Quiz

Directions: How much do you know about how differently men and women use talk? Please answer these questions as TRUE or FALSE by circling your response and test your gender communication knowledge.

TRUE	FALSE	1. Women like to use talk to assert their identity, expertise, and knowledge.

TRUE	FALSE	2. Men like to use talk cooperatively to invite people into the conversation.
TRUE	FALSE	3. Women like to use talk primarily to solve a problem, give advice, or take a stand on issues.
TRUE	FALSE	4. Men like to engage in personal communication with subordinates and peers, and less with the boss.
TRUE	FALSE	5. Women believe that activities are the key foundation of close friendships and romantic relationships.
TRUE	FALSE	6. Men use talk to search for empathy and connection when facing a difficult challenge.
TRUE	FALSE	7. Women like to disclose infrequently. They like to keep issues to themselves.
TRUE	FALSE	8. Men like to verbally acknowledge that they are listening to others.
TRUE	FALSE	9. If there is a problem in the relationship, women like to wait for the men to bring it up.
TRUE	FALSE	10. Men like to touch people to show that they like them. Parents touch daughters less often than sons.
TRUE	FALSE	11. Women talk more than men in mixed sex dyads.
TRUE	FALSE	12. In single-sex dyads, men are more likely to overlap (talking simultaneously but not interrupting or stopping) one another's speech than women.
TRUE	FALSE	13. Men are more likely to use hedges (e.g., "sort of," "I think," "kind of") and more passive verb forms (e.g., should, could, would, may, might).
TRUE	FALSE	14. Men are more likely to use personal topics dealing with family, emotions, friendships while using more details to better involve people in the events being described.
TRUE	FALSE	15. Women are more direct when giving orders whereas men tend to soften their demands by using tag phrases such as, "Don't you think?"
TRUE	FALSE	16. Men are more likely to give praise than women, and more likely to use it before giving bad news.

Here are the answers to the quiz. If you got four or more wrong, you'll need to attend gender re-education camp!

1. False. Men like to focus on topics and styles of communication aimed at asserting themselves, establishing their identity, and making sure people know who they are and what they know. Women, on the other hand, have different goals. They select topics and styles aimed at showing interest in others, learning about their needs, and responding to those needs.

2. False. Men are more likely to bring up topics that focus on competition as a method of proving themselves, gaining attention from others, and interrupting others to keep topics focused on them. Women select more cooperative topics by inviting others into the conversation, following up on their topics, and responding to what others say.

3. False. Men believe that talks should accomplish something such as solving a problem, giving advice, or taking a stand on issues. To men, small talk is boring and stupid, so they often tune it out. But women are more likely to bring up topics that deal with feelings, personal ideas and problems. They believe talk should be used to build relationships with others. Small talk is good because it both reveals and solidifies the relationship.

4. False. At work, women select different communication partners than men. Men communicate with the boss as much as possible to establish their identity. They select more business-related topics, again to compete—to move up the ladder. Women select more personal topics, and seek out other women who tend to value these topics regardless of their relative roles in the company. Consequently, women are more likely to engage in personal communication with subordinates and peers.

5. False. Men believe that activities are the key foundation of close friendships and romantic relationships. They like to cement friendships by doing things together (playing or watching sports) and doing things for one another (trading favors, washing a car, picking up snacks). For women, close friendships and romantic relationships are all about the talk. That is, talk is not just a means to an end, but an end in itself. Topics focusing on feelings, personal issues, and daily life are the way to build and continuously enrich relationships.

6. False. First, men don't like to talk about troubles because they believe it shows weakness. If they do, the goal of the talk is to search for solutions. Men are socialized to use communication instrumentally so they tend to offer advice or solutions. Thus, women often interpret men's advice as communicating lack of personal concern. Men are often frustrated if they hear empathy and support instead of solutions. In contrast, women like to talk about what's troubling them because they want to validate their feelings about these issues. So, the first thing women look for when discussing problems is empathy and connection – old-fashioned listening, and not necessarily advice.

7. False. Men like to disclose infrequently. The rule is, "Keep your issues to yourself. You don't want to look weak or powerless to solve your own problems." For women, the rule is, "Disclose often. Sharing confidences is an important way to enhance closeness."

8. False. Men are silent listeners—women are noisy listeners. Women tend to make listening noises such as "hmm," "yeah," and "I know what you mean," while others are talking to show interest. However, the listening noises don't necessarily mean agreement. For men the rule is, "Be quiet while listening." Affirming isn't part of the listening contract. Men often misinterpret women's listening noises as indicating agreement (versus attention) and are surprised if women later disagree with their ideas.

9. False. Men perceive that the "relationship" is the woman's job or concern so it's not a topic men want on their card. For men, the rule is: "Let's not talk about us." Talking about us means trouble or a problem to be resolved. If you want to be close, let's do something together. If there is a problem, the man will wait for her to bring it up. Men often don't understand that for women the rule is: "Let's talk about us." This means let's celebrate and increase closeness. But if there is a problem, women believe they must take the lead in resolving it because the men simply won't – they'll ignore it.

10. False. Women touch people to show liking and intimacy. Women are often socialized to be deferential and nice to others which explains why some women don't voice objections to unwanted touching. Men touch people to assert power and control. In fact, research indicates that parents touch sons less often and more roughly than they touch daughters.

11. False. Men talk about twice as much as women in mixed-sex dyads. In fact, a woman who talks for more than one-third of the available time may be regarded by others as talking too much. Men assert their power by talking more.

12. False. Women are much more likely to overlap one another's speech than men are. Women highly value cooperation and collaboration in their conversations. For men, overlapping is seen as interrupting. Remember, talk is not necessarily a cooperative act for men. It is an opportunity to assert identity.

13. False. Women are much more likely to use hedges, or words that "dilute" an assertion by saying things like "sort of," "like," "I think" or "kind of." They also use words that hedge their certainty about a concept, such as saying "should," "could," "would," "may" or "might." In contrast, men are less likely to hedge or qualify their speech, or ask permission to be certain in their speech.

14. False. Women are more likely to discuss personal topics in more detail than men as a means of getting people more involved in their lives. Men speak in general terms. They move more sequentially through points,

which is more formal and less intimate while reinforcing the conversational goal of information exchange rather than relationship development.

15. False. Women give orders differently than men. Women often soften their demands and statements. Women tend to use tag phrases such as, "if you don't mind" or "don't you think?" following a comment or request. Men are more direct and less tentative in their communication than women. It doesn't mean the person is bossier or feels superior; the style is simply different.

16. False. Women are more likely to give praise than men, and more likely to use it before giving bad news. Women are frustrated when male managers are slow to give praise.

Summary of Gender Findings

Topic Differences. So, what have we learned about the contents of each person's gender card? First, men and women prefer to include different topics on their cards. Women like to talk about feelings, personal issues and daily life—topics that build more comprehensive relationships. By extension, this relational talk also includes discussions about personal troubles or challenges. Of course, men want to avoid talking about troubles since they don't want to seem weak and incapable of handling these challenges.

Also, women want to disclose personal issues and expect others to reciprocate. That means they also want more specifics on topics. Men, on the other hand, want to be more general about personal issues since going too deeply into them is too "touchy-feely." Women like topics of general interest across people's lives; men want to focus on specific problems or issues in order to use communication as a problem-solving tool.

Style Differences. Second, men and women differ on the styles they use to present their topics. Women appear to have a wider range of ways of expressing liking. They will touch more, listen more actively, and show more expressions of approval and praise. They show more excitement than men, typically.

Regarding formality, men are more formal listeners—they don't provide much verbal or nonverbal feedback when listening. In contrast, women are more responsive listeners. They give noisy feedback and overlap one another's speech to add informality to the situation. Men are also more formal in how they organize conversation. Men will move sequentially through points as a means of using communication to solve a problem while looking like a strong contributor.

Power differences among the sexes are very apparent. For example, even when men are the minority in a meeting or conversation, they are more likely to dominate the interaction by talking more (again, in mixed-sex interactions), and interrupting more. They want their topics to take precedence. Women often form habits that project a lower-power status. They will hedge their thoughts and be more tentative in conversation. They will try to soften bad news first with praise as a means of being less superior and more conscious of the other's feelings.

Do Not Over-Generalize. It's important to recognize that these general findings from communication research do not apply to everyone. There is tremendous variability in each person's gender card. In fact, men and women can exchange gender cards with women talking like men and vice-versa. Or, people can adopt features of another person's card as they wish. Listening to how individuals communicate as they interact with one another is the best way to determine whether individuals have and play a Male or Female Gender Card.

Lessons Learned

- **Meanings are in people, not words.** Thus we must strive to use more concrete, not more abstract language when playing our cards. Concrete language tries to directly identify a referent, whereas abstract language uses generalities. Remember, the style part of your card consists of non-verbal communication cues, as well. Can you keep those concrete to avoid misinterpretation?

- **Check your perceptions to be sure you've understood what the speaker intended.** This is a key lesson because it will help you interpret the card that the other is playing and the card the other is asking you to play.

- **Consider how your language lines up behind your goals.** We are always sending messages about our self-presentation, relational, and achievement goals. Are you creating impressions of yourself and sending relational signals that are consistent with your achievement goals? Using language that is inconsistent with your goals can cause others to play card games you don't want them to play.

- **Changing to more inclusive language can expand our perceptions of the world.** Therefore, **we should be open to new ways of expressing ideas**. Experimenting with new terminology for events, people, groups and other phenomena expands what we have on our cards while also asking others to expand their perceptions of the world. It can also increase our sensitivity to the perceptions of others.

- **Be aware of these rules that are in play at any given point in time and how they impact your card games.** Language is a code system governed by rules and norms. As explained in Chapter 3, norms are usually situationally determined. Procedural knowledge tells you how to handle yourself in particular situations. Increase your sensitivity to procedural norms by watching others.

- **Be aware of your biases, judgments and the stereotypes you apply to the language you use.** Everyone is biased in some fashion because we all have preferences for certain kinds of speech, different kinds of people, or communicating in different situations. The danger when we communicate is that we are unaware of our biases and unwilling to be flexible. That can result in stereotyping, which is thinking someone is inferior simply because he or she is different.

Chapter 3
Social Identity Card Games

Introduction

As we learned in the previous chapters, playing cards means displaying information about the way we want others to see us, what relationships we want to promote, and what achievement goals we want to obtain. When both parties synchronize around those three elements, parties are more likely to understand each other and "win" the Card Talk Game.

Recall that the first set of messages people focus on when they interpret your card is your self-presentation goals. How do you want to be seen by others at that moment? In general, these specific goals are driven by your identity or self-concept. You see yourself—and you want others to see you—in a particular way, and that serves as the foundation for playing the rest of your card. What you wear, how you cut your hair, how you display your gender, and how you phonetically form words all reflect on your identity.

Social Identity Card Talk Games

The Gangster Game. In preparing for this chapter I ran across the following website, which is a step-by-step guide on how to be a gangster: www.hubpage.com. According the website's creator, the first step is talking like a gangster, which involves constantly cursing and using the "F" word as often as possible. Next it is important to use "The Pimp Walk," which is more like a limp. "So, if you can limp, then you're a pimp," the website said. Clothes are also a key element in the transformation. A gangster wears baggy pants that are at least 10 sizes too big, and extra-large shirts that have the Coogi label. The Gangster Card begins with these elements that are aimed at a clear self-presentation.

The Clan Game. Most Americans have little understanding of tribal or clan identity. For us, being an American supersedes our ethnic identities. But in a war-torn country like Somalia, tribal identity is more important than national identity. I had a student from Somalia who described the dangers of what can happen when one has the wrong tribal identity. Somalia is split up into many clans and subclans with the Hawiye clan dominating the capitol of Mogadishu, and the Darod clan spread throughout northeastern and southwestern Somalia. My student was from the Darod clan but lived in Mogadishu. One day a member of the Hawiye clan came to his home and simply abducted his father and brothers, who were never seen again. Frightened, he and his mother escaped the capitol and moved to Nairobi, Kenya. But because my student looked like a Somali citizen he was constantly at risk of being arrested as an illegal immigrant. He finally made it to Detroit where he faced further discrimination as an illegal immigrant. Now that he is a citizen of the United States, his American identity has displaced his clan identity.

The Respect Game. Research in the areas of conflict and violence prevention indicates that conflict escalates into violence largely as a way of showing strength and restoring respect. In some communities one's very survival depends on being seen as strong and respected. When respect is challenged, the person must respond. Generally the game plays out in the following way: If, in a casual social event like a party, a young male bumps into another young male, the person being bumped first looks into the other's eyes to define the event as either a challenge to his respect or as an accident. If the person apologizes or simply looks away, then it is an accident. But if no apology is offered and the person looks into the other's eyes, then it is a challenge and demands a response of some kind. The challenge is typically verbal at first as each sizes up the other to determine the level of the threat. If the infraction cannot be resolved verbally then the situation is likely to escalate to violence, particularly if others are watching. The goal of the violence is to restore respect and an identity of being "large and in charge."

Social Identity: Who Am I?

To understand why we play games related to our self-presentation goals we turn to Henri Tajfel, a Polish Jew growing up in Europe during the rise of the Nazis leading up to World War II and the Holocaust. Fellow Polish Jews were being rounded up and executed simply because they were the "wrong" race. Tajfel went on to pursue an academic career to understand what drives prejudice, discrimination and intergroup conflict, like the kind my Somali student experienced. Tajfel felt the need to move beyond explanations on focusing personality and concentrate instead on the idea that these social ills stem from an individual's social identity. Tajfel defined **social identity** as "the individual's knowledge that he belongs to certain social groups together with some emotional and value significance to him of this group membership" (Tajfel, 1974).

Types of Social Identity. Tajfel argued that identity consists of two separate sets of attributes—what I think of myself *personally that is separate* from everyone else in my group, and what I believe I *share in common* with all the other members of my group. Thus, we have both a *personal* and a *group* identity. Clearly, each person believes he or she is somewhat different or unique in some way from others in the group; perhaps the person believes he or she is smarter, faster or more articulate than anyone else in the group. But the person might also believe he or she shares some attributes in common with everyone else. "We're all loyal, caring, and honest people," a member might say when asked to describe the group members.

This combination of separate and common attributes constitutes the individual's personal identity or **self-concept**. In other words, my self-concept is a psychological understanding of what I believe to be true about myself, both separately from the group and in common with my group. If you were to describe yourself to others, what five terms would you use? How about these?

- Smart
- Caring
- Funny
- Persistent
- Likeable

These might be five terms that you would reveal on a Facebook page, or in an email in response to an acquaintance's request to describe yourself. If these were your five terms how might they impact the kinds of cards you would play, what topics and styles you would apply to them, and how you might play them? If you see yourself as smart, you might build your card with many interesting topics related to your academic interests that would allow you to play with other smart people. If you think you're caring, you might decide to play cards with people who appear to have some social problems so you could slip into the comfortable role of providing social support.

In addition to a self-concept (which combines personal and group perceptions of one's self) we also have a "relational self" or set of perceptions about significant dyadic relationships in our lives such as two great friends, a husband and wife, or a spousal partnership. When these relationships are close, people focus on attitudes and beliefs about what both parties share in common. A partnership might believe that as a couple they are effective parents and excellent friends to other couples they know. It is more of a collective sense of self that grows over time from the closeness of the relationship.

The Significance of Social Identity. Your vision of yourself individually, as a member of a group and as a relationship is the foundation of how you communicate. It guides how you perceive others, how you select people to communicate with, and how you play your cards. For example, playing the Gangster Game is all about projecting an identity that will allow the gangster to hang out with other gangsters and to share their culture with one another. In other words, showing the card is like a ticket to enter the group. If you are proud of your ethnic heritage and it was at the top of your list, then you might want to wear clothes and use language that proudly displays that heritage. That allows you to hang out with those folks on a regular basis. Most students want others to see them as students so they dress in casual student clothes to "fit in."

Because self-concept is subjective, it is neither "right" nor "wrong." It is simply my view of myself. Unfortunately, this subjective view can be significantly distorted or extremely different than how others see you. A person suffering from an eating disorder such as anorexia nervosa or bulimia, has a view of his or her own body that is inconsistent with both reality and with others' perceptions. Such a person typically looks in the mirror and evaluates himself or herself as being too fat. This biased self-perception, in turn, often leads to further attempts at weight loss and devastating physical consequences.

Because social identity is so important to individuals in terms of guiding how they talk, dress, and act when playing cards, it also happens to be the first judgment people make about one another (first impression). It's a simple judgment to make because it's visual. People look at age, skin color, facial features, dress and other personal features to decide if the person is like them or not like them. Then they make a prediction about how the other is likely to respond if spoken to. It's a very quick judgment, but it takes priority over other judgments, including whether you are a nice person or an honest person. Most people, like the person playing the Gangster Game give many cues about how they want to be evaluated as a person. Of course, if the person is not a stranger and his or her identity is known, then other initial judgments are made. But the key point is that social identity judgments are important because they are immediate and influential in guiding behavior.

Origins of Self-Concept. Psychologists have thought for some time that our self-concept comes from communication with others. Since we cannot watch ourselves communicate with others, we instead focus on their reactions to us. Others, in a sense, function as mirrors to our social behavior. As you recall from Chapter 2 when we talked about **Symbolic Interactionism Theory** (p. 22), this is the same reflective process we use in learning language. People let us know if we're funny, caring, smart or useful as we read their reactions to our card plays. This feedback can be negative through overt criticism, gestures, and looks of annoyance or people just avoiding us. Through repeated exposures to this feedback over time, we begin to get a feel for what we do well and not so well. Of course we have to be open to that feedback, which for some is a tall order.

Psychologically what drives the fundamental need to form a social identity? Every person, from birth on, strives to satisfy three basic interpersonal needs:

- **Inclusion,** or the desire to be accepted and respected within some group, family or relationship.
- **Control,** or the desire to impact the environment to get others to pay attention to us so we can get our message across, get fed or get help.
- **Affection,** or the desire to receive intimacy and civility from others.

These needs are not negotiable. We are social creatures. We must be part of a group, be included and accepted for who we are in that social structure, and receive some emotional support from that group. People turn first to their families for this kind of acceptance and membership. However, if our family refuses or is dysfunctional, then we look to peers and others to provide this kind of acceptance. In fact, people will do almost anything that the group demands to be included. Our gangster friend is a good example of the extremes people will go to fit with that identity. In fact, children seldom want to be separated from their abusive parents. Their desire to belong to a family overpowers their need for survival.

What role does social identity play in satisfying these needs? Our identity is the primary tool we rely on to satisfy these needs. And the cards we play and the manner in which we play them constitutes the expression of our identity. We forge and then protect our identity so we can then communicate and present ourselves in a way that the group will accept us. If our social identity does not conform to what the group is looking for as evidenced by the fact that we're playing the wrong cards, or using the wrong topics on those cards, the group will reject us. The Somali student was from the "wrong" clan or tribe in his country. He was unable to play the card of the majority tribe and was rejected by that majority tribe – even risking persecution or the fate his father and brothers suffered.

These are powerful needs. When we perceive that someone is disrespecting us, not listening, or being mean, then we perceive it as an attack on our social identity. "They don't like me as a person. They are attacking me personally." This realization makes people get very emotional since the one gift we hold most dear is our identity. When threatened, we get pretty attached to it, and we are willing to do most anything to defend and protect it.

Self-Concept Structure. The **content** of my identity is the collection of beliefs that I have about myself. It contains the substantive information about me. But these beliefs are also organized in a **structure**. We organize these ideas into a system called the **self-schema**. A schema is the psychological "scheme" or organization for all the beliefs and attitudes we have about ourselves. We have a:

- Physical self (How do I view my physical appearance?)
- Moral-ethical self (How religious, moral or ethical am I?)
- Relational self (How do I see myself as a friend or mate?)
- Professional self (How do I see myself professionally?)
- Family-oriented self (What vision do I have about my place in my family?)
- Personal self (How smart, cute or interesting am I?)
- Social or group self (What social, tribal or clan beliefs and attitudes do I have?)

Each contains a large number of individual beliefs and attitudes. They overlap a great deal, and they are interconnected. So it is not easy to simply break apart this schema. For example, if you think you're attractive physically, you probably also think that personally you're very cute and interesting, and socially you are a member of the "cool" clan. We only truly understand how people are viewing themselves when we step back from the conversation and look at the cards they are playing and the games they choose to play or not play.

Self-Esteem: Do I Like Myself?

Perhaps you have confused self-concept and self-esteem. You might hear someone say, "that person has a bad self-concept." Actually, there is no such thing as a bad self-concept—it is what it is. On the other hand, someone might not like their own self-concept and play their cards accordingly. For example, someone who refuses to play a card in a group might lack self-confidence, we could easily conclude. That lack of card playing is really a result of low self-esteem.

Self-esteem is a positive or negative **evaluation** of one's self. It is the difference between where I am and where I would like to be as a person—my **real self** and my **ideal self**. It is the subjective judgment about the gap between these two selves. For example, let's say you want to be really smart as a key part of your ideal self. Then you take a class at Michigan State University in calculus and fail it. If you needed that class for your major, and you also failed some other classes as well, you might conclude (probably falsely) that your real self is not very smart. This gap might produce low self-esteem about your calculus ability.

On the other hand, your real self and ideal self might match up quite well in your moral/ethical self-concept domain. You would like to be ethical and moral and you see yourself that way. In that particular area there is not big gap so your self-esteem is higher as it pertains to the moral/ethical self.

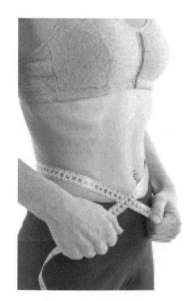

Can you imagine the self-esteem issues the Somali student faced when arriving in Detroit? He might have lacked social confidence because he didn't know the English language well. Yet, he might have felt personally confident knowing that his mother gave him a sense that he was smart, capable, and had successfully navigated several countries. Using confidence that came from his family he was motivated to overcome the gap between this ideal self (knowing English and succeeding in America) and his real self (not knowing much English). Over time, as he learned to communicate very well in English, this gap disappeared, so he was able to play a wider range of cards more comfortably.

Self-esteem is also a product of comparing one's self to others. Students conduct these kinds of social comparisons all the time when they want to know how well they scored on tests in relation to their friends. If you consistently score higher than your friends you might conclude that your real self and ideal self are pretty close together. You're doing fine! These social comparisons may also be the source of sibling rivalries. My older brother was always good at talking with girls and I was less skilled in this area. He was also bigger, and I thought, got more attention from our parents. This self-esteem gap started to diminish as we got older and we grew closer personally. Our relationship self developed and we forgot about all those old growing-up issues.

Self-Esteem Effects. What is the effect of self-esteem on the cards we build, which cards we play, and what games we play?

The higher our self-esteem (smaller the gap between real and ideal selves), the more likely we are to develop and play cards associated with that part of our self-concept. For example, if I am personally and relationally more confident, I am probably going to take risks in disclosing personal information to important people in my life. I am going to open up more when the time is right, and play cards that express riskier and more personal topics.

As self-esteem climbs, people are more likely to take risks in expressing their personal attitudes. They are going to have more topics on their cards and are willing to play them when necessary. If they believe they are smart, they may are willing to play a Political Debate Game with a friend. If they lack professional self-esteem and are supervisors, they may not be able to construct a Supervisor Card, or play it very well.

People with higher self-esteem make better friends and lovers. Friends and lovers listen to one another, but also share their thoughts in a constructive way. It is a balanced give and take. They don't try to attack one another, they are able to empathize and help one another work through their issues. One of the most important cards that anyone can hold and develop is a Friend Card. Being a good friend means that you can show your support when needed and that you are willing to talk about any topics of interest to your friend. The better developed this card is (good listening, honest discussion) the better the friendship becomes.

A healthy sense of self-esteem consists of a small gap between our real and ideal selves. There's always room for improvement. We should learn to live with the idea that we can grow bigger and better cards. We can add topics, we can be flexible in the styles we apply to those topics, and we can learn to play card games more constructively.

Identity and Behavior. How does identity drive behavior then? What is the psychological path that brings our self concept into play with respect to the cards we build and select for playing talk games? The process is actually a three-step flow:

- We create an identity. ("I'm Tough!")
- We develop principles or policies to protect our identity. ("Don't yield to attack.")
- We engage in behavior that implements the policy. ("Resist or fight back.")

Essentially, identity drives the development of principles that we use to protect it. After all, it must be protected because it defines us. The principles are general guidelines for behavior. "Don't yield to attack," protects the identity of being tough. "Tell the truth," protects the personal identity characteristic of being honest. "Wear your pants low," protects the identity of belonging to an urban community. These principles state our intentions to act in a specific way in response to a certain situation.

Facework and Identity

Positive Face. Another way to view identity that is more consistent with the way most people think about this concept and that integrates this idea of developing principles to guide our behavior is the concept of "face." Face focuses on our self-presentation goals when we play our cards. Essentially, there are two kinds of face goals. The first is **positive face**, and it is the desire to be viewed in a positive, attractive and competent way by others. You might play a card that makes people laugh so they will view you as a funny, interesting person. On the other hand, if you are trying to look tough, then you play cards that have topics and styles showing that look to others. The goal is to present a face that gets positive reviews and more respect so the individual can be accepted into the group that values such a face.

Negative Face is the desire not to be controlled or pushed around in any way. It is the desire to maintain autonomy or freedom of choice. Do you remember your mom ever asking you to clean your room? Did she say, "If you have a moment and it's convenient for you, can you please straighten up your room a bit dear?" Or was she more likely to say, "This room's a mess! Clean it up right now or else!" The second example is the full Mom Card shoved in your face with high power and an attempt to threaten your negative face. You have to do something right now, which severely restricts your autonomy, to say the least!

Our positive and negative face goals are frequently negotiated when we play our talk cards. Let's take the Mom Card example. When mom plays her full Mom Card with the second example, she is engaging in a full **face threat**. She is threatening your negative face or desire to do what you want. But, in the first example, mom plays her card very differently. She is giving you the option of cleaning your room; she is asking if you're willing to do it, which avoids a direct negative face threat. Clearly, the full Mom Card with a high-power style attached to it is meant to threaten negative face.

When mom plays that card how do you respond? You might simply comply and accept her right to play that card by playing the compliant son/daughter card. Or, you could reject the full Mom Card and push back: "I'll get to it when I'm done! I'm busy." Or you might respond with: "It's my room and I'll clean when I want!" Mom may not have wanted this confrontation, but nevertheless, she got it. The negotiation is on and the card game is on.

Could mom have played her card more constructively to avoid this confrontation? Perhaps she could have by using a **face support** strategy. Rather than playing the full Mom Card with high power, she might have tried to support your positive face needs by saying: "I am really proud of you for doing so well at your swimming meet. Dad and I are bragging about you to everyone! By the way, I wonder if you could straighten up in here a bit before tomorrow. Thanks, hon!" Notice that mom first plays the Mom Card by bringing up the swimming meet to support Positive Face, which is important to her child. Then she makes a soft request to avoid threatening **negative face** too much. There are options for cleaning up the room. This negotiation tactic still has some minor face threats, but begins by building up or supporting face. That improves the relationship messages while also avoiding a confrontation.

Face Maintenance is a self-presentation strategy aimed at building up one's face to make it less vulnerable to face threats. We try to make ourselves look good by building up positive face, and showing policies to others that it is unnecessary or unwise to threaten our negative face. The purpose of the Respect Game is to build up positive face and avoid negative face threats. The people playing the game must look tough and capable of taking care of themselves in a fight. Most of the time, in casual conversation games, we might brag about something, use big words, or raise topics that we know will impress others. These are attempts to build up our face to ensure that we can accomplish our self-presentation goals of inclusion, control, and affection.

Face Saving involves warding off face attacks. Notice that the child's response to the mom's direct face attack was push back. "I'll get to it when I'm done. I'm too busy." If the face attacks are strong and severe, they are generally met with attempts to save positive face and negative face—to not look bad, or to not allow others to restrict autonomy or control. Thus, by playing the full Mom Card, she invited her child to play a Face-saving Card, which resulted in an argument.

Self-Monitoring: How Do Others See Me?

So far we have talked mostly about how individuals see themselves. And, we have also raised the issue of how we compare ourselves with others. But we have not really explored the important issue of how we take others' perceptions into account in developing our self-esteem. In other words, how do we really incorporate this information about others' perceptions into our self-concept and self-esteem?

The answer lies in understanding that our self-concept really consists of two sets of perceptions: **How I See Myself** and **How Others See Me**. We can call them, the "I" and the "Me." I see the characteristics of my identity by the cards I play. But when others observe me, what do they see? Is there a gap or are they fairly consistent? Are you more concerned about what you think about yourself, or more concerned with others' opinions of you? Your answers to these questions define you as either a **high** or **low self-monitor**. Let's look at this idea more closely and explore its impact in developing your talk cards.

We begin with the premise that most people want to act in a socially appropriate manner. The question is, what is "socially appropriate?" Clearly, people use different criteria to answer this question. **High self-monitors** base their judgments of appropriateness on external factors. These are people who constantly scan the environment to determine what people think about them. How are others evaluating them? Those external factors might be other people's behavior or aspects of the context. High self-monitors base appropriateness judgments on cues they observe from the situation.

In contrast, people who are **low self-monitors** are more "I" oriented. They are mostly concerned with how they see themselves. So they tend to base social appropriateness judgments on internal factors including their own attitudes, moods, and values. After all, they are looking only at themselves while high self-monitors are looking at how others see them.

High self-monitors have excellent cognitive, or thinking skills in that they are very skilled in scanning the social situation to determine what behaviors are appropriate. They monitor the cards everyone is playing and are good at figuring out what games are being played, as well. Second, high self-monitors can better adapt their behavior in ways that are viewed as appropriate in that situation. They are going to play the cards that are going to be most effective in the card game because they see what's needed to win.

Low self-monitors pay far less attention to the social setting and the cards that others are playing. They are focused on their own feelings and attitudes about what they are seeing around them. Because they have more difficulty figuring out what games people are playing, they are far less adept at modifying their behavior to meet changing situational demands. They act the way they feel.

As you might imagine, self-monitoring has a significant impact on card play. High self-monitors can present whatever image they consider appropriate. If they need to play a card that makes them look good in some way, they know how to do that because they are focused on the external situation. As a result, they can present a variety of "selves" as needed when selecting and playing a card. In contrast, low self-monitors react generally to their underlying beliefs, attitudes, or feelings and play whatever card they want regardless of how others might view those cards.

Who is more likely to exhibit the true characteristics of their identities—high or low self-monitors? Clearly, low self-monitors more accurately display their underlying attitudes and feelings than high self-monitors. These individuals talk more and tend to control conversation in an effort to present "multiple selves" that would be viewed positively by others. They also seek more personal and private information when selecting a topic from their card than do low self-monitors. It should come as no surprise, then, that high self-monitors are perceived as more competent communicators than are low self-monitors.

The high self-monitor is more "Me" oriented (How do others see me?) while the low self-monitor is more "I" oriented (How do I see myself?). Which is best? Research seems to suggest that the more of a balance is best with a slight bias toward being more of a high self-monitor. You will be concerned with both how you see the world and how others see it. You will be able to read the audience and the situation more carefully, but not allow the audience to turn you into a social chameleon who is unwilling to express any personal opinions.

To determine if you are more balanced, take this quiz. Answer each question on a scale of 1-10 with *10 being strongly agree and 1 being strongly disagree.*

Self Monitoring Items	Scores 1-10
I would probably make a good actor.	
I have considered being an entertainer.	
I can look anyone in the eye and tell a lie with a straight face (if for the right end).	
In different situations and with different people, I often act like very different people.	
I can make impromptu speeches even on topics about which I have almost no information.	
I guess I put on a show to impress or entertain others.	
I am not always the person I appear to be.	
I may deceive people by being friendly when I really dislike them.	

If you scored over 60 you are more of a high self-monitor and more "Me" oriented. If you scored between 35-50 you probably display a more balanced sense of "I" and "Me." Below 35 and you are probably a low self-monitor.

What are the implications for how you play cards? First, if you are a low self-monitor, you are more "I" oriented. You play cards based on feelings, not what cards the other person is asking you to play. You tend to play the card you want, when you want it. It may or may not be the right card to accomplish your goals, but that's the card that made you feel good at that moment. Second, if you are a high self-monitor, you are more plugged into what the other wants you to play. If you are an extremely high self-monitor, however, you will be cautious in how you play your cards. You will play the one that you think will make you look the best since your self-presentation goals are probably the most important. Maintaining a strong positive and negative face is critical for you.

What Influences Social Identity Development?

What factors shape our identity or self-concept? What shapes how we develop a sense of "I" and a sense of "Me?" Let's look at each of these factors and their impact on how we play our cards.

Culture. Culture strongly influences the development of self-concepts as we know from Tajfel's work, and even from the author of the gangster example at the beginning of the chapter. Once we become a member of that group or culture, we create a self that allows us to continue to be accepted and respected by that group. But, keeping that membership means adding that cultural information to our cards so that others will recognize our membership.

One of the most profound cultural influences is the issue of **high and low context**. This concept refers to how we interpret the cards another person plays. How can we understand the other's message? In a **high-context** message, the only way to accurately interpret it is to understand the context in which the card was played. Slang is a good example. All slang is essentially insider talk— made-up words and phrases that only insiders who live in the culture really understand. To understand someone playing a Gangster Card it's important to become immersed in that culture.

In contrast, a **low-context** message is one in which all the information for interpreting the message is in the message itself. It is essentially context-free. It is standard English. Your speeches and presentations in this course are low context messages designed for anyone who speaks English either as a native speaker or a non-native speaker. The point is that you must be aware of your cultural biases as you construct your cards and work to interpret the cards that others are playing.

Family. Since it is such an important part of our self-concept development, the family is often called a **primary group**. Family is the first group from which we seek to satisfy our needs for inclusion, control and affection. We look carefully at what cards we need to create, what topics should be on them, and what cards we should play to be a member of this group. When we bond with this group it is our first and most important reference point.

Of most importance is the relationship we create with our primary caregiver. We pay close attention to this person and allow them to help shape our cards. Did your parents ever tell you to say some things and not others? Did you have rules about how to label or interpret certain phrases uttered by others? More importantly, the primary caregiver's job is to help us create a self-concept or identity that we're happy with. It is to give us the self-esteem we need to take the risks necessary to play the card games that help us grow. If the mother does not treat her child in a loving and caring way, it is less likely that the child will exhibit feelings of self-worth. Those feelings about the self are thought to influence adult social identity as well as the nature of adult relationships.

Roles. Once we begin moving outside the family context we look to others like peers, teachers and employers to shape our identities. Once we get to school and compare ourselves to other kids, we get a real feel for the shape of our identity. Am I as smart or as attractive as the other kids? Do I get the kind of attention they receive? These issues are important in families, but once we get outside of the family context these issues become even more vital in shaping our identity. We learn to be friends, students, teammates, and employees on our path of life. We create multiple identities that enable us to function in these contexts.

Each role you play requires a unique card. The student supervisor example in Chapter 1 illustrates this point. Those students facing a new role, must learn to create that role through their talk. They must acquire the topics and the styles necessary to "play" the various games that supervisors must play with employees. For example, how should the supervisor play the Job Interview Game? What topics are appropriate to raise, what styles should be used to raise those topics, and what games should be played to learn as much as possible about that potential employee?

Identity Transitions

Your Identity. Your identity will change somewhat over time. You will make many transitions as you age. To really understand your multiple identities take a minute to rank order along the seven dimensions that we described previously. To complete this task rank these dimensions from 1-7 with *1 being the most important and 7 being the least important.*

Self-Concept Dimensions	Rank Order
Physical self (How do I see myself physically?)	
Moral-ethical self (How religious, moral or ethical am I?)	
Relational self (How do I see myself as a friend or mate?)	
Professional self (How do I see myself as a student and ultimately as a professional?)	
Family-oriented self (How do I see my role in my family?)	
Personal self (How smart, cute, interesting am I?)	
Social or group self (What social, tribal or clan beliefs and attitudes do I have?)	

What do your rankings tell you about how you see yourself today? Is your moral-ethical self most important or perhaps your family-oriented self? If you see that part of your identity as most important, what beliefs do you have about yourself as a family member? For example, my role as a dad to my children is probably my biggest priority. I want to get that right. Whatever you select serves as a core driver of your vision of yourself and what's important to develop and to defend. These ratings will change over the course of your life, but right now they present a good snapshot of how you see yourself today.

Finally, as you develop your character as a student, professional, spouse or parent in your personal growth, it is important to see how these priorities will impact some of the key Card Talk challenges you will face as you make these various transitions in life. These transitions will define how you grow. Do you control the growth and make these transitions in a positive way, or will you just let them happen to you? Let's explore each one and how your self-concept impacts each one.

Knowledge. The first transition we make in life is knowledge growth. As soon as you could see or hear you began learning. Continuously learning and seeing connections between concepts is vital for your personal and professional growth. Only when you challenge yourself can you grow in your knowledge and understanding of ideas, places, people and events. How does your identity impact your ability to make these important transitions? If you believe that you can make them, that you are personally able to learn and grow, you can. If you believe that you can work in a team environment with others and take advantage of their perspectives, learning will continue. We live in a knowledge society in which your job will be creating knowledge and passing it along. You are only valuable professionally if you can do this effectively.

Spiritual. The spiritual transitions in your life focus on the extent to which you believe in a higher power. That power may have religious roots, or it may have scientific roots, or both. My son believes that there is a unified force in the universe that binds all things together. He is unable to label that force, but it guides his views of people and events. You may have traditional religious beliefs that guide your views of the world. If you rated your moral or ethical dimension of your self-concept as important, what are the foundations of these dimensions driving its value for you? Should you attempt to explore these further?

Relational. The next chapter will focus on our relational cards and card games. Everyone lives in a web of relationships, some stronger than others. We make many transitions relationally in our lives. We begin as children of parents, and perhaps brothers and sisters. Then we expand our web of relationships with friends, teachers, bosses and others. Of course the big challenge we face relationally is mate selection. Can we acquire the kind of relational maturity to make a good choice? Self-concept is a big driver of this decision. If you see yourself as emotionally engaging, sensitive to others, and able to be a little higher self-monitor, then you may have the ability to make a good choice the first time.

Communicative. A fourth transition is that people change the way they communicate. Their card decks expand, their cards become more complex as they learn different roles and become challenged to speak with individuals from many cultures. This chapter talked at length about how identity shapes our communication strategies. The key in making transitions is keeping ahead of the communication contexts you face. For example, you know you're entering a professional role soon after graduation. You probably already have a job. Do you feel confident that you can play cards with the correct topics and styles needed to connect with other professionals in your area of expertise? Develop them now if you can in internships or professional groups.

Physical. Finally, we make many physical changes in our lives. We typically grow larger (on average people add about 1 pound per year to their bodies after age 20). But more importantly, we generally alter our appearances to adapt to new situations and challenges, and the changing styles and norms in our society. The trick is to control your physical development instead of ignoring it.

These transitions work together, of course. As your communicative transitions evolve, so can your relational transitions. You become more adept at connecting with people and playing the kinds of card games that result in success in social, professional, personal and moral situations. Becoming more knowledgeable also helps develop your communication cards. Your spiritual growth can also impact your knowledge quests. In other words all these work together, driven by your identity to form your character going forward. Travel well on your journey!

Lessons Learned

Take care to understand your own identity. This chapter begins with the question "Who am I." Most of us develop our life transitions quite naturally without paying much attention to the changes that are happening to us. But, for people like Tajfel or my Somali student who were confronted early in life with challenges to their identities they had to know who they were and learn to use it to survive. The point is that all of us should reflect on our identities and see how they help our hinder our ability to make productive transitions.

It is important to understand where your identity comes from. Remember that your social identity is formed around your needs for inclusion, control and affection. So, your identity is shaped largely to satisfy the requirements you believe are in place to belong to your preferred groups. So, pick your groups carefully because they will determine what kind of person you will become as you make your transitions in life.

Make sure you like yourself, but not too much! This seems like a bizarre lesson. How can you like yourself too much? If your self-esteem is high it's because you believe your real self and ideal self match perfectly. There is no gap. That means you don't want to improve. The mere fact that you're in college suggests that you do want to improve and there is a gap so most of you are in good shape. But, the real challenge is to not let this gap get too wide or too small. Keep on learning and growing to make more productive transitions in life.

Face issues are important in Card Talk. One of the first considerations that is important in playing cards is how does it impact the other's face? Most critically, does it threaten the other's positive or negative face? Generally, it's more effective to support the other's face rather than threaten it. So, always think about face issues when playing a card.

Balance in the "I" and "Me" components of your identity helps Card Talk. You will be much more effective in your card play if you are a moderately high self-monitor. If you're too "I" oriented you tend to ignore other's reactions to your card play; if you're too "me" oriented you lack confidence to say what's on your mind. Balance is key.

Being aware of what influences your social identity development. We began this section of Lessons Learned by asking you to reflect on your identity. Take a broad look at this question regularly by asking whether you have sufficiently broad cultural, professional and relational experiences to help your identity develop in productive ways.

REFERENCE

Tajfel, H. (1974). Social identity and intergroup behaviour. *Social Science Information, 13,* 65-93.

Chapter 4
Relationship Card Games

Introduction

In a recent study conducted by the Pew Internet & American Life Project researchers found that 55 percent of teens who use the Internet have created a personal profile online using sites like Facebook and MySpace. Older teens, particularly girls, are most attracted to these sites. They use them primarily as a place to reinforce pre-existing friendships. According to the study, boys were more likely to use these sites for flirting and making new friends. About 48 percent of teens make these sites a part of their daily interpersonal communication routine to keep in touch with friends, make plans with friends, and, in some cases, flirt with others.

Why are so many people using these social networking sites? Quite simply, we want to be plugged in! We want to satisfy our need for inclusion—to be part of a group, or even better, part of a network. Social networking is an easy and fun way to stay connected with current friends or to make new friends, as the Pew study found. The success of these sites stems from their ability to build relationships through Card Talk.

Remember, we learned in the first chapter that every time people communicate they present three kinds of information in their messages: Self-presentation, relationship, and achievement cues. In the last chapter we focused on self-presentation cues. This chapter focuses on relational cues and how we play our cards to accomplish our relational objectives. To begin, let's look at what we mean by the terms **"relationship"** and **"relational communication."**

Relationship Card Games

The Facebook Game. Let's look at a typical Facebook post to get a feel for how people inject relational communication messages in the styles they select. Read this actual wall posting and try to figure out what assumptions this person is making about the relationship:

"Alrighty roomie love----I think I went 0 for 2 today on exams (kill me now) and I am not ready for this next one tomorrow. If you don't mind will you sign me in to 450 tomorrow morning? Sorry but I will be around the rest of the week....oh and tomorrow afternoon too (I have that exam--fingers crossed!) Keep me posted on the interview and I will let you know how things are on my end! Love you and have a great night at work!"

1. Is this a female or male posting?
2. Is the target of the posting male or female?
3. What is the assumed level of intimacy and attraction between the parties?
4. What is the assumed role relationship or status between the parties?
5. What is the assumed level of trust?
6. What is the assumed level of commitment to the relationship?

This posting is from a female to her female roommate who clearly cares a great deal for her, and trusts her to "sign me in to 450" and is showing commitment to the relationship by doing the wall posting in the first place. Looking at the language how can we draw these conclusions? Let's examine the topics and the styles used to convey these impressions as this roommate plays her Friend Card on the posting:

- **Topics.** a) Exam performance, b) Class attendance in 450, c) Scheduling about being "around next week," d) The interview progress for both folks, and e) Having a great night at work.

- **Style 1: Liking.** There are several cues starting with "Alrighty roomie love." And, she ends with "Love you." There are also signs of caring by asking about how well the roommate performed on the interview.

- **Style 2: Formality.** The posting contains many signs of informality beginning with the informal greeting, the shifting around of topics that resemble casual conversation, and the phrases "kill me now" and "I have that exam--fingers crossed!" There are also several exclamation points used in the post to convey emotion.

- **Style 3: Power.** The posting clearly conveys equal power by asking about the interviewing process and offering to share information about her own progress. And, to some extent, the roommate even shows a bit of deference by apologizing for being around next week.

Clearly, the roommate plays primarily a Friend Card, and also shows a bit of her Roommate Card as evidenced by the apology for being around the apartment all week. If it were only the Roommate Card, there would be no need for all the chatter about interviewing. The primary card played is a Friend Card meant to advance all the impressions that: a) she likes her b) roommate and friend, c) trusts her, and d) is committed to the relationship.

Intimacy Games. A second set of games that's very interesting relates to how couples express their intimacy through talk. One of the most important challenges couples face is expressing their thoughts and feelings about their relationship. It is not easy talking about it. In the early stages of the relationship it's important to understand how committed both parties are to one another and their bond together. One common game that couples play to define their commitment is called Love Talk. This game typically begins when one female introduces a topic about where the relationship is headed or how she feels about the relationship. Her goal might be to escalate the relational commitment and the level of intimacy. To accomplish this goal she must pull out her Girlfriend Card and start a conversation about this topic while using styles that look like she wants to escalate the relationship.

For example, she would probably use verbal and nonverbal messages that displayed **high liking** (maybe a low, sexy voice), **low formality** (she might use touch while she's talking), and **low power** (she might ask a question or hint around about how he feels about her). If he reciprocates with his Boyfriend Card and plays along, then the game is on and the Love Talk begins. If he fails to see what she's doing and instead plays his Friend Card, he is essentially asking her to play a different game, perhaps the Sharing Talk Game that will be described next. So, for this game to be successful, he's got to accurately label the card she's playing and identify the game she wants to play.

A second intimacy game is called "Sharing Talk." The goal of this game is to simply talk about events of the day, or general perceptions about issues of common interest. It's an intimacy game because couples use this time to indirectly say they like spending time together. This game might begin with her playing a Friend Card and talking about what happened in Professor Donohue's class today. Style-wise she might use moderate levels of liking, low formality, and low power to have this sharing conversation. Will he pick up on this game and reciprocate by playing his Friend Card and sharing too? We know from Chapter 2 that men are more biased toward viewing communication as a tool for problem solving. When communicating they expect there to be a reason other than "It's time to share." Often women will initiate this game, men will tune out, and women will ask, "Are you listening to me?" The men will say yes, and the **Sharing Talk Game** will continue to some extent. Couples who learn to share their thoughts as a means of exploring the intimacy in the relationship will be more successful in strengthening their relationship.

Relationships and Card Talk

The Facebook Game and the Intimacy Games tell us a great deal about how relationships work. The first point they tell us about relationships is that understanding of "the relationship" is found in two locations. The most commonly understood location that people use to locate their relationships is in their heads. We explore our own feelings and thoughts to form an understanding of, or a set of **beliefs about the level and type of interdependence between ourselves and others**. We look inside ourselves psychologically to define our interdependence. Then we apply a label to all those feelings and beliefs and call ourselves lovers, friends, coworkers, colleagues, etc. This definition process is continuous. We are always reevaluating our thoughts about our relationships since they are so important in our lives.

There are four dimensions to this understanding of our interdependence:

1. The level of **intimacy** and personal attraction parties share (how strongly are parties emotionally bonded, attracted to, or care about one another?)
2. Their type of **role status** (are they friends, coworkers, employer/employee, customer/client, marital partners?)
3. The level of **trust** between parties (do parties feel that the other will act in his or her best interest?)
4. Their level of **personal commitment** to the interdependence (what is the relative importance of the interdependence to the individual?)

For example, playing the Love Game requires that each party in the relationship plays their relationship card like a Boyfriend/Girlfriend, Husband/Wife, or Partner/Partner Card. Then they must discuss topics and use styles that communicate intimacy, reinforce their relational status as an intimate couple, and demonstrate trust and personal commitment. That's a lot to ask for Card Talk to accomplish, but couples must learn to talk like intimate couples to be intimate couples. The feeling and the talk must be consistent with one another.

This issue of consistency brings us to the second location in which relationships reside. Relationships not only live in our heads but they also live fully exposed in the Card Talk message styles we choose to use in framing our topics. **Relationships are also in our talk**. As we exchange messages we deliver lots of cues through our style choices about the relationship we have with that other person at that point in time, or the relationship we would like to have in the future. Over time, as relational messages stabilize, we start to form beliefs about the psychological nature of our interdependence. How much do we like, trust, and care about one another? What is our role relationship?

For example, let's take a look at the Facebook Game. If strangers begin exchanging messages on Facebook, they might select an Acquaintance Card and play the Casual Conversation Game. They would probably stick with safe topics like the MSU events since they share that in common, and select styles that show some liking, some informality, and equal power. But, if message exchange is between a male who is flirting with a female on Facebook, then he would try to change the game from a Casual Conversation to a Flirting

Game. Playing this game might involve talking about more intimate topics, showing more liking and expressing increased informality hoping that she will reciprocate and also play the Flirting Game. If she does, then he might begin to form the psychological impression that she likes him and might want to begin a relationship. These impressions may or may not be the same as hers. In fact, she might be just playing along for fun with no real interest in him.

In essence, this is how we use language to build relationships of all kinds. We build in the style cues capable of accomplishing our relational goals when we select topics from a specific card we want to play. If we see the other person using similar language in response, we come to believe that the other "feels" the same way about the relationship. In the Facebook Game above, the roommates have a conversation playing their Friend Cards with reciprocated topics and styles that serve to confirm a friendship relationship that goes deeper than a roommate relationship.

Interpersonal Communication

I hope you now have a feel for how relationships are actually created and reinforced through language and the talk cards we play. But, there is another important process we're missing in explaining how we form our Card Talk messages to build relationships. We know what topics and styles are present and how the relationship messages are communicated. But, when they were playing the Facebook Game, we don't know how the roommate knew that her message would be interpreted positively. How did she know which topics to discuss and which styles to use?

To her the answer is simple: She's talking to her friend and they have a history. Based on her knowledge of her friend/roommate, she made a prediction about what kind of topics would be most meaningful to her friend, and which styles would have the most impact before she began writing her post. She thought, "I'll talk about these subjects with these styles and I think she'll like that."

This is a key point. **Whenever we formulate messages we make predictions about how the other person is likely to interpret the message before we create it**. Scholars in communication tell us that we make these predictions on three kinds of information in every communication situation:

Cultural Information. The first judgment anyone makes about someone they don't know when trying to predict how someone will hear or interpret a message is **cultural information**. We look at the person's gender, age, ethnicity, clothing and body language and then make a guess about what cultural orientations they might have. We don't necessarily stereotype because that means automatically evaluating someone negatively and in a prejudiced way. Rather, we label people culturally and reach into our past experiences with similar people, and act accordingly.

Once we label someone culturally and decide to play a card, like a Casual Acquaintance Card, and a game like, Casual Conversation, then we have to pick topics and styles. Perhaps we'll talk about the weather using a friendly, yet somewhat formal tone since we're not sure how the other will respond. If the person responds then we can see what card they play in return and if they are interested in playing the Casual Conversation Game. That provides more cultural information and improves our ability to predict what other topics the person might like to discuss.

Social Information. Once we make these cultural judgments, we look for more information to refine our ability to predict how the person will interpret the messages we want to present. We look for cues in both appearance and language to determine what groups or organizations the person might belong to that would make some topics and styles more relevant than others. Are you a student in a specific school, or an employee of an organization, or a member of a club, or a family that I might know about? We also look for other social cues in the specific communication context to determine if the timing is right for what we want to say.

Sometimes people wear clothes that have slogans or logos on them like "Michigan State University," which help define group membership. Most of the time people are pretty open about what groups they belong to and that helps us make better predictions about the topics and styles that would appeal to them. After all, we know that people belong to groups because they share certain beliefs, attitudes, and values. These are tools people use to filter messages and make them meaningful, as we learned in the first and second chapters. If we know what these filters are, we can make better predictions about how they are going to respond.

Personal Information. The most refined piece of information needed to make better predictions is on a personal level. What separates you from all other students, employees, or group members? What are your unique likes and dislikes, attitudes and values? Once we have this kind of personal information we can make very accurate predictions about how our specific messages are likely to be interpreted. Notice that once you have achieved that level of knowledge you have already identified the individual culturally and socially. You know what cultural orientations they have and what group memberships they have. So, now you can speak to them on a personal level like the roommates/friends did when playing their Facebook Game.

Communication at a personal level is called **interpersonal communication**. These are messages that individuals tailor to each other's personal profile. Notice how specifically the roommate tailored her comments to her good friend. Everyone would clearly recognize that the roommate was not speaking to a stranger, or someone who was just a co-member of a club. That was her friend and she knew that when she crafted the post. Thus, any message exchanges that we make using personal information by definition create **interpersonal relationships**. So, sustained interaction between parties that involve personal information will result in interpersonal relationships.

Now that we know how interpersonal relationships are formed and how language works to change them in some way, let's talk about the range of relationships that we create and how we must build cards to manage them successfully.

Types of Interpersonal Relationships

Families. The first set of interpersonal relationships we learn to create are with our family. The first card that we form is a Son or Daughter Card to receive nurturing from mom or dad or some other care giver. Then we might also form Brother and Sister Cards, Niece and Nephew Cards. Creating these cards with specific topics and styles is a challenge because the families have changed a great deal over the years. Instead of mostly traditional families with moms and dads raising kids, we now have single mothers and fathers, grandparents, or even foster parents raising children and serving one or both parental roles. Families now include people who are not related through any legal connection. Some people even refer to their close friends as "family."

Perhaps the best way to think about "family" is to conceive of them as network of people who share their lives over long periods of time, are bound by marriage, blood, or some formal or informal commitment, and who share future expectations of being connected to one another.

Of course, the type of family of which you are a member is going to influence the kinds of cards that you need to develop to thrive in that system. For example, if you are from a **closed family** in which members keep to themselves and are less involved in larger social networks, your communications are probably going to be fairly reserved, and regulated. In these kinds of families decision-making is fairly hierarchical and concentrated in one parent or the other.

For example, if dad is the decision-maker he will be expected to play his Dad Card that is likely to include topics related to disciplining the children, performing tasks around the house, and setting policies about friends and other issues related to growing up. In such a family, a mom is expected to hold a Mom Card that enables her to organize the household, enforce rules, and manage the system. The rules are known, and everyone is expected to follow them. In this family, negotiating maybe frowned upon and conflicts are solved through predetermined rules and are authority based. If a child asks why, the parents might answer, "Because I said so!"

What kind of topics and styles might be expected in a closed family? Certainly, the topics might be limited by the rules. You learn quickly what you can and cannot discuss and when and where you can discuss them. If you live in a closed family, you probably could not talk about your love life to your parents or even your siblings. Styles would also be more limited. While you might be friendly, you would probably be a little more formal, and you would communicate low power. You would need to continuously reinforce that others in the family have power over you as a child.

At the other end of the continuum is the **open family** guided by values for novelty, creativity and individuality. Members of these families have a much more expansive set of cards to play. They express affection in spontaneous, enthusiastic and public ways, vary in their time commitments to the family, and have fewer specific rules with few of them rigidly enforced. Negotiation is seen as a positive and useful tool in this system. Mom and Dad Cards are not likely to be very different in open families since their roles can interchange significantly. In this family, if a child asks why, the parent's answer might be, "What do you think?"

The topics and styles played by the children in an open family would be very different than in the closed family. You could probably talk about your love life with your parents/caregivers and your siblings. You would not need to be as formal or as worried about showing low power. Power in open families is always being negotiated and is much more fluid. As a result, people in these families are more easily able to adapt to challenges that may face the family. The movies *Meet the Parents* and *Meet the Fockers* illustrate the differences between open and closed families. In these movies, the Burns family was very closed and traditional. The Focker family was very open and non-traditional. It is important to emphasize that **no one type of family is inherently better than another**. They vary mostly in process—how they're organized and how family members interact with one another.

Friendships. Once we develop our family cards, we venture out into the world and start to develop friendships. These require different cards altogether. We need to create a Friend Card that enables us to talk with male and female friends, older and younger friends, and friends that we meet at different locations such as in the neighborhood, at school or at work.

How are friends different than family and how will that impact our cards? Of course, friends are created voluntarily. We see people that are similar to us, and if we play a card and person returns with a similar card, we continue communicating and maybe becoming friends. My son is a history buff and loves to talk about war battles. If he finds another boy interested in such subjects they become fast friends. The voluntary nature of friendships is important because the rules for how we must develop and play our cards are very different than for families. Friendships are much more open and flexible, and probably look a lot like open family cards. In fact, kids from open families might consider their parents "friends" since the cards between parents and friends look similar.

Another important feature of friendships is assumed equality. People affiliate with others who are similar culturally, socially, financially and often spiritually. They hang out with people who share their activities and who are willing to help with various tasks. And, once these patterns have been established we also expect friends to act as confidants and provide emotional support. In other words, friends are a lot like open families in the sense that people voluntarily hang out together because they like each other and share lots of activities. They can even act as confidants and support givers.

Intimate Relationships. As we move along in life working to make the various transitions we discussed in Chapter 1, we want to grow in our ability to create intimate relationships with a few select individuals. We need these relationships to satisfy our drive for intimacy that is satisfied by hugs and kisses as children, but becomes more comprehensive as we mature into adults.

Thus, as we mature we tend to think of intimate relationships in terms of emotional bonds associated with closeness, passion and commitment. We are **close** when we feel bonded and connected to someone. We feel **passionate** when we are physiologically aroused and have an intense desire to be with another person. **Commitment** involves both the short term decision to love another person, and the longer term commitment to maintain that love.

If you think about it, **Sharing Talk** and **Love Talk** games can only be played successfully if each party is willing to play his or her Boyfriend/Girlfriend, Husband/Wife, or Partner/Partner Cards. If one person refuses or cannot reciprocate with the appropriate card, the game changes. For example, if a female suddenly plays a Girlfriend Card and initiates a Love Talk Game, she is asking him to play a Boyfriend Card to play along with her. He might not play that card because he doesn't know how to do that. After all, a Boyfriend Card would need to consist of various topics like, "My feelings about you," or, "My feelings about myself and about others." Accompanying these topics would need to be styles that reinforce them. The styles would need to show high friendliness and intimacy, low formality, and low power. It's called being vulnerable and sharing. If he never was a boyfriend and did not understand how to discuss these topics, he could not play the game.

This description of the Love Talk Game illustrates the idea that relationship talk has rules. There are rules about topics, when and how often people must communicate these topics, and what styles they should use for each. If the people in the relationship don't want to be accountable for these rules they are essentially rejecting the escalation of the relationship to a more intimate level. Each partner certainly has to establish priorities in his or her life, and perhaps an intimate relationship is not desirable right now. This does raise the point about how and why relationships escalate. Let's look at various theoretical frameworks to better understand these processes.

Theories about Relationships

A Stage Theory of Escalation and De-escalation. Scholars have spent decades learning how relationships form, develop and end. They have posed several theories seeking to describe and explain these processes. The first framework of interest focuses on how relationships evolve over time by moving through various stages. Let's explore each and see how relationships move up and down the staircase of development. Here are the stages:

Contact: When we first meet someone our goal is to develop an understanding about his or her cultural, social and personal characteristics. We might consciously or subconsciously ask ourselves if we like this person, if we think he or she is physically attractive, and/or whether we should continue this conversation.

Experimenting: Playing the Sharing Talk Game is an indicator that parties have moved beyond the simple contact stage. Now they are experimenting with different talk games, seeking potential similarities, and searching on multiple levels for more information about the other person and deciding if they want to create Boyfriend/Girlfriend or Partner/Partner Cards.

Intensifying: Playing the Love Talk Game reflects movement into this intensifying phase of the relationship. It might involve sitting close and holding hands while talking about the relationship, or requesting psychological and physical favors from one another.

Integrating: Movement to this stage is marked by sharing some kind of physical symbol of unification like a ring or necklace. During integration, social circles may merge, couples may refer to things as belonging to both of them (e.g., "our song," "our restaurant").

Bonding: Public rituals institutionalizing the relationship such as marriage, or even having a child together. However, going steady, engagement, or using the term "dating" are other forms of institutionalization, depending on age.

Differentiating: Couples at this stage find themselves expressing differences about the level of commitment to the relationship. These discussions are often useful in helping them grow as a couple since they are issues that must be sorted out for them to continue to grow as a couple. As a result, couples will often go back and forth between **bonding** and **differentiating** as the relationship intensifies.

Circumscribing: The hallmark of circumscribing is constricted (circumscribed) talk games. Couples no longer play Love Talk or Sharing Talk Games. Their communication focuses on superficial topics that avoid intimate discussions. Topics that address logistics or other non-involving issues are typically very brief. Phrases like, "It's none of your business," are common.

Stagnating: Going through the motions of the relationship by doing the routine activities, but not trying to confront conflict or to communicate in any meaningful way. Since the intimacy is long gone, couples are just trying to survive.

Avoiding: Couples move to this stage when they actively seek to be away from one another or even separate physically. Parties still maintain some contact, however superficial, as a means of carrying on child-rearing or other common tasks.

Terminating: The final stage of coming apart implements the decision to end the relationship. The movement to this phase typically involves undoing the institutional label that formed the relationship, such as a divorce. Parties may be still involved, but the relationship has been totally redefined into different institutional forms.

Each of these phases is marked by parties playing different games at different times. As relationships escalate they work to fill their talk cards with an ever increasing number of topics and styles. They learn to play fun and interesting talk games that signal their desire to escalate intimacy. Love Talk Games and Sharing Talk Games are two examples. Others might be Teasing Games or Couples Sharing Games played with other couples to reify the institutional strength of their relationships. De-escalating games also mark those stages as well. Parties often invent new games like the Fight Game that might include the Hurt Feelings Game or the Lying Game. Perhaps you have seen couples play these games, some of which are fun to watch while others can be quite painful to observe.

Marital Types Theory. Since marriage is common in every society, scholars have for years tried to understand what types of marriages people create. Four types have emerged:

- **Independents.** Independent couples (22 percent of the total) accept uncertainty and change, but do not pay as much attention to schedules and traditional values. They are more autonomous, work to confront conflict and negotiate autonomy issues while also sharing extensively. These folks will work to develop fairly sophisticated card games that are useful in managing a full range of differences. They are more flexible in terms of decision-making and housework than the other types.

- **Separates.** Separates (17 percent) tend to maintain more distance between each other than other couple types. They are typically not together very much and are not very good at the Sharing Talk Game. Also, they are not very skilled in arguing as they tend to avoid conflict. These folks are typically not growing as much in the kinds of topics they have on their cards and are not playfully constructing new card games. Separates don't integrate their physical spaces very much while also maintaining separate schedules. They are also more rigid in who makes decisions and does chores around the house.

- **Traditionals.** Traditional couples (20 percent) need routine. They like consistent card games played in routine ways. They hold conventional belief systems about what husbands and wives ought to do in relationships and actively resist changing those ideas. Yet, they share more physically and psychologically than the other types. While these folks will argue, their disputes are very limited and played out routinely when they happen. Uncertainty and change upset the traditional couples similar to separates.

- **Mixed.** A total of 40 percent of couples represent some mixed type in which the husband and wife differ on their values and talk card skills. One party might be a traditional and the other a separate, for example. This ambiguity often threatens these relationships, particularly if these values clash often.

Relational Success Theory. Clearly, couples fall into routines as they age. Some of these routines help pull them together while others allow couples to drift apart. Talk games play a significant role since couples use these games to express and perform their intimacy and commitment to one another. Other scholars have also conducted studies to better understand the factors that can predict relational success. Results indicate that there are five major predictors of whether or not partners would maintain their relationship. See how these factors might be influenced by playing various card games.

- **Greater Certainty.** When couples have a clear picture about one another's commitment to the relationship and that commitment is high, they are more likely to stay together longer. Card games help with this process. Couples who play the Sharing Talk Game are better able to see these issues clearly.

- **More Extensive Communication.** Partners who share more are better able to stay together. These couples develop rules for sharing such as when to talk, and what games are best at what times. Have you ever seen couples develop communication or Card Talk routines?

- **Support from Family Members.** Support helps couples cope with various stressors. For example, the grandparents can take the kids for a week while the couple takes a vacation together.

- **Support from Friendship Networks.** Couples need to play talk games with other couples so they can share their thoughts and fears. Successful couples reserve time to spend with others on a regular basis. Bowling leagues, church committees or golf outings are good examples.

- **Similarity.** Successful couples find ways to expand the contexts in which they play with one another. They might learn to play tennis together, or volunteer or work out together. The more of these joint activities they learn to perform, the more they can understand and become attracted to one another.

Self-Disclosure Theory. One of the key talk games that successful couples play is the Sharing Game. The card we play is our Boyfriend/Girlfriend, Husband/Wife or Partner/Partner card. Among the key topics on those cards are items that are very personally important to us. They may be attitudes, deep dark secrets about our past, or important feelings. The only way to escalate a relationship is to reduce uncertainty about one another. **Self-disclosure** is the term used to reveal those key thoughts in the context of the Sharing Talk Game.

Most people know they must continue to reveal personal information about themselves but it can be very frightening. Telling another person your most embarrassing moment, what you are afraid of, or your intimate thoughts is intimidating. Nevertheless, we cannot help but disclose ourselves; even without words, our nonverbal communication can reveal to people how we feel or what we are thinking. People who have trouble playing the Sharing Talk Game have difficulty self-disclosing. Yet it is important in escalating relationships for two reasons. First, it makes people more self-aware. By revealing the information I also explain it to myself. And the other person is helping me understand it. Second, revealing information communicates trust of the other partner and commitment to the relationship, which are important success factors.

Not all self-disclosures are equally revealing. The hallmark of self-disclosure is that the information being shared is unique in that only a few other special people know the information. These are personal items that allow the other to better understand key personality traits so the person can judge compatibility. Yet, research tells us that there are rules for playing the Sharing Talk Game and self-disclosing. Personal information must be shared with only a few people, and only in small doses relevant to the topics at hand. If the information comes out of the blue and there's too much of it, the self disclosure will not look very special. People who do "mind dumps" like that can come across as creepy.

Physical Attractiveness Theory. So far we have not talked much about physical attractiveness. Yet you probably have the sense that attractiveness is an important issue in developing relationships. Research tells us that most people will publicly say that they form relationships based on internal factors such as a person's values, beliefs, personality and character. Yet research has repeatedly found that we form relationships with people primarily on the external factor of physical attractiveness and not on character dimensions. We like attractive people better and we believe they have better social skills. We also think they are more fluent, faster speakers and more confident. In addition, people are more likely to date people they find physically attractive, and avoid people they find unattractive.

Why do we do this? First, people are taught from an early age about who is attractive and who is not attractive from parents and peers. For instance, children who are viewed as more physically attractive tend to receive less harsh punishments when they misbehave than less attractive kids. This "halo" effect finds that people are willing to dismiss misbehavior from attractive kids because they find it "cute." Misbehavior from unattractive children is not typically overlooked. In fact, these kids are punished more than attractive children. Later in life, unattractive people are viewed more negatively in general, and are perceived as less interesting and less successful than people who are attractive.

As these studies reveal, people who are perceived as more physically attractive receive far more social rewards than those who are not. Moreover, society views attractive people as being able to provide social benefits. Thus, we prefer to be surrounded by others who are more physically attractive.

Interestingly, people have a strong tendency to deny that they value attractiveness in other people. This denial may be viewed as taboo within our societal norms. By admitting that physical attractiveness is important, people may risk being viewed as shallow and superficial. Furthermore, another study showed that people tend to make negative evaluations of those who rely heavily on physical attractiveness in choosing a dating partner. In general, it appears that individuals want to date physically attractive people, but do not want to admit that physical attraction affects their dates' desirability.

Social Exchange Theory. Based on a rational, economic model of relationships the **Social Exchange Model** views relationships in terms of their costs and rewards. The idea is that we seek relationships with people who provide more rewards than costs. Rewards are both physical and emotional. When we begin relationships with people we may unconsciously think, "Is this worth the effort?" For instance, the term "emotional baggage" is often used with people who take more (emotionally) than they give back. It is difficult to maintain a friendship with a person who takes and rarely gives.

While at its most basic level the concept of social exchange might appear too rational in contrast to relationships based on emotional attachment and intimacy. **Social Exchange Theory** would argue that emotions are one of the factors that we use to calculate our cost-benefit ratio. If someone is emotionally attached to another person that feeling is factored into his or her thinking as one of the rewarding aspects of the relationship.

Summary

Relationships exist in our heads and in our talk. Relationships are not only thoughts we have about other people. We send relationship messages through our Card Talk as we play games.

Relationships about interdependence. We think about relationships in terms of interdependence. The four issues that comprise interdependence consist of intimacy, role status, trust and personal commitment.

Interpersonal communication requires information about the unique characteristics of the individual. That information goes beyond what is known about the person culturally or socially.

We live in many different kinds of interpersonal relationships. We live within families, friendships and intimate couple relationships. The key is that each requires different cards to play these relationship games successfully.

Relationships escalate and de-escalate. Whether we're moving up or down the relationship ladder, we face different Card Talk Game challenges at each level. It is important to know when we are moving from one level to the next.

There are several theories about how relationships function. Each suggests that as we develop the relationship, we create different communication patterns that serve to constrain how we respond to and develop the relationship. For example, more self-disclosure leads to more intimacy typically.

Lessons Learned

Clearly, we all have to deal with and communicate with our families, our friends, and our loved ones. While this chapter only touches on some of the foundations and keys to interpersonal communication, it should provide you with an understanding of these intricacies.

- **Relationships exist both in your head and in your talk.** You feel a certain way about someone then you put cues in your messages reflecting those thoughts and feelings. Thus, guard your language cues carefully. Are you able to send the kinds of cues you want for the kinds of relationships you are trying to create?

- **There are many different kinds of relationships, and each one requires separate cards and conscious thought** about the important games that are expected in those relationships. Do you have the cards and do you know the games?

- **There are several theories about relationships.** In terms of the process of relational development we know that relationships grow in predictable stages. Since shifts to the next level are often driven by changes in Card Talk patterns, it is important to explore whether you can or even want to adjust your card deck to create the kinds of relationships you want.

- **When relationships evolve into marriage they can take different paths**, and these paths have important implications for the kinds of talk cards we can and should play to be successful. Look around and see if you can identify the kind of marriage you want. Then ask whether you have the cards or styles needed to create that marriage.

- **In terms of factors that influence relational success, communication plays a key role in reducing the ambiguity** that can threaten the foundations of the relationship. It seems clear that self-disclosure is a key part of relational escalation, but there are rules for how we do it properly. Do you know the rules to perform effectively?

- **Physical attractiveness is important in relationships** and that people find it rewarding and a key factor determining their desire to escalate. Work to improve your physical attractiveness by transforming yourself into a more interesting person who can also communicate effectively.

Chapter 5
Socialization Card Games

Introduction

The number-one reason people leave their jobs or drop out of universities is that they don't fit into the organizational culture. They fail to become socialized into the new system. The culture is moving one way and the person is moving a different way. Learning what it takes to fit in and then performing according to those rules can be more difficult than the job itself. So much of the adjustment is simply acquiring the Talk Cards needed to play in the new culture. The goal of this chapter is to help you understand what it takes to fit in and then describe some of the card games you are likely to face in pursuing your career.

To understand the challenge of becoming socialized into a new organizational culture consider these talk games. Most of them should sound familiar since everyone belongs to multiple organizations such as family, living quarters, classes and jobs. Each of these develops a unique culture that requires adaptation.

Talk Games that Socialize Members

To help understand how talk actually shapes our ability to fit into the many cultures we encounter, consider these common socialization talk games. Of course, there are an infinite number of these games, but here are a few of the most common ones.

The Name Game. Groups and organizations communicate values to members by playing the Name Game. This game often surfaces when members are playing their organizational role cards. For example, at work, let's say you are having a discussion with your supervisor about who is going to work on a specific project. You are playing your Employee Card, and your supervisor is playing her Supervisor Card. Your employee card consists of many topics about how to do your work. The styles for communicating these topics are relatively friendly, informal, and low power. Responding to her request for names you throw out a friend's name and your supervisor says, "We can't have him on the project—he just won't put in the time and pull in the right people to do the job. He's basically a lazy loner." In playing her Supervisor Card she communicates her values about what counts as performance by naming someone as a competent or incompetent group member. In other words, you get the message loud and clear about what it takes to be a member of the team. So, when you play your Employee Card, you know that you must work extra hard and interact will with others.

The New Lingo Game. One of the more fun card games that people play in groups is to make up new words for stuff. When people use these unique words it shows solidarity for the culture of the group and a desire to continue being a member. For example, a student told me a story about his house mates and how they often made up words. He lived in a house of about 10 guys and they were really close friends. They regularly played beer pong on the front porch. This is a drinking game in which cups and ping-pong balls are used. Beer became such a part of the house culture that they made up a word for anything good that happened to them as individuals. They called it "beer-a-licious." So, anytime they wanted to label someone or something positively they used the beer-a-licious term. As the students each played their Roommate Cards, this new lingo game of making up words and then spreading them reinforced the culture of the group and the closeness of their relationships with each other.

The Funny Story Game. A very common way of spreading group cultural values is recalling funny or interesting stories about people in the group or organization. For example, our academic department places a high value on collegiality and the importance of faculty and graduate students working together on research. So, it is vital that the department establishes activities that reinforce this value of student-faculty collaboration. One of the common group activities is touch football. Most Friday afternoons in the Fall semester graduate students are invited (and expected) to play football with faculty for about an hour or so. These events always produce several funny stories about what happened during the games. When students and faculty retell those stories while playing their Faculty and Graduate Student Cards, they reinforce our value for collegiality. This has been going on for years and stories have been passed down for decades solidifying the value of collegiality.

The Explanation Game. Research tells us that at work people expect their leaders to make sense out of the chaos. In many cases, things that happen around them don't make any sense and they need someone to help them understand what's happening so they can better perform their jobs. Effective leaders know the importance of playing the Explanation Game to keep employees focused and motivated. For example, while playing his Supervisor Card, the individual might find himself in a conversation with a few employees who are playing their Employee Cards. Someone might make a comment about a rumor floating around about a new policy the boss is considering.

At that point the supervisor might say, "Yeah, the boss isn't serious about that. It's all politics. She's just saying that to make a member of the board of directors happy. Nothing is going to change." This socializes members by indicating who is in charge and how change really happens in the organization. It also helps everyone know which card to play next on this topic and with how much style.

The Discipline Game. Supervisors also discipline members, and through this discipline process, send information about what's acceptable and what's not acceptable behavior. How much freedom do people have to do their own thing in the workplace, or how much do they need to conform? One topic that supervisors must have on their cards is disciplining employees who step out of line and do the wrong thing. Other employees see that and learn by example. For example, a supervisor might say to an employee, "That's not how we handle clients in this business. We don't send them emails when we need to deliver bad news. We call them right away and problem solve. Respect for clients is job one!" Sometimes the supervisor will use the situation as a teaching moment for the entire staff, to get everyone quickly on the same page. The supervisor's goal would be to communicate the organization's values and create an effective working culture.

Learning the Culture

In general, when anyone becomes a new member of some group he or she must quickly learn five key elements of the new culture:

- The basic goals of the organization or group the person has just joined
- The preferred means members should use to achieve these goals
- The basic responsibilities of the members in the role that is being granted to him or her by the organization
- The behavior patterns that are required for effective performance in the role
- A set of rules or principles that pertain to the maintenance of the identity and integrity of the organization

How does this actually work in the real world? Most students have been an employee at some point before or during their college career. When you decided to become an employee here's how you may have run down this list:

Basic Goals. The basic goal of being an effective employee is to do your job, get paid, and develop in ways that will help you personally and professionally. I hope you also want to develop a strong network of friends and maybe have some fun in the process. As a result, your self-presentation goals are to look and act like a competent employee in a way that is consistent with your ethnicity, cultural heritage and gender. Your **relational goals** at work are to impress customers, and get to know your boss and the other employees. But, your **achievement goals** are focused on performing well and getting paid. The job is secondary (or certainly should be) to getting a diploma while in school. Nevertheless, college jobs are excellent professional training.

If your job is being an athlete and you came to MSU on a scholarship, perhaps you have dreams of being a professional athlete. In that case your athletic goals will be more important than your academic goals. Or if you came to college primarily to find a spouse or simply to party, then once again, those goals would be more important than your academics. In general, the Talk Cards you create and the games you choose to play in college will hinge upon these goal priorities. If academics are your key preference then you will start to join organizations that will immerse you in your major and have you interacting with others in your major about academic topics. If athletics are your focus you will hang out with other athletes and develop Talk Cards that will help you in that arena. If your job is most important, your Talk Cards will be aligned with work priorities.

Preferred Means of Attaining Goals. An employee quickly learns that there are both formal and informal means of attaining goals. The company tells you how to do your job, what duties are required, what to wear, and how to follow other important rules. But informally, employees learn how to "game" the system. They learn that some jobs are more important to do than others, that some supervisors are more lenient than others, and that some customers are more important than others. The point is that while your employer is generally pretty clear about the preferred way of doing business, employees develop an informal approach to accomplish goals and both contribute to the organization's culture.

In addition to business goals employees must accomplish their social goals. The primary goal is to fit in both with other employees and with management so everyone can work as a team to serve clients. Sometimes this is a difficult task because people may not take the time to get to know one another socially. Some employers create community outreach projects for employees, like delivering holiday baskets to needy families, as a way of pulling together as a team. Athletes are expected to hang out with each other and show that they are good teammates. In general, an organizational culture should create an environment in which people enjoy working together and sharing ideas.

Sometimes other factors intervene in achieving these social goals. Student employees are very busy so there might not be extra time to hang out with other employees. Or, maybe the nature of the job itself is unpleasant and the last thing you want to do is spend more time with others talking about it. Also, you might not have much in common with the others who work at the company making it more difficult to connect with them socially. Or, you may simply be shy and like to keep to yourself. Some may feel they do not hold the Talk Cards needed to compete in the social scene.

If any of these apply to you, then you are allowing limits to be placed on yourself that prevent you from becoming more involved and getting as much as possible from your employment experience. Everyone has limits, but those who recognize them and learn to overcome them and take charge of their experiences are most likely to succeed.

Basic Responsibilities of Being an Employee. The basic responsibilities of being a productive employee are fairly straightforward: show up on time, look good, have a good attitude, and be ready to put 100 percent into the job. The best employees think about creative ways of serving clients and then take those ideas to their boss for potential implementation. If the culture of the organization is effective, it will encourage people to bring new ideas to management for their consideration. That's how innovation happens in many cases.

Of course, there are also important social responsibilities employees are expected to fulfill. In addition to just getting along with the others in the organization, there are other key markers of a socially "competent" employee. For example, if you gave another employee advice on how to fit in would you advise them on how to dress a particular way, hang out with a certain group of people, and develop certain topics on their Employee Card? What other advice would you provide?

Behavior Patterns Required for Effective Employee Performance. The behavior patterns that are required for effective performance in your employee role are many. Think of the job requirements. You must learn the job skills, and be able to perform them in a consistent and professional manner. It's important to come to work on time and do whatever is necessary to forward the goals of the organization.

The behavior patterns most relevant to your development as an effective employee are communication based. Let's focus just for a moment on your Employee Talk Card. I have had the privilege of witnessing many student Employee Cards over the years that have really impressed me. Many students have served as section leaders for this course, which carries instructional responsibilities. That means they must develop a Section Leader Card that allows them to talk with students about course demands. They may explain assignments, deal with complaints, sometimes provide advice on family matters, and generally serve as an example of being an effective speaker. The Section Leader Card is large and student employees must learn it quickly.

Rules needed to maintain the identity and integrity of the organization. What does it mean to be a "good employee?" Each student employee on campus, or off campus, is viewed as representing Michigan State University and the other company he or she works for. If you work for a restaurant off campus you are representing both MSU and the company you work for. Acting in a responsible, ethical manner reflects well on the University and the other company. Each member of the Spartan Family that performs well brings credit to the organization and builds the integrity of the University.

But, there are other informal rules for how to be a good employee as well. Usually companies are organized around some kind of metaphor and the informal rules often emerge from this metaphor. For example, the boss might say, "Let's pull the troops together for a meeting." This is a military metaphor and suggests a rigid, top-down decision-making structure. If the identity of the company you work for revolves around a family metaphor, then what does that require you to do? If a member of the "family" needs help, would you provide assistance? If there's a big social event at the company should you attend or wear something special? Are there certain topics on your Talk Card that reify the family metaphor like how you might tease each other while at work?

This framework for thinking about becoming socialized helps us understand the role it plays in helping us be successful communicators. We cannot be a successful member of any organization unless we work through these issues. What do these key issues mean for how we think about socialization? Let's look at a definition and explore how it impacts our ability to create Talk Cards and play talk games.

Socialization Defined. To summarize these five elements here is a definition of socialization: You are socialized into an organization when you: **a) have acquired the skills, knowledge, values, motives and role requirements; b) that are appropriate to your position in the group; c) that allows you to fit into the group; d) while also perpetuating the group, building its cultural values;** and **e) forming your individual social identity**.

In other words, people fit in when they know what the group needs them to do, when they are motivated to fit in, when and they are able to perform up to everyone's expectations. There is a **cultural fit**, in essence. The person understands the culture of the group and it seems attractive and attainable. When this happens, it reinforces the culture of the group and perpetuates it. More buy-in from more people means the culture grows and becomes stronger.

As people find the group or organization more rewarding and satisfying, they conform more to the requirements of the group thereby shaping how they see themselves. When this kind of buy-in occurs the group becomes a significant source of influence for that individual. It begins to shape his or her behavior in significant ways. The employee's Talk Cards change rapidly to strengthen his or her ability to participate. Think of someone new to a school. If that person talked differently before, they learn quickly to build Talk Cards to help them fit into that new school.

Socialization and Communication

That brings us to the issue of socialization and communication. When we play talk games in a group or organization like the Discipline Game or the New Lingo Game, they serve some important functions for that organization. Here are some of the more important functions:

Messages transfer values from one generation to the next. Each group develops its own unique Talk Cards just like individuals create cards of their own. In other words, group members will often discuss the same topics using similar styles over and over again related to the job the group has to do. I'll bet your family has some common topics like food, family activities, maybe even politics. Family members will use similar styles for those topics.

We talked a lot about sports growing up in my family and played the New Lingo Game by making up words about sport. In our family the word "dogger" meant someone who slacked off and didn't care. The style we used on playing these games was very informal, but confrontational (high power) as everyone tried to assert different opinions. The message my brother and I learned was that to be successful in sports (and in life) it's important to be committed, dedicated, and disciplined. There was no being a dogger at our house!

These are value lessons, transferred through the cards we play and how we play them, that over time, become very important to sustaining the family culture. Our sports discussions communicated the value for hard work, discipline, learning and commitment. When you have these discussions repeatedly, they create a set of values that comprises the culture of the group and it gets passed down from member to member over the generations. We'll describe some family talk games later to which you might relate.

Messages help shape our identities. Listening to these recurring value discussions we quickly learn the "right" and "wrong" way to behave in the group. The "right" way refers to how the group wants us to act, whether or not it is right in any moral or appropriate way. And the "wrong" way refers to how the group does not want us to act. Many times we conform to group requirements even though we know it's not appropriate or good for us. These value discussions shape our identities because we come to create an image of ourselves that is both consistent with these values while also living them.

For example, the Funny Story Game becomes a tool to shape graduate student identities in the Communication Department. The funny stories that are told and retold over the years that emerge from Friday afternoon football shape an identity of collegiality between faculty and graduate students. When the stories are retold the message is, "We work together and we play together, and we respect each other." Our goal is to infuse the collegiality ethic into a student's academic identity in our department.

Messages shape our role expectations. One of the key requirements of finding out how to fit into the group is discovering the expectations others have of our role. The Name Game is aimed at achieving this goal. When we hear labels being applied to people as either performers or slackers we gain a sense of what kind of expectations others have of how we should behave. Does the organization expect a lot from me or not very much? When people take the time to label others based on how hard they work that sends a clear message about how we're expected to perform.

Socialization and Group Climate

When we play talk games we are constantly screening the cues to assess group climate. The "climate" metaphor refers to our "feelings" about the group, just like climate refers to how we feel about the weather when we go outside. Recall that the last dimension of becoming socialized is learning the rules for fitting in. These climate feelings refer to whether or not we like the rules for how the group does its business. There are **four climate elements** we pay close attention to when trying to decide if we want to fit into a group:

1. **Autonomy**: How much individual freedom and flexibility do I have? If I want to wear something weird or tell the kind of jokes I want, or play a card that I feel is necessary, will anyone care? If not, then the rules would

be flexible and the climate would give me a lot of autonomy. If the rules are rigid and the slightest deviation from the norm is not acceptable, then my autonomy would be very low.

2. **Structure**: Who is in charge and how do decisions get made? A second climate assessment that we make is deciding who is running the show. Does one person make all the decisions, or are they shared? Do people have specific roles to play, or do they cross boundaries depending on the task? If there is a lot of structure, then people are very concerned about following a specific chain of command to get anything accomplished.

3. **Rewards**: What behaviors are supported and rejected? What does the group reward and what do they punish? This climate element focuses on values. Does the group value hard work? Do they value honesty and commitment or even loyalty? Effective groups usually make their values clear. If people don't like the values they see, then they are likely to claim that the climate is not right for them.

4. **Support**: How emotionally supportive is the climate? If people are nice and willing to help, we feel that the climate is warm. If no one pays attention to anyone else, then a climate might feel chilly.

How does playing talk games give us information about these four climate dimensions? Take the Name Game for example. If you supervisor calls someone a "lazy loner," the supervisor is first telling you about what the organization values (**rewards**), that the supervisor is definitely in charge of making decisions (**structure**), and the act of calling someone a lazy loner is not very warm and fuzzy (**support**). Playing the Funny Story Game also tells members what the group values while the Explanation Game reveals a great deal about how the organization is structured.

The point is that when we play card talk games we scan them for climate information to help us understand what's necessary to plug into the group. What are the rules, what's my role, and what should I do next to win my membership card?

Learning Socialization Games

The first card talk games we play are with our family members. Moms and dads, brothers and sisters play their cards and you listen and watch. I watched intensely as my parents played the Discipline Game with my brother. He was always getting into trouble so as I watched I certainly learned what not to do, how to act around my parents to get rewards and not get into trouble. They also taught me how to properly name people and events, and shaped the role I would play in the family.

As you become older and move into the teen years, peers play a very dominant role in providing socialization information and ultimately helping you fill in topics and styles for your Friend Card. As you play talk games with peers you develop your Friend Card and learn a great deal about your gender, identity, ethnicity and group membership. For example, if you were a girl and hung out with a lot of boys growing up you probably learned to talk about many "boy" topics. As a result your Friend Card may currently consists of many of those topics. If you did not hang out with girls, then you didn't learn much about those topics suggesting that your identity is probably shaped more by the boys since that's how you talk.

Schools also play an important part in socialization. Teachers play many talk games and teach us more about structure, authority, rewards and support. Schools are the second real socialization challenge we have because we go from one group governed by one set of rules (our family) to another group with a whole new set of rules (school). This change forces us to become re-socialized into a new system that may not be very much like our family structure. School might be more like a job than a family. In fact, one of the main functions of education is to prepare us to enter the workplace by teaching us how to get along with strangers and work in teams.

We also look to various electronic media for information about how to fit in. The talk games of celebrities in TV shows seem very different than our everyday lives. They wear different clothes, talk differently, and live the good life. The TV talk games are meant to provide simple images of characters so we can learn about them quickly, and sometimes too quickly. This oversimplification can lead to stereotyping, which we will talk more about when we get to the media chapter. Media gives us new lingo, transmits values, and tells us what's cool (rewarding) and not cool to believe (Chapter 13).

What group exerts the most influence over you? Is it your family, work or peer group? What Talk Card games do they play? What cards do they ask you to play? Can you play the cards well and win games effortlessly? Do you think that the cards you develop and the games you play are good for you or hinder you in some way? If your cards and games are dominated by your family and they don't translate well to work, you might have a problem. As I said before, we argued a lot in our house so I was used to playing games that way. I quickly learned once I got to school that my teachers and new friends did not appreciate the cards or the games I played. I had to calm down.

Socialization Trouble

My trouble fitting in at school is a good example of socialization trouble. What are some of the main causes of not being able to fit in? The quick answer is a lack of the relevant Talk Cards needed to play the important talk games the group wants to play. Why might people lack the Talk Cards needed to fit in? There are several reasons:

Poor Orientation. People might receive poor information from a member who provides inadequate or poor information. An individual might learn something from an official representative of the group or organization, but real insights from real insiders might be missing. So the person gets only part of the information about what it's like to be a member. Poor orientation results in not knowing which topics to discuss, when to discuss them, or what styles to use in raising the topics. Most groups and organizations present many different faces to a new member and the more information the member can get about these differences the better. Clearly, getting both formal and informal insights from multiple sources is very important to quickly performing a role well in a new setting.

Poor Communication Competence. Even if the individual receives excellent orientation from multiple, reliable sources he or she can still experience difficulty adjusting. People are **communicatively competent** when they can: a) accurately interpret messages from the specific group's perspective, and b) create messages that are consistent and appropriate with their role in the group. Regarding the message interpretation challenge, recall that earlier in this chapter I talked about all the upfront investigative work needed to be accepted into a group. We search for information about what the organization is trying to do and how it should be done.

A key part of that search is examining the cards and card games that people are playing as they work in the group context. **Communication competence** suggests that when people pay attention to the cards and card games, they learn the rules and expectations of the group and how to interpret messages. Having greater self-monitoring skills certainly helps this learning process, but being able to interpret the meaning and significance of group-generated messages is the first step toward competence.

The end result of accurate interpretation is being able to play a card and win a talk game with group members. The more games someone wins, the more likely that person is to be accepted into the group. Each message from that person sounds appropriate and consistent with group expectations. In other words, the person seems **communicatively competent**. When these stars do not align and the person can't accurately interpret what's going on and can't participate in the interaction, he or she is going to have trouble fitting in and thriving in the new situation.

For example, have you ever heard someone tell a crude joke that seemed really inappropriate and made everyone feel uncomfortable? What made that person think that joke was appropriate? Did the person get bad information about what the group is like? Is the person incapable of reading the cards others are playing and thought the joke would go over well? Inappropriate humor is a good example of being communicatively incompetent. It's not that the joke is bad as much as it just doesn't fit the situation and the group.

The Process of Becoming Socialized

Trouble fitting in generally comes early on in someone's participation in a group. Over time people start to catch on as they gather information about the climate and begin playing simple Talk Card games on a limited basis. As they become more comfortable, the "old-timers" might even design "tests" to see how the new members react under pressure and see if the new kid will fit in socially. It is a process that can take weeks, months or even years to complete. Getting into some groups is much harder than others, as we shall see when we talk more generally about culture in the next chapter. For now, let's see what research tells us about the phases of socialization.

Anticipation. In this first phase, sometimes known as **getting in**, both the group and the potential new member develop expectations about one another. When you thought about coming to Michigan State you began to develop ideas about the benefits of coming here, what it would be like to be a student, and how you might fit in with your new roommate and the other students on campus. You wondered about the climate here. What kind of freedoms might you have? What kind of authority would you need to live with? How friendly were people likely to be to you? On the flip side, faculty and staff develop expectations about the ease or difficulty of working with the new students. Greater familiarity by both parties generally results in a smoother transition for recruits from "outsider" to "insider." It is at this phase that good orientation information is valuable to create more accurate expectations of what the job requirements are, the formal and informal rules needed to do that job well, and what the climate is like in the workplace.

Accommodation. After learning all about one another, the new member finally enters the scene and joins the group. This is the **breaking in** phase in which the individual starts quickly gathering climate information to begin the job he or she came into the group to perform. For you, is the job of being a student what you expected? Is it more or less difficult? Is the life of being a student like you expected or is it vastly different? Your answers to these questions reveal how many accommodations you needed to make to continue to be a student. Maybe you study more than you did in high school. Maybe you play fewer video games than before. Perhaps you interact with many more different kinds of people than you ever imagined. The point is you begin to learn what Talk Cards are needed, when and how to play them, and how to change to be a more effective communicator. People who resist the accommodation generally decide to leave the group because the process is just too difficult.

Role Management. Once the commitment is made to continue participating in the group or organization, the individual starts **settling in** to their new role. The person has made the necessary accommodations and is building new cards and playing different games. This settling-in process involves managing the new role to find a path that is most effective. Finding this path requires that the new members resolve two types of conflict: Conflict between work and life interests outside of work (e.g., commuting, childcare arrangements); and conflicts in the workplace itself (e.g., getting along with coworkers or the supervisor). For all practical purposes the honeymoon period has long been over, and the problems associated with the (sometimes) harsh realities of the boss's personality, work conditions and time demands must be resolved or managed.

How successful was the transition to your new role as a college student? If you took the time to get good information about life on campus, scoped your new roommate out on Facebook, and maybe read some of the material for your new classes; it probably went fairly well. For some, the conflict between work life and social life might have caused problems. If you didn't like your roommate then school might have been more stressful. Or, regarding classes, if you got into groups that were unproductive or had professors who were difficult to understand, then the socialization process was more difficult. At the end of the day, taking charge of the process is what matters most. Find out what's best for you and make it happen!

Outcomes of Socialization

I am sure you have come in and out of many groups or organizations on your way to college. The decision to stay or go generally hinges on one or more of four outcomes that we use to judge the success of our socialization.

Satisfaction. Satisfaction refers to how much people become emotionally attached to the new group. Do they like it and feel good in it? Do they have a positive attitude about their membership? Do they feel as if they are being productive and effective in their jobs and able to resolve the conflicts they face in settling into the new roles?

Identification. Another marker of socialization is identification or the extent to which our identity has been shaped by the group. If the group values showing Spartan pride, do you share that value? Do you wear MSU spirit wear? Is your identity now permanently linked to the university? If you remember the Lingo Talk Game described previously in which group members make up and then share new words, then you will recall that this sharing process is a good indication of identifying with the new group. Members of the group now have common Talk Cards; people are formally declaring their membership by frequently using the new cards.

Integration. If you belong to the group you see yourself as having extensive contacts with other members of the group. People hang out together, share information, and work more as a team. Being integrated into a major field of study is an important achievement for a student. By the time you are a junior or senior you ought to know other students in your cohort, key faculty members, and perhaps even corporate sponsors who want to hire people from your major. I always advise students to join some key student organizations related to their major just to take advantage of these integration opportunities.

Communication Competence. A final marker of socialization is being communicatively competent. Members who are settled into the group know how to interpret a wide range of situations and can carefully craft their messages to adapt to these situations. You can just see how much people grow into their roles by witnessing their "voice." I teach a course in sales communication and it is fun to see students progress from the beginning to the end of the course. They learn to develop a professional sales "voice" or style and are able to clearly and confidently articulate their positions. In essence it is the ultimate achievement—the development of the Talk Cards needed for success, and the ability to play those cards to perfection. It is a beautiful thing to watch!

Summary

New members of a group seeking membership must become socialized into the group's culture. Understanding a group's culture is derived from observing and participating in the card talk games that members play as they interact with one another. Decoding these games reveals information about the goals of the organization, and how to perform effectively. When someone is socialized into a group that person has acquired the skills, knowledge, values, motives, and role requirements needed to fit in and perform well.

When new members look to become integrated into the group they examine the messages that come from leadership and coworkers to learn about the organization's values such as hard work, professionalism, or continuous learning. As individuals accept these values and incorporate them into their lives they serve to shape their personal and professional identities. Once this identification process is complete members strengthen the culture of their group or organization—they've bought into the process—and then they pass it on to other new members.

Another key focus of new member integration is the social climate. Individuals constantly analyze the social interaction of a new place to determine how much individual freedom they have to act as they wish, how decisions are made, what behaviors are rewarded, and how emotionally supportive the environment is. As these climate parameters become more and more stable they start to form the organization's culture.

We learn socialization games from many sources. Family, schools, media, and the workplace are some of the most common. Each represents a new group that members must learn to adapt to by learning the card talk games played by members. Members fit in when they have constructed the cards necessary to participate in these games.

Trouble becoming integrated into a group comes from poor orientation, or an inability to develop the cards necessary to play the games needed for success in that organization. The idea of communication competence is that people are competent when they can understand the games being played, and learn to play them well. Your goal as a communicator is to become communicatively competent. Learn to form more accurate interpretations of social events and then how to play cards to succeed in the groups.

Success is all about being satisfied as a member of the group. Are you integrated, satisfied, connected and having fun? Are you performing well and emotionally supported? As you probe membership in more and more diverse groups you will create diverse cards and greatly bolster your communicative competence.

Lessons Learned

When facing a major transition in your life, whether it's a new school, a new job, a move abroad, or even a new relationship, consider what's required to be successful in those transitions.

- **First, be clear about your goals in entering a new group or organization**. What are you trying to achieve and is this group the best place to achieve it? The more information you can gather about the new groups you are about to enter including their goals, rules, etc., the more able you will be to build your Talk Cards and the play talk games essential to success.

- **When you make the transition into the new group, assess the fit**. Are you culturally compatible with the other members of the group? Can you perform the roles assigned to you effectively? It might take some time, but this fit is very important and it's essential that you be honest with yourself about the fit.

- **Pay attention to the talk games**. Each conversation in a new group represents a new card talk game. Whether you are receiving a formal orientation or just interacting casually with folks around the latte machine, people are playing talk games. Each of these games, like the Name Game, displays valuable information about how to become successfully socialized into the group. Pay attention!

- **Assess the group's social climate**. Can you grow within this climate? Can you learn, mature and profit within this new structure? I like to throw myself into some high-risk groups just to see if I can compete. Sometimes I am successful and it's very energizing. I have failed on several occasions, but that's OK. I learn as a result of the process.

- **Grow beyond a single influence in learning your talk games**. As you make new transitions in life personally and professionally, examine the talk games that take you through these transitions. As you learn how to shape your games you will become more flexible communicatively and therefore, more communicatively competent. Remember, you are learning about talk games so you can make more deliberate and productive transitions. Don't just react to the games others want to play; initiate your own games to test the group's climate parameters. Play and learn!

Chapter 6
Culture Card Games

Introduction

If you looked up "hip hop Culture" in Wikipedia, in 2010, it explains Hip Hop as a cultural movement growing from the working-class communities in New York City in the late 1970s. According to the entry, one of the movement's founders, DJ Afrika Bambaataa outlined five pillars of hip hop including: MCing, DJing, breaking, graffiti writing and knowledge. Other elements are beatboxing, hip hop fashion, and slang. The movement began as an expression of African-American urban life through language, art, music, politics, fashion and technology. What began as essentially an urban cultural expression in the United States spread first to suburbia and now extends worldwide through rap music, movies and dress.

Do you know this culture? Have you ever tried to build it into your life or even escape from it? I like talking about hip hop culture because it has endured and grown and has become so interesting and influential. It tells us a great deal about how culture works, directs our lives, and most importantly for our purposes, exemplifies key principles of Card Talk.

Remember in Chapter 4 focusing on relationships we talked about how every message we send contains information about our cultural identity? Every card we play seeks to tell the other person how we want to be labeled culturally and socially, and eventually interpersonally. These parts of our cards help with our self-presentation goals. We want to be seen in a particular way to help us fit into some groups and separate ourselves from others. Over time we create an identity or self-concept that forms the beliefs and attitudes about ourselves needed to sustain this group membership. Let's dive into this idea about culture to better understand its influence.

Culture Card Talk Games

The Business Negotiation Game. Since so many business deals span continents, it is very common for cultures to clash during negotiations. Much has been written about U.S. business people trying to negotiate with Chinese or Japanese business people. Before they become more skilled at these games, the Americans would fly to Japan, and begin meeting with Japanese executives looking to close a deal. U.S. business people are accustomed to completing deals within two weeks or less with intense negotiations over complex details. Yet the Japanese, being people who enjoy the process, are more flexible with time and prefer to get to know their partners better before doing any kind of business deals. While the U.S. people pushed for greater detail and immediate results, the Japanese delayed and wanted instead to focus only on the big picture with a handshake instead of a contract. In Card Talk terms, the Americans played their Executive Cards very differently by trying to play the Business Meeting Game while the Japanese reciprocated with the Get Acquainted Game. They didn't understand each other's cultural orientations and were not able to play the same kind of talk game.

The Trust Game. This same kind of game mismatch can occur when people from more task-based and relationship-based cultures try to work together. For example, police agencies are often very relationship-focused cultures; they learn to stick together to function as a team to deal with crises that might threaten the community. Officers have to earn their way into the police fraternity to be trusted. Outsiders are not trusted immediately and must earn their way into the culture, as well. I once tried to work with a police agency on a project. I played my Professor Card thinking that they would be interested in my ideas. While I was playing the Business Meeting Game, they were playing the Trust Game. Playing their Police Cards, they were listening to me and trying to determine if I could be trusted. They were not particularly interested in my ideas. If I had started playing the Trust Game, I would have approached the project very differently by getting to know them first in a social setting, persuading an insider to vouch for me and be my sponsor, and showing my support for police culture.

The Culture Test Game. Can you prove you're a member of the cultural group that most defines you? If your whole college experience is focused on being an athlete, then you probably dress in athletic clothing every day and hang out with other athletes. You will also be expected to walk and talk like an athlete specific to your chosen sport. In reality what you're doing is showing off your Athlete Card. You want to clearly label yourself as belonging to a specific culture. Think of this process as a test. How can you "prove" you're a member of a specific culture—the MSU Athlete Culture, for example? What tests would you give to someone to prove membership? Perhaps knowing how to dress, discuss certain sports topics, or walk in a particular way would be sufficient to pass your test. Other membership tests relate to how outsiders view the MSU Athlete Culture. If an outsider can easily view you as an athlete, then your membership status is solidified. Once you've been successfully labeled as an athlete, then one of the first things people probably ask you about is your sport. They want to talk about the team so they ask you to play your Athlete Card. They tend not to ask you to play your Student Card by inquiring about your major, expected graduation date and planned career choice.

The Fit In Game. Unfortunately, sometimes being able to pass these culture tests can have significant consequences. Do you recall the story of the Somali student Nairobi who escaped to Kenya from Chapter 3?

To survive in Nairobi he had to play the Fit In Game. He had to look and talk like a Kenyan and not a Somali, or he would be tossed into the refugee camp or worse. He had to quickly learn Swahili, the native language of Kenya, and use a Kenyan accent. Unfortunately, he had to pass this intense culture test every day. After a few years when he turned 13, his mother got enough money to smuggle him to the United States. He arrived in Chicago and took a bus with the smuggler headed for Canada and safe haven with a distant relative. On the way while he was sleeping, the smuggler abandoned him at the Detroit bus terminal. There he was all alone, 13 years old, no money, only a little understanding of English he picked up in Kenya, and in the United States for just a few hours. Again, he was faced with having to rapidly adapt to and pass even more difficult culture tests or face deportation back to Somalia.

After spending time in a homeless shelter in Detroit for a couple of years, he was informally adopted by a teacher at a school he was attending and was able to stay with that family until graduating from high school. He was ultimately voted president of his senior class, graduated with honors, and received a scholarship to Michigan State. Imagine the Fit In Games he had to play successfully in school! Not only did he need to learn English, he had to make friends and continue his education.

His inspiring story of survival and success is first and foremost a testament to his own courage and the courage, guidance and caring of his mother. He used this foundation to make the knowledge, relational and communicative **transitions** necessary to adapt extremely well to his new country and its cultures. He learned how to communicate in order to pass many cultural tests and survive in extremely precarious life-and-death situations in Africa, and how to thrive in new, yet difficult academic and social situations when he came to Michigan. A key to his success was playing his cards well enough to fit in and quickly adapt to his many new environments.

Culture Defined

The word "culture" is often overused as a way of explaining human behavior. After all, it is an appealing concept since its effects are so visible and often amusing, engaging and perplexing. People frequently talk about culture, counterculture, yuppie culture, the culture of poverty, and cultural diversity. All of these usages display a unitary point of reference—a group of people who share common beliefs, attitudes, values, and behaviors over a long period of time. More typically, the word culture is used to mean a **group of people:**

1. **Who believe they share common characteristics.** In other words, members of any given culture are constantly searching for cues or clues about their commonality with one another. When someone plays a card

around friends, that person must pass the Culture Test Game. In most cases, part of being a friend means showing respect for the culture. Is the person using the language, wearing the clothes, and walking the walk as expected? When these consistent behaviors occur, members feel like they belong to a unique group of individuals called a culture.

2. **Who outsiders see as having common characteristics.** The external face of the culture is just as important as its internal face. The culture must be visible from the outside because the insiders want everyone to know how they're different, so they must display their differences clearly and visibly. A shared sense of cultural identity is a vital part of each individual's persona. Common language and dress are critical in holding the hip hoppers, the police, or the Somali tribes together as a group. They want to show their pride and attachment to the culture through language, dress, music and other unique actions.

3. **With a common destiny.** Not only is it important that the outsiders know who belongs to the culture, it is also important to communicate that these members share a common destiny. They share goals, a mission, a set of strategies for accomplishing their goals, and a common fate. If the culture exists to fight crime (the police), or claim legitimacy for a lifestyle (the hip hop group), then everyone who claims membership shares that destiny. This common destiny issue is very important for the police because they must know who they can trust among their peers. Their ability to take risks in life-threatening circumstances depends on knowing that they will be backed up when necessary.

4. **Across several generations.** Cultures are also enduring. They certainly change and shift, but the common elements remain fairly stable over time. Members of some cultural groups take great pride in transferring their language, customs, and rituals to future generations. The Japanese and American executives believe that their cultural orientations are best because they have endured for many years. American business culture has not endured for thousands of years - or even hundreds. Both of these cultural orientations run very deep. I visited Japan recently and came back impressed by their commitment to strongly-held cultural orientations.

Functions of Culture

The Somali student playing the Fit In Game illustrates the importance of achieving the kind of meaningful **social connection** that allows us to make the **transitions** in our lives that help us grow productive self-concepts, as discussed in Chapter 3. Recall from that chapter that we work to make these transitions by forming a self-concept or identity that helps us satisfy three key social needs: **Inclusion**, or belonging; **control**, or impacting others in the group; and **affection**, or receiving social support from the group. Satisfying these needs makes us human; we are social creatures who need to connect with people. The Somali student's goal was to pass all the culture tests imposed upon him by his family, his tribe, his peers, and his teachers to gain membership into the different cultures to satisfy his social needs. He needed to build an identity that allowed him to adapt. Clearly then, culture serves some very important functions for us. Let's take a look at some of the more critical functions.

Linking. When we make cultural judgments about one another, we are looking for people who might quickly and willingly include us in their group. We then apply the membership test and if these persons mostly passes, they become good candidates with whom to develop some kind of relationship—to link up. People who understand your own culture are easier to talk to so it's easier to be yourself around them. Men and women each have unique cultural orientations. We've already talked about their gender cards in great detail. If a man wants to link to a woman he must understand her culture— her talk cards. Men are usually less able or willing to make this adjustment than women.

Common Identity. As social creatures, we need to know that we are not alone. There are others out there like us. That makes me "normal" and a regular social being. People of like cultures seek out one another to give them a common identity and validate themselves as normal people. Also, being a member of a culture provides people with a common destiny. It provides a set of goals, a place in society. As a college student, your goals are pretty clear. You take classes to amass your 130 credits in something cool, interesting and marketable, and then start your future from there. After graduation, students who don't get jobs right away have a hard time adjusting because their cultural identity is up for grabs. Who are they? They are no longer students, they're not employed, they're not parents, and they certainly don't want to be kids living at home again. What are they—unemployed job seekers? That's neither very cool nor interesting, and probably doesn't suit their self-concept.

Interaction Context. Once you pass the membership tests by pulling out and playing a few cards that will convince everyone you belong, what other functions does culture play? Culture gives us rules for how to play our cards and our card games. Remember in Chapter 1 that we talked about regulative and constitutive rules for card games? **Constitutive** rules tell us how to interpret card plays. **Regulative** rules tell us when and how we can play our cards. For example, in some cultures establishing eye contact during interaction with another person who has higher status is considered an insult. It is expected that the lower-status person will look down. During a job interview in this cultural context, if the lower status person establishes eye contact, the interviewer would interpret the person's card style as threatening (constitutive rule). Then the interviewer might tell the person to look away or even dismiss the person (enforcing a regulative rule). In this case, both constitutive and regulative rules were violated because of cultural orientations. The interviewee didn't first respect the culture before selecting topics and styles to play the Interviewing Game effectively.

Value Clusters

These examples illustrate how we use culture to organize our interaction with others. The reason why culture is able to have this kind of significant impact is that members share some very deep-seated values that bind them together. For several years scholars have sought to understand the values that members use to form their cultural orientations. The consensus of this research is that there are the **four value clusters** that seem to discriminate between cultures.

Context. The first cluster focuses on how much group members value togetherness in their groups. A **high-context culture** is a densely layered support network of individuals that emphasizes unity and conformity. The fate of the individual is closely linked to the good of the group. To do anything negative would first bring shame to the group, and second to the individual. The person might then risk being shunned by the group. This is not to say that people in high-context cultures have no sense of individuality, for surely they do—only that the primary goal in high-context cultures is for the good of the group. For people in these cultures the extended family is very important. It would not be unusual for a better-off relative to sponsor the schooling and provide a place to live for several distant, poorer relatives from rural areas. Consensus is the preferred norm, while conflict and criticism are avoided. Japan, China and India exemplify high-context cultures.

In a **low-context culture** the needs of the individual are seen as separate from the group and if forced to choose, individual needs come first. Being immersed in a low-context culture creates **an "I" identity**. Group membership changes a lot in low-context societies meaning allegiance to the group is not as important as allegiance to self. People belong to many different groups for short durations to accomplish specific tasks making membership in any one group less important. Members are loyal to themselves because of these shifting social structures. Debate and discussion that challenge the norms are welcome and regarded as healthy by individuals from any political orientation. England, Australia, Germany and the United States are examples of low-context cultures.

Context has a very profound impact on talk card play. In high-context cultures all the information for interpreting the card is in the context. It creates more of a **"me" identity**. Inside jokes and slang are only funny or sensible to people who understand the unique languages that the group members have developed. In low-context cultures, all the information for interpreting the card or the game is in the message so people can communicate across groups. When you give your speeches you want anyone from any group to understand your messages. The point is that card play in high-context cultures for individuals not familiar with the culture is very difficult. It takes a long time to get access to the group and to understand the communication shorthand.

Individualism and Collectivism. Driving the need to form a high-context culture is a value for **collectivism**, or a desire for group cohesiveness, uniformity and common identity. People from collectivist cultures hold a very insider-outsider view of the world. Everyone within their own group or society has a bond of togetherness and a loyalty to uphold the goals and traditions of the group, family, religion, town or profession. These group members may not trust or even like people from outside their accepted groups, tribes or societies. The prejudice is that members are good, and nonmembers are bad.

Individuals do not hold this same in-group/out-group mentality. They belong to many different groups and value their own individual success over group success. They measure their own value not by what the group accomplishes as collectivists do, but by what the individual accomplishes. They are expected to display their individual personalities and to choose their own affiliations. These folks want to separate themselves from the group and rise above the crowd, not be part of the crowd.

These values also dramatically impact talk card choices. People from individualistic, low-context cultures tend to use more direct, dominating, task-oriented conflict styles, for example. In playing an Employee Card, for example, the individual would feel free to disagree with a less friendly, more informal, and higher power style on the card. He or she might even encourage open disagreement. This is not so in collectivistic cultures. People in these more high-context groups prefer conflict avoidance as a means of showing respect for one another's face or identity. Any kind of disagreement is seen as a threat to positive and negative face, disrespect, and a threat to group cohesion. It is frustrating for a person from an individualistic culture to try to get "straight talk" from a collectivistic person. Collectivists just don't want to risk the face threat.

Card play differences in the Business Negotiation Game illustrate this challenge. When someone from an individualist culture like the United States goes to a collectivist culture like Japan to craft a deal, the U.S. people will expect periods of direct agreement and disagreement. If U.S. negotiators cannot discriminate between the two they will have difficulty figuring out what the Japanese business people want in the ultimate contract.

Power Distance. Power distance focuses on the issue of status or inequality. High power-distance groups and societies value status and social rank. To them it is important to locate someone's status as a member of their social worth. In low power-distance groups and societies, status is less important. People are more informal and are viewed more as equals. People from these low power-distance cultures value independence, loose supervision, consultative management, friendly disagreement, and have a positive view of wealth and reward. Most Euro-American countries maintain low power-distance values.

High power-distance countries, such as many equatorial, Spanish-speaking countries like Ecuador, Columbia, Venezuela, and Mexico; or Asian countries such as Korea and Japan; value conformity, close supervision, autocratic and paternalistic managers, and conflict avoidance. They have a negative association with individual wealth; they prefer coercive power strategies to keep people in line, and they have more centralization and broader acceptance of authority.

You can imagine how power distance might impact card play. In high power-distance cultures playing the Trust Game is difficult for a person who does not enjoy much social status. If the person is not "important", then authorities have less value for communicating with that person making it difficult to establish any trust. As a result, higher-status people generally mistrust lower-status people. There are many scenes from movies (*Aladdin* comes to mind) in which a commoner (low-status person) dresses up in high-status garb to impress, and secure the trust from some upper-class person. The key challenge is to recognize the high power-distance nature of the culture and concentrate on spending time building interpersonal relationships rather than getting down to business too quickly.

Masculinity and Femininity. Fourth, some cultures are more masculine while others are more feminine. A male-focused culture values competitiveness, assertiveness, ambition, and the accumulation of wealth and material possessions. Members of female cultures value relationships, quality of life, and more fluid sex roles; they are not stuck in the idea of man's work or woman's work. They have more flexible ideas about what constitutes appropriate behavior for men and women. If you are a woman and you were told as a child that "Girls can do anything," then you were likely raised in a more female-focused household emphasizing fluid sex roles. If you were told that, "Men should be tough and do what's necessary to get ahead," then you grew up in a more male-focused household emphasizing competitiveness and ambition. Strict boundaries laying out "women's work" and "men's work" or emphasizing competitiveness and ambition characterize a male-oriented culture.

High power-distance cultures tend to be more masculine in their cultural orientation. The idea of status is often associated with gender. It is common to see men in positions of power and women in positions of service. For example, in very conservative Muslim countries such as Saudi Arabia, women are forbidden to drive (although that began changing in mid 2011)and must wear very conservative clothing. In Japan, men are much more likely to be leaders while women tend to work in service positions.

You can imagine how someone from a more feminine culture might react to another person playing a card very competitively. If someone used a very powerful style while playing their card in The Fit In Game in a feminine culture, that person would risk offending everyone and not fitting in very well. That person should use a more affiliative style when raising a topic.

It is important to note that a value cluster describing attitudes and behaviors about masculinity and femininity is a concept associated with gender and not necessarily with biological sex. **Gender** refers to one's orientation about the roles men and women play in society while sex is simply a biological trait. So, both men and women can exhibit **either masculine or feminine** gender qualities. More masculine people will look for opportunities to compete and assert themselves in search of their ambitions, regardless of whether they are men or women. That said, there is a very high correlation between gender and sex so that most men act like the male gender sex role and most women act like the female gender sex role. But, I am sure you know women who act like men and vice versa.

Future Orientation. Cultural groups develop a psychological orientation about time. Some focus more on the future while others focus more on the past and present. In long-term oriented societies, members are more patient focusing on actions, beliefs and values that impact the future: Persistence/ perseverance, thrift and shame. Groups that are more focused on the past or the immediate present think in more short-term time frames. They value immediate stability, protecting one's own face, respect for tradition, and reciprocation of greetings, favors, and gifts.

Some people feel that the United States failed the Vietnam War in 1975 in part because the North Vietnamese have a very long-term view of their culture. They are very patient and measure their success over decades and centuries. In contrast, the U.S. culture is very "now" oriented. Everyone wants results now for instant gratification.

Time is also used in a manner in some countries as a way of communicating power distance. In some Hispanic cultures, the longer someone is asked to wait to see someone the more status they have. It is not uncommon to make an important person wait for a couple of hours to see someone. Only the low-status folks are seen right away. Of course, in the United States time is viewed differently so that lower-status people are asked to wait while higher-status people are seen immediately.

The issue of how a culture thinks of time and punctuality impacts talk card play. In the Business Negotiation Game, it would be important to not request an immediate solution to a problem in negotiating a business deal with someone who takes a long-term view of the business arrangement. The longer-term thinker would want to think about the deal a bit and lengthen out the process because they see the deal as a multi-year arrangement.

Cultural Orientation

These five value clusters, context, individualism/collectivism, power distance, masculinity/femininity and future orientation combine to create some very interesting cultural orientations that are a little easier to remember when thinking strategically about which cards to play as you're interacting. Basically, there are three orientations that will assist you in **winning Card Talk games**. These global cultural orientations focus on how people view time, schedules, information, planning, and interacting. I will talk about the different orientations and then reveal the countries that are most likely to exhibit these characteristics.

Task Oriented. Cultures that value a **task orientation** are more individualistic, low context, low power distance, feminine and more focused on the past and present. They work with strict time limits and time schedules. They have a plan and stick to it. They believe in facts, and obtaining information that is statistical and verifiable. There is a correct, logical procedure for doing things, and a big priority for finishing the job. They are ambitious and competitive, materialistic, and they want it all NOW. Task-oriented people follow rules when they communicate and interrupt infrequently. Countries whose majority populations demonstrate these orientations are the United States, United Kingdom, Australia, Germany and Sweden.

People Oriented. Cultures with a **people orientation** are more collectivistic, high context, feminine, status conscious and future oriented. These cultures don't fixate on time and rigid, formal schedules. They work when it suits them or makes sense. Schedules are flexible and not very predictable. People change plans when they want and may or may not tell anyone about it. They value information that comes from first-hand sources that is communicated orally. It's got to be verbalized to be real or important. So there are no hard facts. Facts can change as people see things differently. Relationships are the most important part of this orientation. Finishing human interactions, but not necessarily tasks, is a key expectation in people-oriented cultures. People-oriented cultures are more confrontational and use highly emotional communication styles. They interrupt often and don't have much use for formal communication rules. Countries whose majority populations demonstrate these orientations are Mediterranean, Eastern European, Latin American, Arab, African, Indian, and Pakistani.

Process Oriented. Individuals in **process-oriented** cultures are also more collectivistic, low context, masculine, status conscious and more future focused. While the task- and people-oriented individuals are more proactive in causing change to happen, these folks are more reactive, focusing instead on following rather than leading. They work with flexible time orientations. Yet they believe in schedules to better structure the process; they prefer small changes to the schedules. When they make a statement, it is a promise, so there is very little need for formal contracts and details. Rather, they are interested in the whole, big picture, not negotiating every little detail up front. They like small changes, not big ones, and use both verifiable facts and first-hand information from others. They react to others in a very quiet way and like to sweep controversy under the rug. Process folks avoid confrontation at all costs and never interrupt since it would be rude. Countries whose majority populations demonstrate a process orientation are Japanese, Chinese, Taiwanese, Singaporean, Korean and Finnish.

Cultural Adaptation

One of the advantages of being a student at a large university like Michigan State is that you run into people from all over the state, the country and the world. The cultural diversity of the university is perhaps its greatest strength. We can only take advantage of this strength if we intentionally try to get to know individuals from these other cultures and perhaps try to adapt to the way they see the world. The best that any of us can do is to learn how to adjust our Card Talk strategy to adapt more quickly and effectively. Let's look at the various steps that people use in adapting to different cultures.

Before we explore the steps it's important to point out that moving through them one after the other is not necessarily required for everyone to adapt to a different culture. Some people jump into a new culture and adapt very quickly with minimal difficulty. Others get exposed to a new culture and become dissatisfied right away and want to leave it immediately and never try to adapt. The adaptation steps in this model reflect a typical process that people might experience if they immerse themselves in that different culture for a significant period of time.

Anticipation. Adaptation begins by gathering as much information as possible to learn about the new culture. Are people from this different culture likely to be more task-, people-, or process-oriented in their basic outlook? Of course, the second part of that information search is self-reflection. Are you a match for those cultural orientations or will you need to learn more to adapt? If you could have listed the top three cultural issues that you were likely to face when enrolling at Michigan State after high school, what would they have been? The Somali student would certainly be able to list more than three issues he confronted when adjusting to life in the United States, Detroit, and Michigan State University. In addition to learning a different language to win the Fit In Game when he arrived from Somalia, he had to learn to adjust to the task-oriented culture typical on campus. Frequently at the end of this anticipation phase, people are excited about becoming a part of the new culture they're about to enter.

Honeymoon. Once the anticipation is over, it's time to jump in with both feet. Since the anticipation process usually ends with a positive attitude and sense of excitement for entering the new culture, the first few contacts in the new culture create a kind of honeymoon experience. The new people see differences as exotic and fun in much the same way as one might feel when visiting an amusement park like Disney World. However, after a while, these differences start to become less amusing; they might even seem annoying. You came to MSU with a sense of excitement, but now the day-to-day grind starts to asset itself. It takes a long time to get to class, people might not be as friendly as you thought, and your roommate is weird.

Frustration. The point at which annoyances outweigh the positives in the new culture is the point at which the new visitor is likely to become frustrated, the third phase of cultural adaptation. We end up taking the positive aspects of the new culture for granted and start focusing more on the elements that are disturbing. On a trip to Hong Kong, I met several American families who had been doing business in China for a couple of years. They are called expatriates, or expats for short. When they first came to Hong Kong they were very excited. But after a while, they started to miss their families back home, a yard for their kids to play in, and extra freedoms that they took for granted in the United States but were not available in China. As a result, they were eager to return home.

Readjustment. The frustration people feel when they stay in a very different culture for a while causes them to develop a coping strategy. Their strategies can evolve in one of four directions. They can: a) Decide to learn the language and customs and **fully participate** in the new culture, b) **make accommodations** to survive in the culture, but make friends only with people from their home culture, c) **fight** any form of adaptation by spending as little time as possible there, or d) **leave** the new culture and return home. Each of these readjustments is an adaptation of sorts to the new culture. For most people learning to fully participate is the best option for gaining the most out of the new surroundings. There is so much to learn from others. Unfortunately, our biases often prevent us from making this kind of fully integrated commitment.

Think about your cultural adaptation to Michigan State University. I see many students at each level of readjustment. Most students get into the culture and fully participate although others never grow comfortable here; instead they attend classes and go home as often as possible. Some become overwhelmed and simply leave. The key is to learn the **Card Talk** as quickly as possible so you can see the world as others see it and gain perspectives you never knew existed. That's probably the real benefit of attending college at a place like Michigan State. It is so impressively diverse that one can't help but be inspired by so many stories of personal achievement in the face of overwhelming odds.

Business Negotiation Revisited

In light of everything we've just learned about cultural adaptation let's revisit The Business Negotiation Game and see how we might develop a better strategy for playing this game effectively. Consider the following issues when deciding how to play your cards in this kind of situation.

Confrontation. If you are negotiating with someone from a **people-oriented culture**, would they appreciate confrontation? They certainly would get upset with a topic introduced using a power-oriented Card Talk style. They value relational harmony and want to preserve face. Any direct face attack with a power play would be rejected. The people-oriented folks would just shut down. Remember that they might not want to negotiate in the first place and risk any kind of confrontation. They might prefer indirect communication mediated by someone they trust rather than direct negotiations. It would be vital to get information up front to learn about their negotiation preferences and their problem solving styles before charging ahead.

Information Sharing. What if the people you're negotiating with don't like direct, open information sharing or they don't like a lot of facts and figures at all? They could be **people-oriented** and want to focus on build trust before sharing any proposals that reveal information about their preferences. Or, if you are more people-oriented and your business counterpart is more **task-oriented**, then you would be expected to directly share information and be specific with facts. Again, learning the preferences of the other negotiators would be important.

Influence. Sometimes people from **task-oriented** cultures will try to directly influence or try to push their counterparts in a specific direction. They will not be afraid to use their power when necessary. If this kind of culture clash happens, it will often result in an impasse or a significant conflict spiral. Those people valuing **people- or process-oriented** cultural perspectives are not generally amenable to this kind of direct influence. They will only respond to less direct influence attempts, or trying to form more creative solutions to the problem. It is generally a bad idea to walk into any negotiation with only one preferred outcome. That sets you up for failure, particularly in a **multi-cultural** setting in which strong-armed tactics are viewed as disrespectful.

This small case study of The Business Negotiation Game illustrates two key points about the importance of understanding the cultural orientations of your co-negotiators. First, **test the other's culture**. Most people learn about the other's cultural orientations by seeing what card they play and guessing what game they're playing. Remember, when the other person talks first, he or she is playing a card and asking you **to play the same card, as well. If they are playing a Friend Card, they want you to play a Friend Card, as well. That helps locate the other's cultural orientation. If they do that repeatedly perhaps they are more people-oriented and less** task-oriented. So, figure out what card the other person is asking you to play and then decide about their cultural orientation.

Second, **planning and flexibility** are very important in any communication situation, but particularly in a negotiation. Just like the **cultural adaptation** process, anticipate who you are negotiating with, their cultural orientations, their key issues and their most important needs. Then see how you match with these preferences and orientations. Remember that a win-win card-talk game is one in which both benefit and creatively address their needs.

Summary

Culture is defined as: a group of people who believe they share common values, beliefs, and behaviors, are viewed by outsiders as having common characteristics, and who share a common destiny.

Culture serves many functions. It helps us link with others, create a common identity, and guide our interaction. Not understanding another's cultural orientation is very confusing and inhibits effective communication.

Culture is shaped by adherence to certain values. These values relate to how people value the context in interpreting information, how they view the individual in relation to others in the group, the extent to which they value status and power, and whether they are more masculine or feminine in their orientation. Views about time are also critical in defining cultural values.

These values create broad cultural orientations. They combine into shaping people's perspective as being more task-, people-, or process-oriented. These orientations have important implications for how people should play their cards.

Ultimately understanding culture is about effective adaptation. There is a process for how people typically adapt to different cultures. Sometimes the process is easy and people move through the phases quickly. More typically the process is very difficult as the individual tries to reconcile his or her own preferences with the preferences of the different culture.

Finally, planning is the key to working effectively in a multi-cultural environment. The more you plan and think through the communication challenges you will face the more effective your Card Talk will be.

Lessons Learned

What are the lessons learned from all that we have discussed in this chapter? Here are several that come immediately to mind.

- **Culture is about tests.** For any culture in which you claim to be a member, others will constantly subject you to tests to earn your membership. Do you hold the cards indicative of membership? Can you play the card games in a way that gives you the right to continue holding your membership status? Do you know the tests you'll be expected to pass and are you willing and able to make the commitments required to pass them?

- **Cultures take different forms.** Some are task oriented, others are more focused on relationships, and still others prioritize process concerns. As much as possible learn about the cultural forms, you are likely to encounter when you visit a place that has a very different orientation than your own. Learn the tests you'll be required to pass and make sure you know how to pass. Passing these tests is difficult because cultural expression is generally difficult for us to change easily.

- **Reserve making snap judgments.** Keep an open mind about the values and orientations that differ from your own. It is easy to become judgmental about how others view time or tasks since they may not make any sense to you. The strategy is to listen first then understand and ultimately adapt. You many never embrace the differences but you can at least learn from them.

- **Cultural adaptation is easier with a mentor.** Find someone who is a respected member of the culture and earn that person's respect. Then, this person will vouch for your credibility giving you entrée into the new culture. Cultural insiders can provide a very rich perspective on their culture and if you are at all curious, they will be pleased to educate you.

- **Be adventurous.** Learn the card games that you'll be expected to play and immerse yourself into the local communities to learn how "real people" play their unique cultural games. Most large cities around the world are very westernized. Get off the beaten path and get lost. This gives you the best way to learn about yourself and about others.

Chapter 7
Persuasion Card Games

Introduction

One of the more interesting sets of Card Talk games I have observed is in the context of hostage negotiations. I have studied communication patterns in this context for years by analyzing interactions between hostage takers and police negotiators. What makes these games interesting is their diversity. The first game the police seek to play with the hostage taker is the Getting to Know You Game, the purpose of which is for the police negotiator to establish a relationship with the hostage taker so they can ultimately work out a surrender deal. Then the police negotiator will switch to various bargaining games to try and trade food or other necessities for hostages. The final set of games involves giving up and coming out, which is very intense. Everyone gets emotional at the end of these episodes since one wrong move could be fatal.

I am fascinated by these because they illustrate some key principles of how persuasion works to change people's minds or alter their behavior in some way. In fact persuasion is very common in most communication contexts. We have seen persuasion at work in many of the games from other chapters, like the Business Negotiation Game from Chapter 6. That's the focus of this chapter—how people craft persuasive messages to effect change.

The quest to determine the key factors that cause people to change their minds has generally dominated the study of communication from the ancient Greeks to the present. Aristotle, one of the ancient Greeks, argued that people were persuasive if they were personally credible, presented emotionally engaging topics, and crafted logically reasoned arguments. From that time forward, scholars have been interested in why and how people change their minds. To understand how persuasion works, let's present some Card Talk games that people play in which one person is trying to promote change.

Persuasive Card Talk Games

The Soft Sell Game. Everyone has experienced a sales pitch at some point. The typical game is fairly easy to identify. We go into a store to purchase a specific item and an individual comes to help with the decision. If that person immediately starts to show a Salesperson Card, which stereotypically involves someone aggressively pushing products, the resulting interaction is often a real turnoff to most people. As a result, salespeople who are professionally trained to avoid the "hard sell" approach and instead take a "soft sell" approach. The soft sell process involves just being friendly and helpful—developing a relationship with the customer, or being a resource with no selling involved. Similar to hostage negotiation, the seller's relational goal is to play a Friend Card first to stimulate conversation, develop a friendly relationship, and learn the buyer's needs. Then, at some point in the process, the seller can use this knowledge to show a little bit of the Salesperson Card and start making recommendations for other purchases. "I know just the tie that would go with that shirt."

The Buckle-Up Game. We have also been exposed to many attempts by public health officials to encourage us to engage in healthier, less risky behavior. The federal government has spent millions of dollars trying to persuade motorists to use their safety belts when driving. Most of the commercials you see on TV tell you to buckle up because it's the law. The commercial plays the Police Officer Card that simply tells you to buckle up or risk getting a ticket. The slogan is, "Buckle Up or Pay Up!" Of course there are similar campaigns aimed at persuading people to stop smoking or taking drugs, or engaging in risky sex. Instead of playing a Police Card or even a Public Health Officer Card, these campaigns might present, for example, a typical teenager playing a Friend Card to tell you about the dangers of these bad behaviors.

The Party Pickup Game. Perhaps you have been to a party or social gathering and gotten "hit on" by someone interested in a more intimate relationship. The game often begins with a pickup line like, "Girl, you must be tired because you've been running through my mind all day." This approach is not generally successful because it is a play that would be on a typical Sleazy Guy Card—it's tacky and immature. The better strategy is to first play a Friend Card, simply initiate conversation, and get to know the other person informally. If the person reciprocates with a Friend Card a pleasant conversation might follow that ultimately evolves into a friendship or even more.

The Persuasive Speech Game. When you give your persuasive speech in class you must play a card. Many students get in front of the class and simply play a Student Card to accomplish their persuasive goals. Is that the right card to play to win acceptance? Students are typically receivers of information and are not usually seen as experts who are qualified to give information on any subject. My advice is to play an Expert Card instead. Begin by presenting your credentials as an expert in your subject and who is passionate about the issues. Start by playing the wrong card, as in the other examples, and your effectiveness drops dramatically.

Definition of Persuasion

Persuasion is defined as a specific communication situation that involves: a) a source creating b) messages that intentionally seek to c) arouse meanings in the targeted receivers of those messages that result in both d) changing their attitudes, beliefs, values and behaviors, and e) a clear path to comply. Let's take a closer look at these five elements.

The Message Source. Each of the social influence games described above tells us something about the source. The first judgment that a targeted receiver makes about complying with another's request is to assess the source's credibility. A credible person is perceived as **knowledgeable**, **trustworthy**, and **dynamic**. Playing the hard-sell Salesperson Card initially fails because it is not genuine and trustworthy. The same is true of the Sleazy Guy Card. The first impression is negative thus no one listens further. The source must read the situation and determine which card to play that is most likely to be effective in that situation for those target receivers. They must play the card in a dynamic, non-boring way. Dull people are generally not very persuasive.

Effective Messages. After the target receivers sign off on the credibility of the source, they look to the source's message. Is the message attention getting, emotionally engaging, logically and clearly argued, and easy to understand? If the answer is "yes" to this question, then the intentional nature of the message is clear. The source is trying to persuade the receiver to change. For example, in the Soft Sell Game, the clerk shifts from playing a Friend Card to playing a Salesperson Card when they suggest additional items to purchase. That shift signals the intentional shift to a persuasive situation. If the seller's message is clear, logically reasoned, and compelling, the buyer is likely to take the additional items if they can afford them. But, if the messages are not clear, or the source never changes from playing a Friend Card to a Salesperson Card then persuasion is likely to fail.

Arouse Meanings. As we know from Chapter 2 focusing on Language, messages are symbolic. They seek to **create meaning** or **build an image** in the target receiver's mind. In the Party Pickup Game, what meaning is conveyed with the bad pickup line? In the Buckle-Up Game, what meaning is triggered when the officer says, "Buckle up or pay up!?" The key point here is that the target receivers will interpret the messages at this third step. They will apply their own set of **filters**, or psychological beliefs, attitudes, and values, when they receive they message. In other words, it is not enough to know if the message is clear, logical and well reasoned from the source's point of view; the only thing that matters is how the audience interprets the message. Knowing their filters is a must. If the audience does not like police, then they are likely to interpret the message as a threat and might react emotionally to the Buckle-Up Game. Or, when giving your speech, you may offend an audience member by introducing a certain fact or opinion. That's why knowing the audience's filters is so important.

Changing Attitudes, Beliefs, Values, and Behaviors. An **attitude** is a judgment about likes and dislikes (e.g., "I like football"). A **belief** is a judgment about the truth or falsity (e.g., "Football is dangerous"). **Values** are about what's right and wrong (e.g., "Football should be banned"). And **behaviors** relate to a person's actions, including their communications. If the intended meanings are aroused in the receivers, they are more likely to change their thoughts and actions. In the Soft Sell Game, the clerk wisely begins with a Friend Card just to learn about the customer's needs. Showing that card increases the chances of completing a deal because it improves customer's attitudes about the store, and his or her belief that the store is a place to shop.

A Clear Path to Comply. Finally, the last judgment that a target receiver makes about the message is the ability to comply with the final request. Is the path toward compliance clear or does it have roadblocks? The receiver's thinking goes something like this: "Do I know how to comply, am I willing to comply, what will happen when I comply, and what will others think of me if I comply?" The Buckle-Up Game is a good example. If the receivers finds the source credible, the messages clear, and change his or her minds to believe that buckling up is a good thing, then the question is can the receiver comply? The receiver might think to him or herself, "Yes, it's easy to buckle up—it just takes a couple of seconds. Yes, I am willing to buckle up and I believe that buckling up won't make me uncomfortable while driving. But what if my friends make fun of me for buckling up?" If this thought sequence happens, then maybe the person will be less willing to do it. The path to compliance is blocked by the perception of personal rejection. However, if the path is clear and the person believes that friends won't be a problem, then buckling up is more likely. They will be officially persuaded at that point.

Psychological Motivations for Change

These examples and the definition of persuasion suggest that there are several psychological reasons that people will change their minds. Let's review a few of the reasons that seem most influential in driving change.

Psychological Needs. Many individuals try to influence others by either threatening to withhold key psychological needs, or appealing to these needs in some way. Recall that we talked about social needs in Chapter 3 in the context of defining self-concept. Social needs are included in this list, but they exist within a much broader framework and function hierarchically. That is, once the first set of needs is met, then the second set becomes important and so on. These needs include:

1. **Physiological needs.** Survival needs for food, water and air.

2. **Safety needs.** The need to be protected from harm and become physically and emotionally secure while having structure and order in life.

3. **Belongingness and love.** The need to achieve the relational goals of socialization and inclusion with people and groups and form bonds with others for reasons other than meeting physiological or safety needs.

4. **Self-esteem.** The need to accomplish the self-presentation and achievement needs of being viewed as competent (positive face), able to accomplish tasks well, to and enhance status and reputation.

5. **Self-actualization.** The need to make some type of lasting contribution to the world and "be all that you can be."

Notice how these needs are referenced in the Card Talk games listed above in the context of persuasive appeals. The Soft Sell Game appeals to our self-esteem needs. The Buckle-Up Game references our safety needs. The Party Pickup Game relates to our need for belongingness and love. The argument is that if you do these things, you can be safe, be loved, feel good about yourself, and even make a lasting contribution to society. These arguments have been used since the beginning of time and they are all needs-based.

Psychological Balance and Consistency. Right alongside our needs is a psychological drive for internal consistency. People strive to live a stress-free life and reduce any inconsistencies that they may encounter in their lives. Everyone holds many sets of beliefs, opinions, attitudes and ideas about people, places, objects and issues. We like to keep all these diverse cognitions consistent and in balance with one another to maintain a stress-free state of mind. Cognitions related to one another that are inconsistent cause stress and we work very hard to eliminate those inconsistencies.

For example, you might like horror movies but your best friend hates them. This awareness creates an inconsistency or imbalance in your mind that somehow needs to be consciously addressed. You can choose to: a) Live with this relatively trivial inconsistency, b) change your mind (or your friend's mind) about the movie preferences, or c) change your mind about the friendship. Of those three, which would you choose? Most people choose the easiest path to consistency, which in this case, would involve learning to either live with it, or changing movie preferences. Eliminating the friendship would not usually be an option.

Appealing to the need for consistency is a common tactic in persuasion. In playing the Soft Sell Game, the clerk might say, "This outfit makes you look sharp, just like your friend." In other words, it is inconsistent that your friend would value her attire more than you do. The easy fix to create consistency is for you to buy the outfit so you can look good, too. Another example is the Persuasive Speech Game. In that game, you might tell people that their actions should be consistent with their words. If they say they want to help save the rainforest, then they should join your organization dedicated to that cause.

Learning and Reinforcement. Attitudes and behaviors are shaped by conditioning processes or getting positively/negatively reinforced for thinking and behaving in particular ways. This is how we learn. Our actions bring about a change—positive or negative—in our environment. If we study and then get a good grade, we may learn to study. The positive outcome (the good grade) reinforces the behavior (studying). Similarly, negative outcomes cause us to decrease the behavior that is associated with it. If every time we ask for a date we're turned down, we may stop asking for dates or stop using the same ineffective approach. Over time this learning molds our behavior by wanting to do more things that result in positive reinforcements and fewer things that result in negative reinforcements.

Learning plays an important role in trying to influence someone. When the Party Pickup Game is played well, each play made from a Friend Card is reciprocated. Each person receives a pleasant response from the other, positively reinforcing the prior comment. The friendlier the play, the more reinforcing it is, and the more it continues. When the sleazy pickup lines are used, they are met with a very negative reaction which, hopefully, causes the person using the lines to take stock and try a more genuine approach. The general strategy is to make plays from cards that the other is likely to find rewarding.

Fear and Emotion. Emotional appeals are often used in persuasive messages to arouse feelings of pride, love, pity, nostalgia, concern, anger or fear. The Buckle-Up Game is often played by using a fear appeal. Perhaps you have seen commercials in which viewers are shown how people die when they get into a crash and are not buckled up. The dummies get thrown from the vehicle and die instantly. You can probably think of many other fear appeals you have seen showing the negative consequences of drinking and driving, unsafe sex, smoking or taking drugs. A fear appeal stimulates emotional reactions by linking negative consequences with a failure to accept the message's recommendation. "If you don't buckle up, you'll die." An effective fear appeal has several important elements:

1. **The fear appeal establishes a threat**. For example, the "Crash Dummies" TV commercials demonstrate the threat of what will happen to our bodies if we don't buckle up.

2. **The fear appeal shows that the threat is real for the receiver. For the fear appeal to be effective,** listeners have to see that the threat could actually happen and that they are vulnerable. For example, several safety belt campaigns show testimonials from real people about their friends dying in traffic crashes. The people and the stories are real to show that the threat is real.

3. **The fear appeal should show that the proposed action will stop or reduce the threat.** Buckling up will solve the problem is the message from the crash dummies. The commercials show the dummies in a crash with and without the belts. The dummies are fine when they wear belts and all smashed up when they're not worn.

4. **The fear appeal should show that the proposed action is easy.** Not only will the belt solve the problem, it is easy to use. It only takes a couple of seconds to snap a safety belt. And the belts are adjustable to make sure they're comfortable for any body size.

5. **The fear appeal should show that the proposed action is doable.** Cars used to be made without seat belts. To tell someone to buckle up and that it's easy is great, but if there are no seatbelts in the car the proposal is not very doable. An effective fear appeal should show the steps necessary to comply in a way that makes each step seem capable of being performed.

To summarize, when someone plays a card to persuade the other to change, it evokes a **psychological response**. The message might threaten or reinforce a basic human need; it might stimulate a perceived inconsistency; or it might evoke fear and emotion. Research in these areas tells us what the likely response will be. If the card threatens someone's need for security, the other might want to know how to avoid that. If the card **creates inconsistency**, the other will want to know how to resolve it easily and quickly. The same is true of a fear reaction. When the audience is scared, they want to know how they can feel secure once again. The key is knowing in advance what kind of psychological reaction you are likely to get from the listener when you play a card. That means understanding as much as possible about the listeners' attitudes, beliefs and values—their **filters**.

Social Motivations for Change

In addition to psychological reasons to change, there are many social reasons why individuals might choose to comply with a request to change. In terms of psychological needs, we've already seen that the need to be included in some group or belong to that group is fundamental for everyone. That need is a private, internal drive innate within everyone. As the individual looks beyond his or her specific personal needs to the environment, some additional social motivations begin to asset themselves. Let's look at these social motivators.

Social Norms. Perhaps the broadest form of social influence is a social norm. A **norm** is a behavioral expectation, or social rule that members of a group or society use to define appropriate and inappropriate attitudes, beliefs, values and behaviors. As we reflect on what we think or do we try to figure out if it is acceptable or not to people that matter to us. "Is that how we do things around here?" is a question that reflects whether we're operating within the rules or outside the rules as we perceive them. Remember in the first chapter when we talked about constitutive and regulative rules for playing card games? These rules are really social norms and they tell us when we are in bounds or out of bounds with respect to our card games. One of the funniest movies I have ever seen is *Borat*. The movie was all about someone from another culture constantly breaking the rules, but people excused him (at least initially) because they perceived he did not understand the rules.

Group Conformity. These norms become particularly powerful when they are made explicit within specific groups or collections of people. As they become more explicit, they produce pressure to conform to the norms—to adhere to the rules. As discussed in the chapter on socialization, we all need to be a part of groups and need to feel accepted by others. At times, however, the need to be accepted can result in taking on the attitudes, beliefs, and behaviors of the group members without considering whether doing so is a good idea.

In a classic study on **group conformity** by Solomon Asch (1956), participants were presented with three lines drawn on a piece of paper and asked to judge which of the lines matched a fourth line in length. The study was conducted in a group setting, where all but one of the participants was a confederate, or someone working for the experimenter. The only real participant was the last person to answer. One by one, the members of the group answered that the same wrong line matched the fourth line. Results showed that most of the participants were influenced by the group and conformed to the majority opinion, even though it was obviously incorrect. Only about one-fourth of the participants were not influenced by the group. In this setting, the norm became very explicit and was repeated over and over again. The same principle applies to dress, language. To be a part of the hip hop culture it is important to conform to these norms, again to show respect to the cultural values.

Social Contagion. Sometimes group conformity becomes so intense that people just cannot resist the pressure. **Group contagion** occurs when individuals within a group behave in a way that would be unlikely if they were not in the group. For example, people are unlikely to stand up in the middle of an auditorium, throw their arms up in the air, and sit back down on their own initiative. But when the "wave" comes around the football stadium, people conform. Within a group, individuals become uninhibited and follow the lead of others. **Contagion** can cause harmless behavior like the wave, as well as disruptive behavior like the crazy social events following some Spartan sporting events when everyone turns out in the streets to celebrate. People get caught up in the moment and do things they would not normally do.

Persuasion Theories

Social Influence Strategies. Several prominent scholars have combined these psychological and social motivations to build models explaining how communicators broadly try to socially influence others. For example, psychologist Robert Cialdini finds that there are essentially six strategies that people use in various combinations to influence one another:

1. **Reciprocity**: One of the more powerful social norms is reciprocity—the expectation that people repay in kind when they receive a gift or favor.

2. **Consistency**: People align their behavior with their stated commitments, particularly when they are public and voluntary.

3. **Social Proof**: People want to be part of the crowd and conform to peer pressure. The use of testimonials from well-liked or famous people often activates this conformity.

4. **Liking:** People like those who like them. Liking increases when people uncover real, genuine similarities between one another. Genuine praise also increases liking.

5. **Authority:** People defer to experts. Exposing expertise that an audience respects builds its perception of the speaker as a subject authority.

6. **Scarcity:** People want more of what they can have less of. When persuaders indicate that an item is scarce or only available for a limited time, they're appealing to scarcity. And research shows it works.

What psychological motivators are at work in these strategies? Scarcity appeals to the fear of withholding physiological or safety needs if the scarce items are perceived as key for survival. **Social proof** deals with our drive for inclusion and the need to belong. **Consistency**, of course, focuses on the need to restore balance and eliminate uncertainty in one's life. **Liking** appeals to reinforcement as we want to be around others who give us rewards of some kind.

The social motivators are also plentiful in these strategies. The idea of social norms is very prevalent in these strategies. Social norms and group conformity are behind the **reciprocity** and **social proof** strategies. Finally, the need to defer to an **authority** figure is a learned reaction as we get reinforced for adhering to authority and punished for not complying.

Theory of Reasoned Action. A second theory widely used in persuasion attempts is a good example of how psychological and social factors combine to influence people. **The Theory of Reasoned Action** argues that persuasion is a result of careful, reasoned reflection about the speaker's key points. The theory contends that:

1. Listeners' intentions to comply are driven first by their general attitudes and beliefs toward the behavior the speaker is seeking to alter, and their specific desires about how much they want to change their behavior.

2. After looking first at their own internal thoughts, listeners then turn to their social surroundings. If they perceive that others who are important to them (e.g., friends and parents) want them engage in the behavior, they are likely to change their behavior.

If the speaker is successful in attracting the audience's attention with the message then the listeners first think about whether they agree with the speaker and like what the person has to say. Secondly think about whether the change would be popular with their friends. Again, the psychological properties of satisfying needs and getting rewarded for compliance along with the social elements of conformity with norms are reflected in this theory. The key implication for playing card games is good arguments are needed to first change peoples' attitudes and then make compliance a popular, socially acceptable choice. Take careful note of the order of these recommendations. Make good arguments and then make them appear popular.

Elaboration Likelihood Theory. A third theory does not take for granted that people will automatically listen carefully to a speaker's message. In fact, this theory says that the amount of persuasion that the speaker achieves depends on how well the audience really listens to the key arguments. If they listen, they are more likely to change their behavior. The key elements of the theory include:

1. The more listeners **elaborate on**, or think about a issue, the more they will change their opinions about that issue.

2. Listeners can listen, or mentally elaborate on an issue in two ways. **Central elaboration** means that they weigh the issue carefully and extensively—they give it full consideration.

3. **Peripheral elaboration** means that they use a simple decision rule to judge the message, such as appearance or credibility. If they believe the speaker is not credible, the messages are not interesting, or the concept is too weird, they will not listen, nor will they change their minds about the issue.

Basically, the **Elaboration Likelihood Theory** argues that people must find the speakers and the information sufficiently rewarding that they are willing to listen and pay full attention. So, picking out a topic on a card aimed at influencing others should be done very carefully. The topic and the style must be attractive and rewarding to the audience if the idea or the persuasive attempt has any chance of success.

Social Norming Theory. This theory builds directly on the powerful idea that people need to conform to social norms.

1. When deciding how to behave in most situations, individuals try to locate a **social norm** to help guide their behavior. What's normal, what are the rules and expectations that are guiding the behavior of other group members? Once the individual locates those norms they are motivated to comply with them to fit into the group.

2. Once the individuals have located the norm, they look to see if the norm provides a lot of flexibility in how to act, or is very restrictive. If the norm is perceived as flexible, people feel they have permission to behave sort of any way they want to behave. However, if the rules are perceived as restrictive, the individuals will have a difficult time breaking them.

The Buckle-Up Game is a good example. If people perceive that hardly anyone wears a safety belt, then there is very little social pressure to conform with a speaker's request to wear a belt. "After all, no one else is doing it so why should I," reasons the listener. But if the listener thinks that nearly everyone else is buckling up, then the listener would feel weird not complying with the request to buckle up.

Which Theory is Best? None of these theories is the best in any absolute sense. Each one is used to understand different persuasive communication card games. For example, the **Influence Strategies** are used often to explain how advertising seeks to influence buyers. **The Theory of Reasoned**

Action is used to help health professionals design health campaigns. The theory tells us that a two-pronged approach is needed—attitude change plus social pressure—to change the public's health behavior. **Elaboration Likelihood Theory** is more narrowly focused on explaining how specific attitudes change in response to persuasive messages. In contrast, **Social Norming Theory** is used when it is clear that the audience is misinformed about some important social norm like drinking or engaging in other risky behaviors. The theory points the way for how to change the perception of those norms and reduce risky behavior.

Message Composition

When selecting a topic from a card to play we often don't think much about the structure of the message we use when we play the card. But research tells us that the structure of the message is important for it to be effective. Essentially, the structure of the message depends on how the audience is likely to perceive the message. Let's take a look at some of the key structural issues that will determine your message effectiveness.

One-sided versus two-sided messages. A **one-sided** message presents only those arguments that favor the recommendation that the persuader is making. This type of message is best used when the audience is already in favor of the proposal or they are not well informed about the issue. For example, if the audience is not familiar with the organization you want them to join in your persuasive speech, there is no reason to tell them any negatives about the organization.

However, if the audience has a negative feeling about your organization or your cause, you may want to use a **two-sided message** that presents arguments for your position and refutes or disparages arguments that oppose your group's position. Two-sided messages are best used when the audience is well informed about the issues being addressed or when the audience initially opposes the position being advocated. In these cases, in addition to presenting the advocated position, the persuader will want to counter the possible negative positions by refuting them. The Soft Sell Game is a good example. Once the seller learns that the buyer knows about competitive products it will be important to show how the seller's product outperforms the competition.

Explicit versus implicit conclusions. A good persuasive message will suggest one or more beliefs or attitudes that the audience should agree with or behaviors that the audience should adopt or avoid. The proposed conclusion can be either **explicit**, laying out clearly what the recommendation is that should be adopted or held, or it can be **implicit**, leaving the audience to draw its own conclusions based on the evidence provided by the persuader.

The Party Pickup Game is best played by making the conclusion implicit. The goal of the game is to simply spend time getting to know one another. There is no specific proposal that the person can advocate, or at least any proposal other than, "Let me get you a drink," would probably be inappropriate.

On the other hand, a message attempting to persuade listeners to vote a particular way on a technical proposal related to health care insurance may be more difficult for them to process; it is a difficult, complex issue. In this case it is more difficult for listeners to draw their own conclusions, particularly if new and unfamiliar evidence is presented. The persuader would need to provide an explicit recommendation.

Primacy versus recency. In situations in which two speakers have the opportunity to present opposing viewpoints, is it better to go first or second? The answer depends on the topic being debated. For certain topics, the audience will remember what they hear first. This idea is called a **primacy effect**. When a topic is controversial, it is better to present your arguments first because the audience is more likely to recall the first arguments it hears. Similarly, when the topic is more interesting, when your arguments are stronger than your opponent's, or when the audience is quite familiar with the topic, a primacy effect is more likely to occur. Thus, it is best to present your arguments first in these situations.

In contrast, when the topic being debated is not controversial, uninteresting, or unfamiliar, then a **recency effect** is likely to occur; that is, the audience is likely to remember what it heard last. In addition, if there is a long delay between the messages from first persuader and those of the second persuader, the audience is more likely to recall what it heard last. Remember this when you are playing The Persuasive Speech Game. Give your most persuasive reasons last because most of your presentations will not be controversial. The audience is most likely to pay attention to what you say last, so make it good!

Analyzing the Audience

Throughout this entire chapter we have talked at length about what listeners are likely to feel, to know or believe to be true. The point is that knowing your audience is **ESSENTIAL**. Whenever a card is played with a persuasive message it is important to know: a) The size of the audience, b) demographic information about the audience in terms of their education, income, cultural orientations, age and knowledge of the issue, c) their interest and level of commitment to the issue, and d) whether they agree or disagree with the issue.

Consider these recommendations:

*   If the **size** of the audience is large it is important to be very dynamic to keep them engaged in the message. If it is small, refer to individuals by name or get the audience involved in your presentation to connect with them as individuals.

*   Understanding the **demographic** characteristics of the audience is important because of the filters they are likely to use in interpreting messages. If the **cultural orientation** of the audience is important—that is they are celebrating their ethnicity, or commitment to a cause—then

reference to the cause or showing respect for the ethnicity is vital. The speaker will need to first earn the respect of the audience before delivering a persuasive message.

- If the audience is **hostile** to the speaker's message, the best strategy is to simply reduce any interference the audience might present and get them to listen to the message. Hostile audiences do not like to listen to opposing views.

- If the audience is **critical**, but not hostile, then certainly a two-sided message is vital. Recognizing the audience's opposing views not only shows respect for the position, but shows an understanding of the issues. The main goal is simply to create doubts in the audience's resistance to the persuasive message

- If the audience is **uninformed** about, but interested in the topic, the goal is to provide sufficient information to educate them about the issue so the message can be processed. It is also likely that the speaker is unknown to the audience requiring that the speaker build credibility by talking about credentials, or similarity to the audience so they will listen. Building a sense of excitement about the issue is also important.

- For a **well-informed** audience that agrees with the speaker, the key is being well-prepared to reinforce the group's position with evidence that will be deemed credible. After all, they know a lot about the issue, so being prepared is important.

Careful consideration of the attitudes currently held by the audience helps you to tailor the message appropriately. A good persuader, whether addressing one person or a thousand, will know about his or her audience and adapt the persuasive message according to the attributes of the audience. One way of planning a persuasive campaign is by interviewing a variety of people who are similar to the recipients of your persuasive message. You might want to ask them:

- What are the words, ideas or concepts that come to mind when you think about your topic?
- Why do you think some people support your position? And why do you think some people are against your position?
- Who do you think is for your position? Who do you think is against your position?

You may then probe further, trying to understand how your topic and the position that you are advocating are related to other issues, and how different positions and related issues are tied to different social groups. This knowledge is tremendously important if you are to wage an effective campaign of any kind, but vital when the audience is diverse and the issue is controversial.

Summary

Persuasion involves sending messages that arouse meanings that encourage change. Persuasion is a very specific goal to achieve because everything must line up. People must pay attention to the message, it must resonate with the receivers, and receivers must be able to comply with it. That's a lot to ask.

There are many psychological motivations for change. Not only do basic needs drive our desire for change, but mentally we are also wired to keep all of our attitudes and beliefs consistent with one another. We are motivated to pursue positive reinforcement, avoid punishment, and resolve our fears. Messages that stimulate these reactions are likely to be successful.

We are also driven to satisfy our social motivations for change. We like to conform to social norms, and sometimes get caught up in a contagious event that makes us want to follow the crowd into extreme behavior. Again, messages that move us in these social directions have proven effective.

There are many important theories of persuasion. Collectively they tell us that persuasive messages are likely to be effective when people are given incentives to attend to the message, are given good arguments to change their attitudes and are made aware of social pressure to change.

Creating persuasive messages is dependent on audience needs. When audiences are uninformed, a one-sided message with explicit conclusions and important arguments given at the end of the message works best. When audiences disagree or are informed, then two-sided messages with implicit conclusions and important arguments at the beginning are best.

Above all, analyze the audience. When the audience is well understood it is much easier to craft persuasive messages that will be effective.

Lessons Learned

Throughout this chapter we have taken the position of the sender or source of messages. But, as you know, card games involve multiple people with multiple perspectives. When you play a card the other person must also decide what card to play in response. Persuasion is all about understanding how to structure your card to elicit the intended response from the other player. Based on the concepts in this chapter, here are some obvious lessons learned:

*   **Persuasive card play requires careful thought.** Make sure you understand the audience's views of the topic, what message is most likely to accomplish the goals and what cards should be played in the persuasive context. Persuasion requires careful thought.

- **Plan the kind of psychological reaction that will best motivate the audience to change.** In structuring the message, decide if it is best to reference needs, create inconsistency, deliver positive reinforcement, or simply scare the audience into action.

- **Plan the desired sociological reaction to effect change.** Referencing social norms can trigger conformity needs that are very powerful in changing the audience's behavior.

- **Any persuasive attempt should be theoretically driven.** Decide which theory best matches the occasion. If the audience is hostile, the Elaboration Likelihood Theory tells us the goal is to encourage central processing of the message—getting people to simply listen. If they are receptive to the message, creating logical arguments to change attitudes and build social pressure to conform to norms is likely to be most persuasive.

- **Message structure is important.** Based on audience analysis decide whether the message should be one-sided or two-sided, whether the conclusions should be explicit or implicit, or whether it is best to go first or last with the most persuasive argument.

A Word about Ethics

Once you know something about persuasion, you have a tool that can be used honestly or deceptively. As we have discussed, one component of source credibility is trustworthiness. Anyone known for being deceptive will, in the long run, lose trustworthiness and, therefore, effectiveness as a source. Although there are certainly moral and religious reasons for being honest, there is also a very practical one: We simply do not believe those who have deceived us. In the long run, we should expect deceptive practices to fail. So, be ethical and moral, always!

REFERENCES

Asch, S. (1956). Studies of independence and conformity: 1. A minority of one against a unanimous majority. *Psychological Monographs, 70* (416).

Maslow, A. H. (1970). *Motivation and personality.* New York: Harper & Row.

Chapter **8**
Conflict Card Games

Introduction

Conflict games are particularly challenging, largely because they are emotionally draining and very stressful. Most people tend to avoid conflict. This avoidance often results in parties sidestepping important issues that are critical to discuss for the health of their relationship. In other words, conflict is about change, or a shift in direction. That shift can be troublesome and threatening, but it can also be an opportunity for growth. Let's look at three conflict card games and explore both their dangers and opportunities. These games examine communication challenges at the interpersonal relationships, organizational, and international levels.

The Sniping Game. When intimate couples fight, they are often not very good at it. One of the least productive talk card games they play is the Sniping Game. It involves one person trying to pick a fight with an intimate partner. Perhaps she is really upset about something. She walks into the room where he's watching TV and she yells as loudly as possible, "You bastard!" Then she stomps out of the room. He might sit there and just respond with, "What?" The idea is that she takes a shot to "kill" her target with a remark and then quickly exits. The danger in sniping is that it risks irreversibly damaging the relationship. The opportunity presented by her sniper attack is an opening to address key issues dividing them. This opportunity will only present itself if she stays in the room and tries to work through her concerns.

The Job Review Game. Imagine that you are a veteran employee of a company. You just got called into the boss's office for your annual job review. You anticipate that it will be tense since you and the boss have not been getting along very well. As you walk in to her office the boss seems upset. She begins the conversation by pulling out her full Boss Card and shoving it in your face by saying, "What the hell do you think you're doing? Don't you know that we're in trouble here and all you do is keep sending me bad information about what's going on in the field? That doesn't do me any good. You better straighten up and do your job!" The **danger** in yelling at the employee is that she risks alienating him from working there while also threatening a positive working relationship. The **opportunity** created by her outburst is raising some important issues about his performance and the goals of the organization. Like the Sniping Game, these opportunities will only surface if she calms down and shifts the discussion to the specific issues causing her outburst.

The Diplomatic Slight Game. Politicians play lots of Card Talk games. In 2010, Vice President Joe Biden traveled to Israel for a diplomatic mission aimed at stimulating peace talks between Palestinians and Israelis. One of the big issues impeding peace is the development of Jewish settlements in East Jerusalem, which the Palestinians claim as their capitol. The day Vice President Biden arrived, the Israeli Prime Minister announced more government-supported settlements in East Jerusalem, which U.S. officials took as a slap in the face to the Vice President's peace mission.

A few weeks later, the Israeli Prime Minister visited Washington and President Obama did not have dinner with him, which the Israeli press interpreted as a rude **diplomatic slight**, or insult. Normally the President would have a state dinner with the Israel Prime Minister, but President Obama chose not to. Was he trying to send a message by playing his President Card? The **danger** presented by President Obama's diplomatic slight is a less cooperative relationship with Israel. The **opportunity** presented by the slight is increased motivation to help each country decide what kind of relationship they want to help bring peace to the Middle East: To take advantage of that opportunity they would need to address the issue directly and not run from it.

Conflict Defined

To understand these games let's first see how they qualify as conflict. There are five elements to defining a Card Talk exchange as a conflict:

An Expressed Struggle. Each of these games reveals a struggle that all parties recognize. We are not talking about conflicts that only one person acknowledges. These conflicts are out in the open. All parties involved must see that a conflict has emerged and have a stake in its outcome.

Between Interdependent Parties. Notice that in each of the examples, individuals are highly involved with one another; either as relational partners, employer/employee, or as individuals involved in a diplomatic exchange. One of the factors that feeds conflict escalation is the difficulty of walking away. The more **interdependent** parties are the more they can **impact** one another personally and even economically.

With Perceived Incompatible Needs and Interests. All conflicts involve issues related to both social identity needs *and* material interests. Let's first explore the social identity component since it is the most challenging to address. Recall from Chapter 3 focusing on **Social Identity** that we talked about how people build an identity to enable them to satisfy their social needs for **inclusion** (being respected by the group), **control** (getting people to listen), and **affection** (getting people to be nice). Every time someone plays a talk card, we evaluate the extent to which the card supports or threatens these three needs. Would you feel disrespected and personally offended if your boss yelled at you like in the Job Review Game? If so, then you would feel that she attacked your **social identity** because she denied your needs for inclusion and affection. **Needs-based conflicts** like this one become very emotional quickly because people feel personally attacked. Your positive and negative face needs have been denied and you may try to strike back to restore them. This **attack-defend cycle** is what makes conflict escalate.

Also notice that in the Job Review Game the boss raises the **material interest** issue of how the employee is communicating with her. She complains about not getting sufficient information. If she had raised that interest without first attacking the employee's social identity, they could have talked about it more calmly and constructively. But, she chose to yell. In conflict, satisfying our social identity needs is mandatory. **These needs are not negotiable**. We must satisfy and defend them. Material interests are different. **These issues are negotiable** since there are many ways to resolve them. All conflicts contain issues related to social identities and material interests, and therefore, ave the potential of getting out of control if parties only focus on identities. The key is to keep the conflict focused on the material interests and away from social identities.

And Perceived Interference. Not only do parties perceive that they have incompatible identity needs and material interests, they also perceive the other is actively **interfering** and standing in the way of satisfying these needs and interests. After all, if you perceive that the other is showing disrespect, then that person is interfering with your right to be addressed in a respectful, honest, and pleasant manner. This perceived interference was a big factor in the Diplomatic Slight Game the politicians played. By announcing settlements in East Jerusalem, the United States perceived that the Israelis were actively interfering with the peace process. The Israelis refuted this perception by claiming the announcement was purely coincidental with the Vice President's visit. Whatever the case, perceived interference played a big part in the dispute.

Problem Solving vs. Conflict. It is important to note the difference between problem solving and conflict. **Problem solving** involves the first three parts of this definition. We have a problem when we have an expressed struggle between interdependent parties who perceive incompatible needs and interests. In problem solving, there is no perceived interference since both parties are trying to help each other resolve the differences. However, a situation **escalates to conflict** when the **perception of interference** becomes clear and obvious. Most interference appears in the form of social identity attacks. Showing disrespect, not listening, or being rude is a sign that the other is less interested in helping you address your material interests and more interested in attacking your **positive** and **negative face**.

Conflicts Are Stressful

Social Identity Protection. People often run from conflicts because of the potential dangers involved and because they are personally threatening. This sense of personal threat is created by the sense of perceived interference. Take a look at the conflict games described above. All of them involve someone "yelling" at someone else. In each case, this yelling (metaphorical yelling in the case of the Diplomatic Slight Game) is viewed as a personal attack. In the Sniping Game, the woman attacks her boyfriend, probably in response to something that he did that she perceived as an attack on her social identity. In the Job Review Game, the boss yells at the employee and in the Diplomatic Slight Game, the Israeli Prime Minister perceived that President Obama disrespected him. When social identity needs are violated though, it's like telling someone that he or she is not a good person. To protect our social identity we often strike back to restore positive and negative face needs. We want to look good and we do not want to be controlled.

Disputants can reduce stress by simply **granting positive and negative face** needs and focusing on material interests. This is not a simple task because face issues are always present in communication and they are particularly important when parties perceive any interference from one another. Later in this chapter we will talk about using constructive conflict strategies for taking advantage of the opportunities presented by the conflict.

Surprise. Conflicts often arise from some triggering event that was completely unintentional. Although it may seem that we have done nothing to provoke a dispute, people in conflict with us can usually point to an incident that set them off. We are perceived to have done something that was unacceptable. As in the Diplomatic Slight Game, the offending event was a statement about settlements in East Jerusalem. This announcement caught the U.S. Vice President by surprise without any warning that such an announcement might be coming.

Scarce Rewards. People often become emotional when they are afraid. Fear becomes a factor when people really want something and they cannot get it. Or when people are trying to protect something they already own they become afraid. You can imagine that the boss's yelling at the Job Review Game was driven in part by the boss being afraid of losing an important contract. That fear probably caused her to get emotional and attack the employee. Conflict can also emerge from being denied resources others have which people feel they need or deserve. When people believe they have been deprived relative to others, they can respond aggressively. Those who have resources will likely defend their right of ownership and resist giving them up without compensation.

Personal Values. Values are a person's thoughts about what "should be." In a sense, values are goals that we want to achieve and we often expect others to pursue them as well. This means that when another's behavior is perceived to be inconsistent with our own value system, conflict can occur. If you think about it, our values are very personal. We often integrate them into our self-concept and they become a part of our identity. Anyone who attacks your values attacks you personally. In the Sniping Game, the woman probably yelled at her boyfriend because he violated some key value that she held strongly and she took the violation as a personal attack. Conflicts over values are difficult to manage because people often view values as non-negotiable. Moreover, we often imagine that individuals who hold different values from our own are extremist and biased.

Strongly Held Beliefs. Beliefs are perceptions of what's true or not true about someone or something. Where values are focused on what "**should be**," beliefs concern what "**is**." People become attached to their beliefs, and will often only look at things that are consistent with those beliefs. When others challenge strongly-held beliefs, individuals become very emotional. Again, it is almost perceived as a personal attack. The United States **believes** that settlements in East Jerusalem will hurt the peace process. Thus, any announcement like the one delivered by the Israelis is filtered through that belief. Combined with the fact that it was a surprise announcement caused a great deal of emotion.

Relationship Differences. When individuals display a card style that implies a different definition of the relationship than was expected, conflict can become emotional. For example, in the Sniping Game, the woman clearly was upset about something. The most common conflict in intimate relationships is the issue of commitment. One party is perceived to be more committed than the other party. In this case, she may have been more committed than she perceived he was, causing her to snipe him in a cursing fashion. Relationships are very personal since we give so much of ourselves. Interdependence grows and grows as people become more involved socially and intimately. As a result, **any conflicts about relationships can be emotional.** There is so much at stake personally, socially and even economically.

Opportunities Created by Conflict

It is difficult to grasp that conflict stirs up about as many **opportunities** as dangers. Most people have difficulty seeing these opportunities simply because of the personally threatening nature of conflict. It takes a great deal of courage to face conflicts in a way that exposes the opportunities. Let's look at several opportunities that the three conflict games present to the disputants.

Facing Important Problems. Perhaps the most important opportunity created by conflict is that it often forces **individuals to become aware of their problems and respond to them**. It is a force for change. Just as pain makes us aware that we need to take care of our body, conflict signals that something is wrong in our social world. It alerts us to take action before things worsen. Can you hear the pain the woman playing the Sniping Game is expressing in her voice? Her style is very negative and forceful. The opportunities she presents include redefining their intimate relationship and perhaps strengthening it. He may or may not choose to play the game and take advantage of her caustically stated offer. If he does play his Boyfriend Card in return and asks her about the problem using a **positive, low-power style,** he will keep the issue focused on the material interests and less on face needs.

Providing a Tension Release. Second, **conflict can serve as a release for tension**. The sniper also releases some tension by playing the Sniping Game. The issue she was facing was probably causing her a great deal of emotional trauma. Getting it out in the open helps relieve the tension, while also giving her an opportunity to face the issue directly rather than stew about it.

Exposing Problem Solving Alternatives. Third, **conflict can make us aware of alternative ways of doing thing**s. The Diplomatic Slight Game provides a key opportunity for each of the significant parties in the Palestinian-Israeli dispute to address the issue of settlements. Since this is such a key **material issue** in building peace, the perceived slight presents an opportunity to take on this issue directly. What are some options to both manage the settlement issue while still working toward building a Palestinian homeland, a goal articulated by all sides in the conflict? Expressing diverse and often conflicting viewpoints is a necessary ingredient for effective decision making.

Strengthening Relationships. Finally, **conflict has the potential to strengthen relationships**. The willingness to confront a problem signals a commitment to the relationship. The Job Review Game played by the boss would certainly freak out the employee. Being confronted in that manner violates a number of social identity needs for respect and threatens both positive and negative face. Yet the opportunity she presents is a commitment to address vital material interests related to the business. The boss could have avoided the talk, but she cared enough about the employee and the relationship to try, however clumsy and de-motivating the attempt was. **People who do not care about a relationship are unwilling to expend the energy that is required to solve a problem**. They would rather avoid the issue until a better alternative comes along. Such neglectful behavior can be the prelude to the end of a relationship. In this case he needed to have the courage to face his boss and say he did not appreciate the tone of her accusation, but wanted to know what she was talking about. That is a constructive beginning to a dialogue about how to deal with the issues.

Capitalizing on opportunities presented by conflict involves trying to move up levels of dealing with the conflict by first managing it, then resolving it, then ultimately transforming the conflict into a new, more productive relationship. Let's look closer at these different forms of conflict outcomes.

Forms of Conflict Outcomes

Conflict Management. The term **conflict management** means that scholars and practitioners alike have come to realize that in many cases disputes are rarely resolved. To be resolved implies that the issue is no longer meaningful or relevant to the parties. In reality, many conflicts do not come to such a neat conclusion. Frequently, the end result is simply a standoff. People get tired and just stop fighting. Or the conflict is just too complex and people agree to confront it later. In effect, **conflict management** is focused on the ways in which individuals try to control their disputes—to keep them from getting worse or holding them off until another time. The Diplomatic Slight Game was never resolved in any meaningful way. The parties simply acknowledged their frustrations and concerns about the issue of settlements in East Jerusalem but there was no attempt to formally address the settlement issue and certainly no formal resolution.

Conflict Resolution. On other hand, when parties are ready and motivated to address their issues, they enter into a discussion that specifically focuses on the dispute with the intention of resolving the issues. The process might involve a third party mediator or someone to help define the issues and develop strategies for dealing with them. This is the point at which **conflict resolution** begins. Both parties have taken ownership of the conflict and develop a plan address it. When she played her Boss Card in the Job Review Game, the boss certainly expressed her frustration. If the employee simply walked away, he would have avoided the conflict. This would have managed the conflict for him. If he stayed and started playing his Employee Card and talked about the material interests with the intention of identifying and dealing with her concerns, then he would be engaging in **conflict resolution**.

Conflict Transformation. Disputants might be satisfied with resolving the issues and walking away from a dispute with some specific agreements for doing things differently. For example, the employee might agree to change his approach to the job and the boss might agree to change her style of communication and her task demands on the employee. Those actions would simply resolve the conflict. But, they would not have **transformed** their attitudes about one another or used the conflict to **restructure** the workplace to make it more productive. When people use the conflict and take advantage of the opportunities it presents, the conflict can be very **transformative**. They can confront both their social identity-based issues and their different material interests and create an entirely better outcome.

For example, during much of its post-colonial history, the country of South Africa lived under a system of **apartheid** or legal segregation in which the Afrikaner National Party Government, ruled by whites, forced Blacks (people from sub-Saharan Africa or Indian descent) to live separately in extreme poverty during this period there were horrific crimes against the Black population. When **apartheid** ended in 1994, the new **National Unity Government** had to decide whether or not to prosecute those who committed crimes against the blacks during this period.

Nelson Mandela, the newly-elected president, decided not to prosecute since the country would be bogged down for decades focusing on the past. Instead of having his country suffer under the burden of **conflict resolution,** Nelson Mandela and Archbishop Desmond Tutu decided to create the **Truth and Reconciliation Commission** and work toward **conflict transformation**. The Commission allowed people to go free if they openly confessed their crimes in public and asked for forgiveness. The effect of the Commission was to **transform** the society because they confronted their past head-on and decided to build new relationships among citizens that would allow their country to grow and prosper.

Constructive vs Destructive Conflict

This discussion about the dangers and opportunities of conflict and the possibility of transformation suggests that conflict is not necessarily something to be avoided. It is something to be channeled into embraced and handled effectively. Conflict is an opportunity. When is conflict constructive and when is conflict destructive?

Destructive Conflict. Conflict is more likely to be destructive to the disputants' relationships and to their ability to resolve or even manage their conflict when they approach a dispute using a **negative frame of reference**. A negative frame of reference is an attitude that says, "I want to protect what I have at all costs; I want to do what it takes to win the conflict and prove that I am right and can't be pushed around." It is not about standing up for your rights, which is certainly appropriate; it is about trying to defeat the other person as a means of saving face or looking tough. **Sniping** with no intention of following up is a personal attack aimed at making the other person look bad. It is an attempt to get even and restore **positive face** by standing up to the other person.

A **positive frame** of reference takes a different approach. Whereas a negative frame focuses on conflict **dangers** and tries to minimize them by striking back at the other person, a **positive frame** focuses on **opportunities**. It says, "Hey, I might as well focus on what I can gain from the situation and look ahead to a better future rather than trying to protect the past." As we shall see later, it is the foundation of **constructive conflict**.

Now that you know about what motivates **destructive conflict**, what does it look like? **Sniping** is one of the best examples of destructive conflict brought on by a negative frame. It is one of several negative conflict management games that can trap people into a negative downward spiral. In addition to sniping, here are several other cycles that research tells us will negatively impact a relationship:

- **Skirting** is avoiding controversial topics. Avoiders and accommodators often ignore or try to get around tough issues by changing the topic or blowing off a comment with humor.

- **Personalizing** involves accusing the other person of causing the conflict with some negative personality trait such as being inconsiderate, insensitive, or uncaring. This is destructive because it assumes the person cannot change and shoves 100 percent of the blame in his or her direction.

- **Complaining** involves repeating old problems over and over again with no attempt to really get to the underlying issues and resolving the problems. It is similar to sniping, but at least it brings up some specific concern whereas sniping is simply throwing insults at another person to cause emotional pain.

- **Aggressing** means attacking the other person either physically or psychologically so the aggressor can bolster his or her positive face or even repair negative face. Attacking someone usually involves accusing them of lying, cheating or possessing some other character flaws.

Constructive Conflict. In contrast, constructive conflict is focused on at least resolving the conflict and possibly using it to **transform** the relationship or some other important outcome associated with the parties' interdependence. It begins with a **positive frame**, or attitude that looks at conflict opportunities as a potential force for change.

There are two major elements associated with **constructive conflict**. The first is recognition. For conflict to be constructive it begins by **recognizing the impact** the conflict has had on the other person both materially and emotionally. This begins to pull the focus away from the individual and reflecting on their own wants and fears, and more toward looking at the other person and what he or she is going through with the conflict.

This **recognition** sets up the ability to collaborate. The process of **collaboration** involves each person recognizing the other's goals in the conflict and helping work toward achieving those goals. It means building creative solutions that can get both parties what they need from the conflict and possibly transform the conflict into really satisfying outcomes for both parties. It begins by not only having a **commitment to learn** from the other person, but **understanding the important problem** that is driving the dispute that he or she must solve to transform the conflict.

As you look at the Job Review Game, what is the boss's main problem? Perhaps the boss is simply frustrated with the lack of progress in the business and she's taking it out on the employee. It might be that the boss feels disrespected on some issue. The employee's job is to figure out what is really troubling the boss and addressing that issue. Notice how much that involves **recognizing** the conflict from the boss's perspective.

The second element of constructive conflict is **empowerment**. When we are empowered we have the skill and courage to take on the conflict. I feel I can talk about my issues and stick with the discussion to resolve and possibly transform the conflict. Some key communication skills necessary for effective Card Talk games are:

- Listening to the other's position;
- Speaking respectfully by talking about your views on issues and keeping away from personal attacks;
- Being able to generate creative solutions to both parties' problems; and
- Working through a specific process for structuring the discussion so it does not get off track.

Generally when people begin a conflict talk card game like the Sniping Game or the Job Review Game, they will begin by identifying their differences. They will talk about how they see things differently and how they want different things. That's constructive. Parties need to understand their differences. Once those discussions have taken place, they can begin to address the future and what brings them together. That process of integration is about identifying issues and generating options to address those issues. Do not get concerned if you are beginning a conflict and you are focusing on differences. That's to be expected. Once those differences have emerged, then the issue is: How can you integrate your interests and come up with creative solutions to **build value** that both of you can use to create positive change?

In fact, constructive conflict is all about **building value**. Value is perception in your mind consisting of two elements: a) How well was I able to solve my problem and b) the cost of the solution. If both parties were really happy about how you jointly solved your problem and the hassles were minimal, then you created value. Building value takes a **commitment** to spend the time necessary to create these **win-win solutions**.

Conflict Communication Style

This discussion lays out a path toward dealing with conflicts **constructively**. Personally, to take advantage of conflicts, you must first be willing to a) **confront** the conflict and, b) use a communication style that allows you to listen attentively and work through the issues. These are the key elements of empowerment. Below is a short survey of your **Conflict Communication Style**. For each question give yourself a score of 1 to 5 using the scale below:

1 = Strongly Disagree, 2 = Disagree, 3 = No Opinion, 4 = Agree, 5 = Strongly Agree

Conflict Communication Style Questions	Score
1. I try to act in a friendly manner when confronted by a conflict.	
2. When in a conflict, I try to repeat back key points the other person says.	
3. I seldom interrupt the other person during a conflict.	
4. I am extremely attentive to the other person's ideas.	
5. I am an open communicator when communicating during conflict.	

6. I make sure to be well prepared on the issues before I discuss them.	
7. In most conflict situations, I explore the full range of issues.	
8. I usually give many good reasons why the other person should accept my ideas for dealing with the conflict.	
9. I try not to rush to a conclusion before the issues have been explored.	
10. I make a conscious effort to understand the other party's most important problems and issues.	

If you scored **under 20**, you are **not confident** in your communication style in handling conflict. If you scored **above 40** you are **confident**. If you scored between **20 and 40** you are **unsure** about your conflict communication style.

These 10 items assess your ability to manage relational and material issues in conflict. The **first five** items of this short survey focus on **building relationships** by being friendly, attentive, and open as a communicator. If you can achieve these objectives you are more likely to create a more collaborative climate in which to deal with the conflict. It also means you are probably able to manage your emotions and concentrate on the material issues.

The **second five** items address your ability to **understand the issues** in the context of the other's most important problem. Are you generally prepared when entering a conflict? Can you explore the full range of issues, develop them, and make sure they solve both parties' main concerns?

If you scored well on this survey then you are probably more able to confront conflict constructively. The first step in achieving this goal is being able to move through the **stages of conflict** constructively. Let's take a look at these stages and see what the process looks like.

Stages of Conflict

Stage 1: Pre-Confrontation. The pre-confrontation stage constitutes the time between first discovering an event that might have triggered the conflict and initially confronting the other person about it. In some cases, this stage is very short. You see a person do something and you immediately tell him or her about it. A quick response often occurs when you are in charge of someone else's behavior. A parent might play a Dad Card when he sees his child doing something wrong or dangerous. "Hey, Samantha, don't play with the man-eating tiger. He's dangerous." **Impulse** may also cause a person to react quickly. Sometimes another person makes you so frightened, angered or irritated that you play your card without hesitating or thinking. When she played her Boss Card and shouted at the employee in the Job Review Game, she may have done so impulsively.

If you can, it is generally best to take some time to delay confronting the conflict to plan how to handle it constructively. Planning is useful because it allows you to prepare and makes you feel more empowered. What is the checklist that is useful to have in deciding how to confront a conflict; what do you plan for? Consider this list of items that will help develop the conflict more constructively:

- **What are your goals for the conflict, both materially and relationally?** When it's over what would you like to get from it? Prioritize your goals from the most to the least important, and concentrate on maybe three or four or your most important goals.

- **What are the main issues in dispute?** What are the issues you are most concerned about, both related to your material needs and your relational needs? In the Job review Game, the boss is concerned about the employee's performance and more specifically about the quality of the information she is receiving. She also seems to have an issue with trust and perhaps respect, as well. The employee will also have issues.

- **What data can be gathered about the issues?** What do we know about each issue to better assess the problems that need to be solved? Have these issues been a problem in the past? To what extent have prior solutions worked?

- **How should you work through the issues?** Generally it is best to start with some easy issues and then progress to the more difficult ones. The key is not to mix them up. Work through one at a time. It is important to show some progress and show that both parties can work as a team and get something done. That is the key to **building value**.

- **What are some options for addressing each issue?** For each issue it is important to create several options and to determine which ones are most likely to be effective. Disputants should also be ready to develop **criteria** about which options would be more useful than others. Otherwise, all options look the same. Why are some better than others?

- **What is the best time to deal with these issues?** Determine when to talk about the issues and make sure to pick a time that allows sufficient time to talk about the issues and negotiate outcomes. It might also be useful to have an agenda so you can provide some structure to solving the problems. Some conflicts must be handled on the spot; others benefit by picking a date in the future.

Stage 2: Confrontation. A confrontation is the initial statement by a person that something is wrong, or there is an issue to address of some kind. It might the statement that kicks off the discussion and defines the card game as some kind of conflict episode. In the Job Review Game, the employee comes in and gets blasted by his boss! This is a fairly typical confrontation. Most are brief and end in a matter of minutes. In many cases, a person says something, the other responds, and it's over. Perhaps because people have a sense that prolonged arguing can be damaging, they try to keep disagreements short. This brief encounter might just manage the conflict without resolving it. **Planning** might help prolong the episode so it can be addressed more productively.

Although they are usually brief, a confrontation is a **sequence that moves** from an opening statement through extended responses to a closing statement. The opening of a confrontation typically involves a statement about what you wish the other to do or stop doing. The phrasing of the opening statement is critical because it sets the tone for the rest of the confrontation. Starting a confrontation with an insult, command, or accusation attacks the positive image that most people have of themselves and can prompt defensiveness. The boss' outburst in the Job Review Game is a good example. Rather than start with this more destructive approach, she should have used a much friendlier opener to put the employee at ease and solicit his help in solving the main material interests. **Part of the planning process ought to involve thinking about this opening confrontation**.

Stage 3: Reaction. Once the differences have been expressed, both parties then react to one another's statements. In some cases, an explanation is provided for the negative behavior. In effect, the person gets the opportunity to explain his or her side of the story. However, there may also be defensive reactions. A person may respond to the opening statement by denying that anything happened, stating that he or she was not responsible for anything that might have happened, or by blaming the person who is complaining.

Even more destructive, the person may counter-complain by stating that the confronter has engaged in other actions that are equally bad. In effect, the tables are turned on the confronter. Equally upsetting, the person may simply ignore the confronter's complaint. Generally, confrontations are more productive when **individuals acknowledge rather than ignore complaints** and when they provide information about the problem, rather than trade accusations.

Stage 4: Resolution. At some point, people in a confrontation must bring it to a close. One or both parties may admit some degree of guilt and **apologize**, promising never to repeat the action. In other cases, the two individuals may agree to **drop the topic** until some other time, or may even agree to never talk about it again. They may simply "agree to disagree" and leave it at that. Often, parties simply stop talking and leave the interaction hurt, confused, and/or angry. **Simply because the initial confrontation has ended does not mean that the conflict is over**. The goal in achieving conflict resolution or transformation is to extend the resolution stage long enough to work through the issues and the options for solving the problems.

Stage 5: Post-Resolution. Even though a confrontation may be very short, the effects can be **long lasting**. Individuals carry with them memories of what was said that they replay later. They can dwell on perceived insults and become angry. They can think of things they should have said or done and plan their attacks for the next confrontation. Furthermore, conflict may cause individuals to actively question the viability of their relationship. When the confrontation has not gone well, **this mulling makes matters worse**.

If, however, the confrontation ended with the possibility of a resolution, the post-confrontation stage may be **positive and even transformative**. If you played out the Job Review Game over time, there are two possible resolutions. The employee might return an insult, or he might try to constructively work through the issues. Of course, he would not have had time to plan, but he could try to work through the issues on the spot. Since the boss created some relationship problems by insulting the employee, they would need to repair their damaged relationship and work to prevent any future blow-ups. Or, they may simply quit thinking about it. The issue is over.

Summary

Conflict is a struggle about social identity needs and material interests. The key to achieving positive outcomes in conflict is to keep the discussion focused on material interests while **granting one another's needs** for inclusion, control and affection.

Conflict is about danger and opportunity. Each conflict presents both dangers and opportunities to disputants. If they look at a conflict with a **negative frame** and focus only on what they can lose, they will focus on dangers. If they approach the conflict with a **positive frame** and focus on what they can gain, they will start to see the opportunities.

Conflicts are stressful. The stress can be relieved by not attacking one another's **social identity**. Such attacks only cause parties to lash out in an effort to restore positive and negative face.

Conflict presents many opportunities. These opportunities include facing important problems, tension release, exploring creative solutions to problems, and strengthening relationships.

Conflict outcomes range from avoidance to transformation. Disputants can give in to the danger approach and **avoid** conflicts to manage their own stress. They can try to **resolve** the conflict and create specific solutions to address their main problems. They can also **transform** the conflict into a much larger solution that is effective and enduring.

Destructive conflict is relationship focused, whereas constructive conflict is focused on resolving material interests. Avoiding destructive conflicts involves **NOT GETTING STUPID**. Getting stupid means becoming **totally emotional** and resorting to attacks in the form of skirting, personalizing, complaining and/or sniping.

Constructive conflict is about recognition and empowerment. Recognition involves understanding the conflict from each party's perspective. Empowerment means that each party possesses the skills and abilities to work through the conflict constructively.

Your Conflict Communication Style is a key element in empowerment. If you are confident in your style then you are better able to work through the issues that are vital in taking advantage of the opportunities that the conflict presents.

Conflict evolves in stages. The more we try to follow this structure the more likely it is that we will work through the conflict constructively.

Lessons Learned

- **Plan your conflict approach carefully, when you can.** If you know that you will be having a conflict or negotiation over some issue, like buying a computer from someone, or even having a relational discussion with a friend, planning is very useful. Most of us do not like doing it, but research tells us that planning makes conflicts go more smoothly.

- **Communicate in a manner that is sufficiently direct so that your concern is clear, but not so direct that it is offensive.** When you play your card, use polite language ("Please turn down the video game."). Include reasons for your request ("I have to study tomorrow and the noise from the game is making it hard for me to concentrate."). And, include pre-apologies when possible to show respect for the other's face ("I'm sorry to bother you, but the stereo is too loud."). If those fail, you can move to more direct language, but avoid offensive language (like saying, "You suck!"). Offensive language inflames people, as you probably know.

- **Try to understand the other's perspective about the dispute.** Remember the issue of recognition. Recognition helps each party see the dispute from the other's perspective and that helps parties be more integrative in their approach to the issues and solutions. Ask the question, **"Why does he think I'm wrong?"** In doing so, you may discover your perceptions are incorrect. Even if you conclude your initial thoughts are right, you can at least anticipate what the other person may say and be better able to respond.

- **Be clear and committed to your goals but remain flexible as to the means of achieving them.** Typically, there are several ways to meet your needs and you should generate as many alternatives as you can. That way, you avoid becoming committed to a single but potentially losing course of action. Also, you might find one that is acceptable to the person with whom you are in conflict. As a result, everyone wins.

- **Be aware of issue linkages.** Work to remove links that create resistance, and add those that will facilitate agreement. Try to link your proposal to something that the other supports to help you reach an agreement. One common technique for doing this is called "logrolling." When logrolling, a person makes concessions on an issue that is less important in exchange for another person's concession on a more important issue.

- **Be sensitive to the need that others have to appear strong and capable, but be less sensitive to their attacks on you.** This advice can be difficult to follow. It runs contrary to our nature. We must be respectful to individuals we do not like. When we must communicate negative information to another, we must do so in a manner that does not threaten their image. Negative feedback should be delivered so that it does not blame the person, is specific about the problem, and is considerate of their feelings.

- **Always acknowledge another person's complaints.** This does not mean that you have to agree or comply with him or her. You can disagree or present your view of the matter; just do not simply ignore the other person.

Chapter 9
Coordination
Card Games

Introduction

The April 9, 2010, edition of the *New York Times* reported that two days earlier, a 27-year-old diplomat from Qatar, Mohammed al-Madadi, went to the lavatory of the plane that he was riding from New York to Denver and briefly smoked his pipe. He left the remaining tobacco in the trash container and returned to his seat. Smelling smoke, the flight attendant confronted al-Madadi about illegally smoking in the restroom, which he denied. The flight attendant alerted a federal air marshal on board, who then confronted al-Madadi about the smoking. Again, he denied it, but admitted he had a pipe. Al-Madidi then made a joking reference to trying to set his shoes on fire.

Authorities feared a repeat of the December 25, 2009, attempted bombing of a Detroit-bound airliner by a Nigerian passenger who tried to explode a bomb hidden in his underwear. This Nigerian man later said he had been trained by the al-Qaeda affiliate in Yemen.

Within a few minutes after confronting al-Madadi, top Transportation Security officials were on a conference call. The Federal Aviation Administration alerted the pilots of the thousands of flights then in the air of a possible terrorism threat, an FBI team assembled in Denver, and airport authorities positioned fire and safety equipment for the 6:45 p.m. landing. NORAD, (the North American Aerospace Defense Command) scrambled fighter jets to accompany the plane for the final segment of its route. While the plane was still in the air, intelligence agencies checked records not only for al-Madadi but for all the other passengers as well, considering the possibility that a team of terrorists might be on the flight.

This is an amazing example of a how a highly coordinated system of agencies and individuals functioned to prevent terrorist attacks. Before September 11, 2001, there was no system that enabled agencies, pilots, NORAD, and others to take actions that might prevent a coordinated terrorist attack. Hence, the United States was vulnerable to attack because there was no plan to coordinate information resources to make effective decisions and take quick action. Now that system exists and apparently it works quite well.

What does coordination have to do with Card Talk? So far we have focused on how individuals communicate with one another. This chapter begins to expand our vision beyond individuals interacting to groups of people connecting with one another. Again, anytime people send a message they play a card. Imagine lots of people playing cards within the context of a larger group, organization or social network, as the example above illustrates. Not only did the people in the al-Madadi incident play their professional cards, they chose to interconnect their messages to form a network. That is what we are going to talk about now—the process of building communication networks.

Coordination Card Games

Before we define coordination and talk about its elements, let's describe some typical talk card games that are played out in the context of people sharing information.

The Blogging Game. In 2009, Jeff Jarvis wrote a book called *What Would Google Do?* I recommend it to anyone trying to understand the revolution in information sharing that has dramatically altered the way in which every organization does business. The book lays out how Google has learned to exploit the **power of the Internet** by providing free content and services that results in the creation of vast networks of people engaged in common enterprises. For example, Google owns **YouTube** in which people form networks to share videos and other types of entertainment. Based on who you connect with and what you search for, advertisements are targeted specifically to you and the things you like to buy. It is a very powerful marketing scheme, perhaps the best ever developed.

Jarvis became interested in blogging when he experienced frustration with the service he received from Dell on his broken computer. He created a blog that ranted on about his experience. In just a few short days thousands of other unhappy Dell customers read Jarvis' blog and shared their negative service stories as well. Google enabled this sharing just as Facebook is another platform that allows the sharing of personal information. By playing his Customer Card in a blog, Jarvis created a powerful angry customer network that ultimately resulted in Dell changing its service policies.

The Decision-Making Game. In 1985, the space shuttle Challenger exploded about 70 seconds into its flight, killing all eight astronauts aboard. I still remember the day it happened and watching the video over and over again. Perhaps you've seen it on YouTube. The Challenger exploded because the O-rings connecting the sections on the booster rocket failed and allowed fuel to escape during takeoff, which ignited and destroyed the rocket. The O-rings failed because they contracted from the freezing weather in Florida. Building and launching the space shuttle involves many different organizations spread over many different states. The rockets are built in California and other states, the shuttle is launched in Florida, but the launch is controlled at a base in Texas. The National Aeronautics and Space Administration (NASA) office that is in charge of the shuttle program is in Washington, D.C. In several meetings before the launch, engineers in California and Washington state advised their superiors against launching in cold weather. None of that information was received by the decision makers at NASA in Washington or in Florida or Texas. As a result, the decision makers decided to launch the shuttle.

The Prize Bull Game. Richard Feldman and Robert Putnam wrote a book called *Better Together* about how communities have created networks of people to complete important community improvement projects. One of my favorite stories in the book is about a group of merchants in Tupelo, Mississippi (the birthplace of Elvis Presley, by the way) in the late 1940s who desperately wanted to build their economy. Each of these individuals played their Business Leader Cards and had several meetings over the course of many months. By pulling together and discussing their options, they decided to purchase a prize bull and begin a dairy farm. The farm became very successful, which led to many other enterprises coming to Tupelo. To this day, Tupelo is an still an economic engine in Mississippi.

What Is Coordination?

Each of these examples provides insights into what happens when individuals play certain talk cards in the context of large networks of individuals. They end up with varying levels of success in **coordinating** their thoughts toward taking some action. As we shall see, if they had played different cards the outcomes might have been very different. To understand why some of these efforts were successful while others failed, let's first try to understand the nature of coordination itself and what makes it work or fail to work.

Coordination is the process of creating **interdependence**. As people evolve into a team, or need each other to perform some task, they coordinate with one another to accomplish their goals. People exchange both tangible resources such as information, ideas and money, sentiment or the desire and motivation to work together. Coordinating to exchange these resources allows people to build the networks they need to achieve quality outcomes. The point of this chapter is that achieving quality outcomes requires creating the right kind of coordination to avoid outcomes like the shuttle disaster.

Types of Coordination. There are actually three ways to coordinate. **Pooled coordination** involves assembling resources into a central location for later use. If a team of five students was charged with writing a group paper, and each person wrote two pages and stapled them together, that would be an effort at pooled coordination. This approach is useful when people do not need to rely on one another's opinions about the task, and they simply need to assemble what they have into some common location. The Blogging Game is a good example of pooled interdependence. To complain about their computers people were simply piling their gripes into a website. The group of bloggers complaining about Dell did not really have any task to perform other than building a collective awareness of frustrations with their Dell computers.

The second means of creating interdependence is called **sequential coordination**. This method of working together involves passing resources from station to station over time. Think of an assembly line. In the group paper writing example, if the first person wrote two pages then passed them to the second person who built on these ideas by adding a few additional pages, and passed the four pages to the third person who added more material and so on, then they would be using **sequential coordination**. The Decision -Making Game was played using sequential coordination. People at lower levels of decision making had some thoughts and passed them up through successive layers of management who filtered the messages, or just did not pass them along. The results were disastrous, unfortunately.

The third means of creating **interdependence** is **reciprocal coordination**. In this approach, all five people writing the paper would simply sit in a room together or use some online chat tool to share thoughts with one another and decide how to write the paper. Everyone is free to connect with one another to generate ideas in real time in a reciprocal fashion. The key advantage of this approach is that everyone has immediate access to everyone's thoughts, which is very useful in adapting to changing situations. If something changes in the environment a quick meeting can be called and people can decide what to do in response. The Prize Bull Game worked well because people got together in Tupelo and created a plan. That planning would not have been possible using just a pooled or even a sequential approach. The decision to launch the Challenger shuttle should have been done in a **reciprocal** manner with everyone having information about the changing weather conditions in the same room making the decision. Using a sequential approach does not allow people to change rapidly.

Sentiment and Resources. Regardless of what kind of coordination strategy a team uses, its success hinges on the ability to effectively exchange resources and sentiment. Let's look at these two needs more closely. **Resource exchange** involves sharing both information and other, more tangible resources such as personnel, money and inventory. When people give these items to one another, it demonstrates that they are serious about working together. Oddly enough, information is not often perceived as adequate for building interdependence. Perhaps members believe that **information is cheap**, and is really not tangible. The common perception is that if others are serious they will contribute money, personnel or other tangibles to the task. Information is not enough.

Sentiment exchange is the desire or motivation to coordinate. For example, in the Prize Bull Game the merchants of Tupelo made a structural shift in their community by deciding to work together in a reciprocal way to grow their regional economy. Developing that kind of coordination was not easy. It took a few very persistent people to go door to door and visit each merchant and persuade them to join the group. In other words, they had to develop an interest in teaming up. Perhaps out of desperation the merchants developed a **sentiment** toward coordination; they knew they needed to coordinate to grow. Building motivation began by sharing information, money, and other resources and focusing on the tangible benefits of building a dairy industry. If the merchants had not made the case for the potential rewards, then the sentiment to coordinate would be lost.

Two other elements in building sentiment are also key. The first is **open communication**. Individuals working in groups must be open with one another and willing to share any information that might be relevant to the task. Secondly, that openness builds **trust** and encourages more openness. Trust is the perception that the other party is working in your best interests and will always be reliable in helping. We will see later that a **lack of openness** causes people to make poor decisions and mistrust one another.

How Coordination Works

Creating the Network. To perform some task like deciding to launch a rocket or create a dairy farm, a network of people forms. These are examples of **task networks** in which the goal is to get something specific accomplished. I receive several **Facebook** requests weekly to join a group to protest something or contribute to a cause. However, most **Facebook** requests are simply aimed at building **social networks**, the purpose of which is to make social connections that keep people up to date on one another's personal events. Sometimes these networks form rather quickly while others take forever to gel.

Developing a Coordination Strategy. Once the network is created the group must decide on a **coordination strategy** to accomplish its goals. Is either a pooled, sequential, or reciprocal approach best? It would have been great if the NASA people had asked this question prior to deciding to launch the shuttle. Unfortunately, they simply used the **sequential** approach in which a lot of information was lost as it passed from one station to the next. They needed a **reciprocal** approach in which everyone with key information had an opportunity to share it.

Developing Links. Once the network is in motion and people are playing their cards and exchanging information, they develop **communication links**. A **link** is a two-way channel of communication—a pipeline that connects at least two individuals. Links have three properties that are important. First, how strong is the link? A **strong link** is one in which the individuals use it frequently to exchange information. That frequency is related to the purpose of the network. If the network is social, perhaps an exchange of daily information is frequent whereas a weekly exchange would be infrequent.

Second, what is the **content** of the information exchanged through the link? The content might be **task-related** in which people are making a decision about launching the shuttle or creating a dairy farm. Or, the link might be **social** in which people are updating one another on personal information. The link could also be used to share ideas about improving **innovation** within the team. These three kinds of links often form very different looking networks. The task and innovation links tend to form networks around the roles people serve in the groups. Managers talk to other managers and employees talk with other employees. Communication is more horizontal. **Social networks are more fluid**. People share information up and down the organizational hierarchy depending on who their friends are and what information they have to share.

Third, what **channels** are used to create different networks? Since the NASA people were spread out, they used the phone to communicate across their various sites because the Internet and email had not yet been invented. For creating the dairy farm, the Tupelo merchants used face-to-face communication for their networks. If you examine the various networks in which you participate, you will notice great differences in channel use. You may use face-to-face for your **task networks** and more **electronic communication** for your **social interactions**, for example.

Network Descriptors

Now you have a picture of the three kinds of networks that form when groups of people communicate (task, social, and innovation), and an understanding of the three kinds of coordination they use within that network (pooled, sequential and reciprocal). We have learned that the shuttle disaster might have been prevented if NASA had used a **reciprocal approach** rather than a **sequential approach** in sharing task information. And, we now have an understanding that the Tupelo merchants were successful because they used reciprocal face-to-face networks to build **sentiment** to create a dairy farm and build their community.

If you think about what these networks might have looked like as they were evolving, they probably had very different appearances. Imagine the NASA network in which people inside the different contractors communicated frequently with one another, but there was very little communication between contractors. The people in California talked to each other but they didn't interact frequently with people in Florida, Texas, or Washington. That network would look like a series of little balls of activity that were not connected.

Now imagine the **Tupelo** network. If you plotted the connections between merchants as they planned the dairy farm, the network would look very busy with lots of frequent connections between people on all three levels. These people shared information about the **task**, about **innovative** ideas, and about **social** news since they all knew one another in this small town.

We can use three terms to describe these network differences: **integrativeness**, **reachability**, and **dominance**. A thoroughly **integrated** network is one like the **Tupelo** model in which everyone shared information in a reciprocal manner, in contrast to the sparsely integrated **NASA** network in which few groups talked outside of their own companies in their own states. **Reachability** refers to how easy it is to reach any one person in the network. In a thoroughly integrated network like the Tupelo merchants, each person was immediately reachable by any other person in the group. They used reciprocal coordination, and all were busy working hard at building the dairy. But, in the sequentially organized NASA network, people were very separated. If a person in California wanted to reach someone in Florida, he (they were mostly men) would need to go though people in Texas and then in Washington. In this case, reachability was low.

Dominance refers to how much the links are controlled in a central location. In a **completely integrated** network, each person is immediately reachable by any other person. In that case **no one individual dominates** the network. Everyone has the same number of links. But, imagine a network in which one person connects with everyone else in the group, but the other members of the group only talk individually with that one person and no one else in the group. The **person with multiple links** would dominate the network since that person has a disproportionately large number of links in comparison with everyone else. Perhaps you know someone who is in touch with everyone else, but the other members of the group do not talk with each other very much. That person **dominates** the network.

Do you think that social networks are more integrated than task networks? Do you think task networks are typically dominated by fewer people than are social networks? The answer is "**yes**" to both questions. Social networks tend to be more egalitarian. Everyone talks with everyone. There are few restrictions and few rules. In contrast, task networks are more regulated. People who are knowledgeable or are given leadership roles tend to dominate the structure of the network giving it a very different structure.

Because social networks are more integrated, people are more directly reachable, and there is less domination. Wise managers will nurture these social networks and help them grow. Some businesses are creating opportunities for employees to volunteer for community projects on company time to build social networks among the volunteers. These networks open up communication in general and create trust among members. When it comes time to coordinate managers can take advantage of this sentiment because people know how to work together as a team to get work done.

Communication Roles

Not only is it important to understand how individuals are linked in networks, it is essential to understand the roles they play in communication networks. There are basically three communication roles that people can play in any given network. The first group of individuals, labeled **non-participants**, has relatively few communication contacts with others. They are members of the organization but they just do not contribute in a noticeable way. Another word for these individuals is **isolates**. They are isolated from others, basically doing their jobs, but they just do not connect into the action very often.

The second group, labeled **Participants**, are very frequent communicators **with others in their group**. These within-group communicators form intense interaction patterns that serve to label them as an active group. These individuals stay within their groups and do not venture out often or connect with people from other groups.

The most important communication role in a network is the **liaison**. These individuals link two or more communication groups, while not being a member of any one group. Serving as **linking pins**, liaisons make sure that groups communicate with one another when needed to improve coordination. They bridge relations between units within an organization. A good example of a liaison is an account executive at an advertising agency. That person directs all efforts of the advertising agency to serve the client. They link the different units in the advertising agency with other units in the client company. They are generally very skilled communicators and may be perceived as friendly and attentive. **Liaisons** generally promote a **positive working climate** and are often responsible for the successful coordination of organizational functions. They also tend to **dominate networks** since they like to communicate and they are good at it, as well.

Liaisons are important when organizations get bigger and divide into more and more groups. A critical job is pulling these groups together to help organizational members better coordinate so they can **adapt to change**. Without them, the organization would be a collection of groups, each going off in its own direction. Typically, liaisons are the most efficient integrating mechanism because of their strategic positioning. Due to their **centrality** and their direct linkages with others, liaisons reduce the probability of message **distortion**, reduce **complexity**, and increase the **timeliness** of communication.

Before its shift toward more collaboration the Tupelo, Mississippi community had very few liaisons that could successfully bridge the different business groups in town. It was not until a couple of key merchants stepped up and started talking to people in different groups that progress accelerated. Soon there were many liaisons that **bridged key community groups** resulting in more and more merchants supporting the dairy farm project. These connectors kept **communication flowing** between community groups and created a whole new communication culture of collaboration.

Inside organizations, why do some people emerge as liaisons and others do not? Quite simply, liaisons are natural communicators; they like to develop open communication relationships with others. And people like to talk to them. They initiate conversations more, opening up communication between diverse groups and they can quickly and creatively process information. In fact, many of the characteristics of a liaison (i.e., **openness, trust, sensitivity to others, and getting a wide array of input**) have also been used to specify the characteristics of more effective managers, and more generally, of open communication **climates**.

The key point is that when more managers become liaisons, the organization is better equipped to adopt **coordination strategies** that better fit the tasks at hand. They **connect** more groups and can better detect the need for change. Organizations need linkers. If NASA had more of them, the **Challenger Shuttle** mission might have turned out very differently.

As networks evolve in communities like Tupelo and organizations like NASA, they begin to develop an overriding communication structure. These structures can either help or hinder an organization's ability to do its job successfully. And, sometimes, leaders **can not see, or do not think about the**

structure they are creating, so they cannot control it. It is useful at this point to introduce this concept and talk about how best to manage the structure to strengthen the organization.

Your Communication Networks

Let's take a look at the roles you serve in the different groups in which you participate. Below are listed a number of different groups in which students might participate. Next to the ones to which you belong, indicate:

- Your role in the group (**isolate**, **participant**, or **liaison**)
- The level of communication integration among group members (**high**, **medium**, or **low**)
- The type of coordination the group uses most often (**pooled**, **sequential**, **reciprocal**)

Organizational Network	Your Role Isolate Participant Liaison	Integration High Medium Low	Coordination Pooled Sequential Reciprocal
Your immediate family			
Your extended family			
Your workspace			
Your dorm floor/apartment			
Comm 100 recitations			
A student organization			
A religious group			
A Facebook/MySpace group			

Now, look at the patterns and consider these questions:

- Do you play a consistent role in these groups? Perhaps you are a liaison in your extended family, at your job, or in a class project.
- Are most of the networks highly integrated or not very integrated? If you are generally an isolate in a highly integrated network, why aren't you participating?
- If the coordination is mostly reciprocal and the networks are not highly integrated, why not? Is there something preventing people from talking with one another?

Network Communication Structures

Over time, network communication patterns begin to stabilize. People find a role they like to play in their communication networks and stay there. Liaisons keep connecting, whereas non-participants remain isolated and avoid interacting with others. Traditionally, researchers have focused on network patterns of information exchange and the manner in which those patterns shape their relationships.

For example, the Internet and smart phones allow managers and team members to communicate directly with one another on a routine basis in real time. This **direct communication** changes the relationship between the parties so that everyone has nearly equal status. Before web applications and email, employees were often forbidden to talk to managers several layers over them. They had to go through supervisors and others to communicate. Customers had the same problem. The information explosion has changed all that. We now live in a world of instant access; that is what employees and customers expect.

Downward Communication. When the communication network is structured so that people in upper levels of management push information down to lower levels, that is called **downward communication**. This type of communication is meant to control the organization and the operations of its personnel. Typically, downward communication messages, since they are official, are very formal, and usually in writing. The most common form of downward communication content deals with **job instructions**. These are usually very direct messages that instruct an employee to perform a specific operation at a particular place. Other types of downward communication might include messages aimed at orienting individuals to the goals of the organization.

Probably the biggest failure in downward communication lies in **feedback about job performance**. Often organizations fail to adopt systematic means of providing members with feedback, such as appraisal interviews about job performance. Employees want to know how well they are doing and where they need to improve, but many organizations operate under the guidelines that no news is good news. According to several studies, excellent companies have the opposite philosophy. They believe that **positive employee recognition** is the best motivator. We know from many studies that **feedback** is essential to improve performance and commitment to the organization. If people have no idea how well they are progressing, they lose interest in the organization, and become isolated in their own interests.

Upward Communication. The opposite of downward communication is **upward communication** (communication from workers to bosses). Upward communication in "**command and control**" organizations like the military tends to be formal, in writing, and flows along the formal chain of command. Without adequate upward communication from workers, management cannot react quickly enough to prevent minor problems from developing into major problems for the organization. Upward communication is often very difficult in these formal "**command and control**" organizations because there are many layers of management between people at the bottom and people at the top. Also, these layers cause status problems. People at the top think they do not have to listen to people at the bottom; so upward communication is often not valued.

However, in more team-based organizations, upward communication is essential. These organizations have only a few layers of people who respect one another's opinions; so information tends to flow more freely. One of the most significant changes that NASA experienced after the **Challenger** disaster was to significantly increase upward communication. Suddenly, people were talking to each other so they might avoid the kinds of communication breakdowns that led to the problem.

Horizontal Communication. The third kind of pattern is termed **horizontal communication**. It occurs at the same level or sideways along the organizational chart. This type of communication is informal, face-to-face, and personal. Since it is much faster and more attuned to the personal needs of communicators, horizontal communication also tends to be used more to coordinate activities. For example, the networks that sprung up in the Tupelo community were essentially **horizontal networks**. Merchants and community people just started talking to one another about how to tackle a particular problem, what tasks each will perform, when the tasks will be performed, and how to keep each other posted as to their problems and progress. This type of communication is very common in a **team-based business style**. Individuals figure out who they need to talk to and simply contact those individuals.

What's exciting about the revolution in communication technologies is that they have significantly flattened out organizational structures by increasing horizontal communication. Most companies have only one or two layers of management and make it clear that a healthy flow of information is important to the health of an organization and its ability to respond quickly to customer needs. In the **Blogging Game**, networks form very rapidly around customer complaints and became very powerful. People from all walks of life contribute and made a pretty loud noise that Dell could not ignore.

Communication Culture

In Chapter 6 we explored how culture impacts communication. But we talked about culture mostly from a national identity standpoint. People from different countries display different communication preferences that are important to know when interacting cross-culturally. This same concept relates to people in organizations. Over time, as their networks become more stable, people develop organizational cultures, as well. Consistent with the discussion in Chapter 6, we define organizational culture as **the framework of beliefs, values, and patterned behaviors that members use to create, maintain and modify their communicative interactions**.

Communication culture serves two key functions: **understanding and regulating**. First, culture helps members to **understand** their work environment, especially the attitudinal and behavioral expectancies. If downward communication is the norm, then the culture probably places more value on complying with authorities than on creating new ideas and sending them upward to management. We might say that this kind of organization has created a **"culture of compliance"** rather than a **"culture of innovation."** So downward communication is understood as more appropriate and upward communication is viewed as inappropriate and maybe even disrespectful.

The second function communication culture serves is **regulating** behavior. If upward communication is interpreted as **disrespectful**, then the organization will likely have rules about who can talk to whom. In these types of places, people are only allowed to talk with their immediate supervisors and no one above the supervisor. The network paths are carefully regulated.

Government agencies like NASA typically create highly regulated cultures that permit only downward communication. To understand the role this highly regulated culture played at NASA, it is important to talk a bit about its history. NASA began after World War II when scientists in Alabama were given the green light to experiment with rockets. These Alabama scientists were viewed as the **"brains"** of NASA. Because they thought they were better than others, they often shunned interaction with other NASA groups. This culture of not valuing input from other states doomed NASA to a series of isolated units incapable of **reciprocal coordination** and adapting to change. This culture lasted for several decades beginning in the early 1950s until the Challenger tragedy.

In NASA's defense, culture is a difficult element to change because people become comfortable within a culture and often resist change; however, after the Challenger disaster NASA was ready for a change. Directors wanted to open up the organization and create a more highly integrated agency capable of building a more responsive program. That could not have happened without a significant cultural change.

Summary

This is a difficult chapter to understand because many of the concepts come from a field called **Systems Theory and Cybernetics**. Look up these two terms in Wikipedia if you want to understand how to take advantage of the tremendous power in communication networks. Here are the key points of this chapter:

The type of coordination that works best depends on the work to be done. When the task requires creative adaptation to change, reciprocal coordination works best. When people just want to collect their opinions for later use, then pooled coordination works best. But, reciprocal coordination is more expensive because it takes more time and resources to implement.

Coordination forms networks. Networks build links among members. Links can be strong or weak, focus on task, social or innovation topics, and be formed and maintained through multiple channels. Social networks tend to be more integrated horizontally, whereas task networks are more vertically integrated going up and down the organization as people need to get their work done.

Networks vary according integrativeness, reachability, and domi-

nance. When an organization is dominated by liaisons working to connect groups of employees, then that organization is likely to be more highly integrated and people are more reachable. Liaisons play a very important role in organizations.

Reciprocal coordination produces highly integrated and reachable networks with low dominance. Sequential coordination is not good at integrating people and making them quickly reachable. So, reciprocal coordination is better for adapting to change.

Networks form communication structures that cause information to flow downward, upward, or in a horizontal way. Often organizations get stuck in these patterns so when they get challenged by a new job that requires changing communication patterns, it becomes very difficult for them.

Organizational culture is a key element in performance. Communication flows create cultures that help members understand how to interpret behaviors and how to regulate their own behavior. These cultures can either help or hinder the organization in accomplishing its task.

Cultural issues played a role in the Challenger tragedy. Since a culture of not cooperating had emerged among NASA units, the sentiment needed to coordinate was not available. That lack of sentiment created a bottleneck in upward information flow and a disincentive for individuals to perhaps play a different card to break away from this tradition and try to build some sentiment.

Lessons Learned

- **The coordination model must match the task.** When the task calls for a reciprocal model then the network must step up and build that model to be effective. That change requires that someone play a Leadership Card and help the team move in that direction.

- **Do not let bad habits dictate the coordination model.** Many times teams or organizations will take on a new task using the same kind of coordination model they have used in the past. In essence, they are making the task fit the coordination model, and not the other way around.

- **Keep information flowing freely smoothly.** It is probably best to err on the side of keeping information flowing smoothly. Information is the raw material of creativity. When it flows, it stimulates creativity. That means constantly monitoring the culture to insure that people want to coordination and share.

- **Nurture the liaison role.** There are many studies indicating that when organizations encourage a few natural linkers to span organizational boundaries and get to know people from multiple units, the organization is better positioned to coordinate more effectively. Helping people create a Liaison Card would be very helpful.

- **Create communication policies that prevent information overload.** The danger of too much information is that it can bury people. When they must manage hundreds of emails a day or labor under constant meetings, they have little time to look forward at big picture issues. It is important to play that Leadership Card and establish policies about how the network should function best to achieve organizational goals.

- **Make innovation talk and upward communication a priority.** Adapting to change requires creativity. But, people will not offer new ideas unless they are asked on several occasions to do so, and they see that the new ideas are actually used and valued. Stimulating new ideas creates a culture of exchange and a sentiment to grow.

- **Information is the currency of the knowledge organization.** This currency should be carefully audited and monitored just like money is watched in organizations. Information that is not managed properly is at best squandered and at worst crippling to an organization's ability to function effectively.

REFERENCE

Jarvis, J. (2009). *What would Google do?* New York: Harper Collins.

Chapter 10
Decision-Making Card Games

Introduction

Chapter 9 makes the point that effective coordination is essential for making great decisions. The Decision-Making Game illustrated the point that once the Tupelo, Mississippi merchants were able to start functioning like a team they were able to make good decisions that ultimately helped to pull them out of their poor economic conditions. The structure they established allowed them to exchange the information required to understand the problem, weigh the options, and select the best choice.

What we skipped in that discussion was a more in-depth analysis of the group decision-making process. Once people start talking there is a whole dynamic that emerges in terms of how the group forms, exchanges information, develops leadership, manages conflict, and ultimately makes a decision. The key issue for you is learning how to control this process to make teams and groups productive. Left on their own, groups can devolve into chaos, as we saw from the Challenger disaster in the last chapter. The whole system collapsed and people lost their lives as a result. The purpose of this chapter is to help you pull back the curtain and see how groups communicate and ultimately make decisions.

To illustrate how groups make decisions, let's look at some typical decision-making games that the many college students play as they move through their college careers.

Decision-Making Games

The College Selection Game. One of the first games you play in your pursuit of higher education is the College Selection Game. Once you make the decision to attend college then the question is where to go. That decision is often complex since there are many factors to consider. Among the most common questions are: Which universities fit your interests best; what does the campus atmosphere feel like; what are the costs and opportunities for employment after graduation? Maybe your parents took you on a college road trip to visit various campuses and talk with recruiters. After these trips you probably sat down with your parents to decide whether or not to apply to the schools you visited, and if accepted, whether or not you should attend. Did your parents lead this discussion while playing their Mom and/or Dad Card and you playing a Son or Daughter Card? Or, did you play a College Student Card and lead the discussion by laying out the pros and cons of each school?

The Move-in Together Game. Do you recall in Chapter 4 when we talked about **Intimacy Games**? Intimate couples often discuss the nature of their relationship and what its future might hold. After couples have been dating for a while and find that they are spending more and more time together, they typically face the decision about whether or not to move in together. In fact, about 60+ percent of couples live together before marriage and it is becoming more common everyday. Unfortunately, couples who move in together before marriage are more likely to get divorced than couples who do not engage in pre-marital cohabitation. So, with the increased likelihood of divorce associated with pre-marital cohabitation, playing the Move-in Together Game well is important. It's a big decision!

Playing this game well requires two sets of cards. In addition to the Boyfriend/Girlfriend Cards to discuss the relationship issues, parties also need a Roommate Card to discuss the logistics and economics of the move. Research indicates that couples are generally biased toward playing their Roommate Cards because what generally drives this big decision is economics. Couples say that since they are spending most of their time at one place they should just get rid of the other apartment and move to that one place.

Is this really the best way to make an important decision like this? Couples should also play their Boyfriend/Girlfriend Cards and discuss the **pros and cons** of waiting until marriage or some other formal commitment is in place and the relationship is on solid ground. Unless all those issues are discussed before hand, making a snap decision to move in together is generally a bad idea.

The Class Project Game. Many classes require students to complete team projects, such as paper or big presentation. These teams are often three to five students in size. Professors typically do not assign roles in these teams so students must decide themselves on how to manage the team's affairs. The typical team struggles with how to proceed and often no one wants to step up and take a leadership role. Students try to play this game with their Friend Card and get by with casual conversation. But, at some point, someone will need to step up and start to organize the group and bring the team together. That requires a Leadership Card to facilitate the meetings and keep the team on task and working effectively. Students typically criticize these assignments because they do not like the responsibility of the leadership role and the group fails to gel resulting in just a couple of students doing most of the work.

To help build a Leadership Card and be effective in a group setting that ranges from making decisions with parents, intimate partners, or classmates it is important to know:

- What does effective decision making look like?
- How do groups function effectively?
- What are some typical barriers to effective group communication?

What Is Group Decision-Making?

Group decision-making is a term that we will use to refer to the process of two or more people picking a solution from a set of alternatives. Decision-making is actually part of the **problem-solving process**, because in the course of solving problems, groups make decisions all the time. Typically, when engaging in decision-making, group members develop this set of alternatives themselves. However, sometimes group members have the job of picking one out of a pre-determined set of alternatives. These alternatives may have been developed by another group or another individual. In either case, the process of selecting an alternative, out of those possible, is the process we will call **decision-making**.

Requirements. For groups to be involved in a decision-making communication event, they must meet four criteria:

First, the group must have a **choice among realistic alternatives**. If you were playing the College Selection Game and your parents were telling you that you had to go to MSU, but they still let you look around at other schools, then you really did not have a choice. But if everyone entered the game with an open mind and you could pick freely among a few schools, then you would have realistic choices.

Second, the group must **take some action** or make a change from the status quo. In playing the Class Project Game your group is required to complete the project; you must take any action or risk failing the assignment. If the group is not required to take any action then members are not in a realistic decision-making mode. They are simply interacting with one another perhaps to just exchange information.

Third, there must be **consequences**. The decision must affect the group or the task in some way. In other words, the process is not academic; rather it's real and everyone knows that the decision will impact the group in some way. There are consequences. The Move-in Together Game has very serious consequences for the relationship. It not only impacts the couple making the decision, but it impacts their families and possibly their children, as well.

Fourth, everyone must be **committed** to live by the changes that the group selects. There is a commitment to action and a desire to actually change. When you began playing the College Selection Game, you were committed to first go to some college after high school, and probably to select one you visited. There would be no reason to just take a tour of colleges around the state or country if you did not intend to go to college somewhere.

Meeting all of these criteria means you are in a **group decision-making context**. But are groups always best for making decisions? Is it possible that groups make worse decisions than individuals working alone? Let's examine this issue in more detail before we move on.

What Makes Groups Productive?

Can you make better decisions about important issues in your life without consulting anyone? What factors **favor groups over individuals** in making better decisions? You can imagine that sometimes assembling a group gets in the way. We've already talked about the Class Project Game and how most students prefer to work alone. But, would working alone produce a better product, aside from just being more convenient for you? Here are the key factors derived from research that determine when groups are more effective than individuals.

Clear Goals. Individuals can outperform a group when the group **is not clear about its goals**. Individuals do not have to deal with anyone else in working toward a goal—only themselves. But groups consist of many members each of whom might have a different goal.

To deal with this problem the group must develop clear, achievable, and measurable goals, and that task typically falls to the group leader. The Class Project Game is a good example. Students must select a project capable of getting a good grade. That is a clear goal that is both achievable and measurable. It might be easier for the student to take charge of the project and to decide the project's goals without group input, but would it produce a better result? When this happens the other students often drop out of the process and let that one student take over. They did not have any ownership because they had no input.

To prevent this kind of collapse, one of the first tasks that the group should tackle when playing the Class Project Game is defining goals. What does the group really want to accomplish and by when? If the group has a **designated leader** then that person should facilitate that discussion to move it along in a focused, productive manner. The chapter talks about how to manage this process later. But for this game, the group only has a chance to perform better than an individual if it collectively establishes clear, attainable goals that members accept and are excited about

Coordination of Effort. A second factor that can make or break a group's effectiveness is **coordination of effort**. To understand this phenomenon we turn to researcher Max Ringelmann, who published an article in 1913, in which he sought to determine if individual efforts can be summed up to yield group outputs. He wondered if in games such as the tug-o-war, every individual on a five-member team could maximally exert 50 pounds of "pull" on the rope, whether all members pulling together would be able to exert 250 pounds of pull.

What Ringelmann found was that as more members were added to the team, **individual effort declined**. While one member was able to pull 50 pounds, adding another member does not guarantee that both can pull 100 pounds together. Indeed, the number is less than that. One person might consistently pull when all other members are concentrating more on getting a firm foothold, or a better grip on the rope. Thus, all members are not exerting maximum effort at the same time; they are not coordinating their effort in the best possible manner. Some people are working at cross purposes from others.

The College Selection Game provides a good example. Perhaps you were not too excited about looking at other universities to attend. You only wanted to apply to Michigan State. But your parents wanted you to add a few more schools to the list just for comparison purposes. Perhaps you visited these schools, but just sat there in meetings with the recruiters not saying much and letting your parents do all the talking. Then, when you got home to discuss the schools, you again sat there and did not say much. You did not pull your weight because you were not particularly motivated to take these trips and consider other schools. So you played your Son or Daughter Card and allowed your parents to play their Father and/or Mother Cards and dictate the flow of the discussion.

Motivation to Perform. As you can see from this last example, a third reason why groups underperform is motivation. Ringelmann claimed that in cases where individuals are given the opportunity to slough off work on someone else, they probably will. In other words, members may not work as hard on their parts of the group assignment if they perceive that others in the group will "cover" for them. If there is **no sentiment to coordinate** or no team spirit focused on **achieving the goal** as we learned from Chapter 9, the group will often fall apart. Or, if there are no **consequences** for failing to meet one's responsibilities, the group is likely to underperform. **Sentiment** and **consequences** are keys in getting people to perform their duties.

Open Communication. Groups work better than individuals when the tasks they are asked to perform are very **ambiguous** (there is no right or wrong answer). For these tasks people can bounce ideas off one another and get the creative juices flowing. Of course, members must be willing to communicate for that to happen. They must feel as if the climate of the group is such that they want to contribute. In other words, sometimes members are rewarded for speaking up and contributing and other times they are punished. That kind of climate can happen in the Move-in Together Game. What if the couple has a history of not talking about important subjects like their feelings about each other, or the consequences of moving in together? They have created a **climate of not discussing these important topics**. That climate compromises the decision making process and puts the couple's long-term viability at great risk.

Role Development and Clarification. Groups also produce better outcomes when everyone is clear about his or her role. Two of the more important roles in a group are task and social leadership. **Task leaders** help develop the agenda, keep everyone on track, keep information flowing, and keep everyone involved. We will talk about effective leadership in the next chapter. **Social leaders** play a different role. Their job is to make sure everyone in the group feels comfortable and respected. They keep things light, ask people if they are happy with how things are progressing and keep people connected with one another. They are the **liaisons** that we talked about in the last chapter on coordination. They link people with their own good nature and interest in talking about others' lives. When groups have both task and social leaders they are generally more effective.

Clear Problem Analysis. One of the key challenges the task leader faces is encouraging the group to shape an understanding of the problem they are trying to solve. Why is this situation a problem, what is the problem, why is it happening, and what can be done to solve it? A common strategy to better develop a course of action is called a SWOT analysis (Strengths, Weaknesses, Opportunities, and Threats). Applied to the College Selection Game, the family working together would list the top three universities of most interest and first explore their strengths and weaknesses. What programs do they offer, what is the atmosphere, what are the costs? Then the family might prepare an analysis exploring opportunities for attending each one including scholarships, likelihood of acceptance, and the prospects of employment after college. The threats analysis might focus on factors that would prevent attending including admission policies, transportation, and funding. Completing this analysis is vital for an effective decision. Typically a **SWOT Chart** may look like this:

Strengths	Weaknesses
Michigan State: Diversity of academic programs, social life, Comm 100 *Central Michigan:* Low cost, close to home, friends attend there *Northwestern:* Quality of academics, small classes, no multiple choice tests	*Michigan State:* Large classes, spread-out campus *Central Michigan:* Limited programs of interest, campus too boring *Northwestern:* Students too liberal for me, Chicago craziness, not safe to walk around
Opportunities	**Threats**
Michigan State: Academic scholarship offer, job opportunities, study abroad *Central Michigan:* Sports scholarship offer, internship opportunities *Northwestern:* Chicago career	*Michigan State:* Need a car but cannot afford it, admission policies difficult *Central Michigan:* Friends are distracting, student loan policies are restrictive *Northwestern:* Tuition costs, admission policies

A Conflict Resolution Plan. What happens if the group members disagree? This is an important question at the beginning of the discussion. For those of you who pursue student leadership opportunities, your leadership should include some kind of plan for when members disagree. The plan might include taking an "**issues time out**" to explore the source of the conflict and work through it, having a vote on key issues, or asking an outside advisor to remedy the dispute. If the group has a social leader, that person needs to be watchful for issues capable of upsetting group progress and bring them to the task leader's attention.

A Willingness to Disagree. One of the significant threats to group decision making is "**Group Think**." Group members tend to conform to the decisions of others. People often don't like to stick out their necks and be different from the group. Over time, this desire to conform tends to close down discussion while also preventing new information from entering the group. I conducted a study several years ago about the optimum level of disagreement in a group for it to function effectively. The research found that at least **10 percent** of the interaction should show some kind of disagreement for the group to be productive. But, more than **30 percent** disagreement and the group risks disintegrating. That's too much conflict. Did you feel comfortable disagreeing with your parents during the College Selection Game? It is difficult to disagree with others in general, but particularly difficult when talking with parents.

Sufficient Time to Deliberate. Information is the lifeblood of group decision making. If the group cuts the process short, there is little time for members to share what they know about the problem and to analyze the problem carefully. Less information means lower quality decisions. Rushing through the process also limits the number of options the group is willing to consider. For any group decision, there should be **at least three options** that are viable and well sorted out. Sometimes groups become dominated by one person who favors a particular approach and cuts off discussion of other options. The **task leader** must prevent this kind of domination since it restricts information flow.

Culture of Trust and Respect. The culture of the group, as we learned from the last chapter focusing on coordination, can have a dramatic impact on the willingness of members to participate. **Establishing trust**, or the perception that others are acting in one another's best interests, enables everyone to contribute freely and openly. Imagine trying to play the Class Project Game in which members created coalitions aimed at ganging up on the leader. **Coalitions** are small subgroups of members who have a separate agenda about what they want to accomplish. Sometimes these coalitions cause culture problems in groups such that people are afraid to open up or trust one another to problem solve effectively. The point is to watch out for the development of these coalitions so that trust and respect are not compromised.

Celebrating Success. It is important to celebrate success as a means of building sentiment or team spirit. If you celebrated your admission to Michigan State University, that was a good idea. Or if you went out for pizza after the big class presentation with your group, you probably felt better about your group experience. These are important milestones to celebrate. Leaders should be sure to take the initiative to acknowledge the hard work of members in accomplishing group goals.

Group Decision-Making Phases

For the most part, groups do not play these communication games in random, haphazard ways. While it may seem that way at times, groups generally go through a series of phases in reaching a decision. Scholars have attempted to identify the patterns of communication that typify that process. Most scholars agree there are four phases that define the process. Let's look at each one and see how they transition one from the rest.

The Orientation Phase. Card Talk in groups often exposes the game-like qualities of group communication. In initial interactions of a newly formed group, members may have difficulty determining which card to play from their hand. Playing the College Selection Game is a good example. Normally kids let their parents make most of the big decisions about things like which schools or religious places to attend, where to live, cars to buy and so forth. Parents play their Mom and Dad Cards while the offspring play their Son or Daughter Cards and go along with the decisions. But, picking a college is different. It is often the first big decision a teen makes and marks the shift from child to adult and from just son or daughter to college student. Now it's time to add a College Student Card to the young adult's hand and take the lead in making the college selection.

The question is can the teen develop the College Student Card and use it in the decision-making process? Topics on the card will include career or personal goals. It will also include information about the various colleges. **Styles** on the card are more **formal** and with **higher power** to asset leadership. During initial meetings when the teen shifts to the College Student Card he or she is asking the parents to play their Advisor Card and not their Mom or Dad Cards. Are mom and dad willing to make this switch? For any new group these Card Talk issues are important to resolve. What cards are people playing and what topics do they want to raise on those cards? Orientation is a time of **social exploration** before people get down to business.

The Conflict Phase. After the orientation phase, groups start to get a little more comfortable with one another. They begin expressing opinions about the problem and what should be done to solve it. This is the phase in which the SWOT analysis would be conducted. When the student plays his or her College Student Card and begins filling in the sections on strengths, weaknesses, opportunities, and threats, the parents might not be able to resist playing their Mom or Dad Cards and jump in with the kind of criticisms parents might make like, "So you want to go to MSU because it's a party school!? If they were playing their Advisor Card, parents would not ask this question in this way. They might raise the issue but it might phrase it like, "Tell me what about the MSU social life appeals to you."

You can see why this is called the **Conflict Phase**. While creating the SWOT analysis and developing options, people will disagree. And that disagreement is necessary if it doesn't get out of control. In fact, if the group is functioning productively, the members will avoid **Group Think** and express opinions that may disagree with one another. Remember the goal of disagreeing between

10 percent and 30 percent of the time in the group? The purpose of that level of disagreement is to insure that the group can pick among multiple options about what to do.

These multiple options are essentially attempts or bids to take over the direction of the group. If the parents insist on playing their Mom and Dad Cards and not letting their teen create a College Student Card, there will be disagreements about which options are best. These disagreements really become resolved when: a) the Card Talk issues become resolved and b) the majority of members support one person's opinions. Reaching that consensus is the point at which the conflict phase ends and the group is ready to make their decision.

The Emergence Phase. During the **decision emergence phase**, conflict declines. By this point, differences have been ironed out, positions have been raised and refuted and Card Talk issues have disappeared. Or, individuals may become quiet as a way of showing their support or even their lack of disagreement. Coalitions that formed to support one position or another disband and specific details of the agreements start to form.

For example, in the College Selection Game, the parents might play their Mom and Dad Cards and gang up on the prospective college student during the **Conflict Phase** regarding a specific college choice. If the student plays the College Student Card and succeeds in persuading them to adopt his or her choice, then a decision will emerge. The parental coalition will break up in this case and rally around their student. At this point the decision has been made and members are ready to reflect on their success making it possible for the group to enter the **Reinforcement Phase** of the discussion.

The Reinforcement Phase. When the group starts reflecting on their success they enter the **Reinforcement Phase**. At this point, group members congratulate one another for their success to celebrate their accomplishments. This is an important phase to embrace for a leader because it helps build group sentiment or morale. The group has been successful, it worked and it can do even better things in the future. It gains team confidence. If task and social leaders are paying attention, they take great pains to celebrate group gains.

How does knowing these phases help you play talk card games more successfully? First, these phases reflect the **natural evolution of a group**; the group naturally wants to progress in this manner and fighting that progression might hinder its ability to perform. Secondly, knowing that groups perform best when they progress through these phases means that the leader does not try to cut off disagreement in the **Conflict Phase**. The leader uses the conflict to sort out the issues so it can move to the **Emergence Phase**. If there is no conflict then the leader has to generate some by proposing different options and playing the "devil's advocate" or intentionally stimulating disagreement. The key lesson is that a leader should keep an eye on the process. Groups can only perform if the process is allowed to work.

Theories of Group Decision-Making

So far, we have talked about when groups perform better than individuals working alone and the phases groups experience as they progress. Now let's take a little broader look at understanding why groups perform as they do by describing some important theories of group communication behavior.

Structuration Theory. When you read the section on phases you probably thought, correctly, that these phases seem really linear. Group meetings often seem more disorganized than the phases suggest. One explanation for your observation is that groups jump around from phase to phase in response to the different rule structures they create as they interact. In Chapter 1, we described how talk games are governed by **constitutive and regulative rules**. Because people play talk games over and over again, they know how to create (or constitute) them and how to keep (or regulate) people from playing them inappropriately.

When couples play their Boyfriend or Girlfriend Card in the Move-in To-gether Game, the discussion will probably be similar to other games they have played about important topics affecting their relationship. They have some experience playing intimate Card Talk games so this new game will have similar regulative and constitutive rules that apply to the new game. What's different about the Move-in Together Game is that it is more difficult to play because they would need both Boyfriend/Girlfriend Cards and Roommate Cards to keep the game on task. The former card is needed to address the **relation-ship** issues (e.g., are we right for each other, are we committed to each other) and the latter card is needed to deal with the **logistical** issues of moving in together (e.g., who pays rent, how will we divide utilities). If they just play one card and not the other they will fail to discuss the full range of issues needed to make a good decision. But, they will try to use the same rule structure for playing this new, more complex game as they have used for other games about their relationship.

An important concept in **Structuration Theory** is the **duality of struc-ture**. On the one hand these rule structures serve as "recipes" for how something is done. There is a recipe for how to have a conversation about important topics affecting the relationship for the couples trying to decide to move in together. They will try to access that recipe when playing the Move-in Together Game. On the other hand, these rule structures are also the prod-ucts of our interaction. We use the rules to understand the game and then as we talk we are recreating the game at the same time. The duality of structure, then, refers to structures being both the **medium** and the **outcome** of our interaction.

This duality idea is important because when we play a talk game we must be aware of both how we're playing it and what the impact of playing it will be. If the parties don't play both Boyfriend/Girlfriend and Roommate Cards well in this game, they will fail to have a productive discussion.

This duality idea also explains why sometimes groups do not progress through phases in a simple and linear manner as they play their various games. As members are involved in the game they might move quickly into another phase, but get the feeling that they're missing something—the outcome they are leading toward will not be successful. So, members double back to an earlier stage that they may have skipped altogether.

For example, our intimate couple may use their Boyfriend/Girlfriend Cards to play a game of "**Let's Talk About Us**." If they feel able to take the relationship to the next level one might suggest moving in together. Then, the game shifts to the Move-In Together Game, and both must add their Roommate Cards to discuss these more complex issues. That shift would require them to double back to an **Orientation Phase** or a **Conflict Phase** to do a **SWOT** analysis of the problem.

Because this switching around happens often it is useful to explore it a bit. The specific path that a group takes depends on various factors or **contingencies**. These contingencies may cause the group to deviate substantially from the ideal linear sequence described previously. These contingencies include:

- **The nature of the task:** when talk games focus on controversial or emotional topics, like values, or games that are ambiguous in that the need for a specific decision disappears, the group is not likely to follow a specific sequence for communicating. Only when the group's task is specific or factual and everyone is clear on what is needed does the group move toward a more linear path.

- **The quality of the leadership:** If the leader of the group does not participate in the interaction and lets the group do what it wants, group members are less likely to keep on track and follow any given sequence. Leaders with an agenda who encourage open communication are more likely to see the group move through a more linear structure.

- **Whether the task is novel:** If group members have little experience with the task they might not know how to proceed so they jump around a great deal.

- **Group sentiment:** When group members like each other a lot they are more likely to play their Friend Cards, which has the effect of people stopping frequently for personal stories and jokes. While this is fun, it tends to force members to jump around in completing the task, unless the leader keeps people on track.

- **Group size:** Larger groups with specific leaders are more likely to use a specific path than smaller groups. When groups are smaller, it is easier to deviate into different phases because any single individual can have more influence over the direction of the interaction than in a bigger group.

- **Cultural norms:** Some cultures, as we have seen in previous chapters, do not like conflict. So, they are more likely to avoid the **Conflict Phase** in their groups. They might simply jump to **Decision Emergence** to conform to the leader's wishes.

Hidden Profiles Theory. A second theoretical perspective tries to explain why some groups are better at making higher-quality decisions than others. Aside from being able to manage the various structures that groups create as they interact, this theory focuses more specifically on what happens when people fail to share information properly.

The theory begins by making a distinction between different kinds of information that people use when making decisions. When members interact they use both **common and unique information**. Common information includes facts that everyone knows. If you are playing the Class Project Game and trying to decide what topic to select for the project, then each member is likely to have some information available about the facts of the situation such as the course syllabus. The syllabus says that the topic should conform to certain criteria and the paper should be a specific length and include a PowerPoint presentation. Everyone knows these facts.

Unique information includes facts and perceptions that only each individual group member has. The sum total of this hidden information is called the **Hidden Profile**. For example, in the Class Project Game, each member is likely to have an opinion about the class, the project, and the professor. Since most people have many opinions and perceptions of the situation, each person typically has an abundance of **both common and unique information**. The question is which type are they most likely to share while playing the Class Project Game?

Research indicates that people are much more likely to emphasize **common information** and not share their **unique information**. The reason is that they may not want to share their unique opinions and risk getting criticized or being made to look foolish or incompetent. They may not want to challenge the opinions of the group leader. Or, they might be reluctant to disappoint anyone in the group by stating a different point of view. There are lots of reasons why people are reluctant to share as we know from the last chapter on coordination when we talked about the dangers of **Group Think**. The result is that groups who are reluctant to share tend to make poor-quality decisions. The **hidden profile** is not revealed, so the group can not get access to the information it needs to be successful. The group lacks a complete picture of the situation hindering its ability to develop options for addressing their problem.

Sometimes group members are more willing to share **hidden information**. When there is a right answer to the task, like figuring out a math problem in a group setting, people are more willing to share unique information. In this case people probably feel that their opinions will not be judged harshly because they are simply trying to solve a puzzle. But, when the decision involves a judgment about the best thing to do, as in the Class Project Game, people are generally only willing to discuss common information.

Finally, the theory indicates that people's **initial preferences** often dominate the discussions and determine if people are willing to share their hidden information. When people have strong preferences they may try to push them on the group. If they are forceful, members will often give up and side with this person even if they have hidden information that contradicts the leader's preference. The leader might have high status or be very popular and members may want to defer to that person. This tendency often limits discussion to **common** information thereby compromising the quality of the decisions.

Communication Process Theory. A final theory of interest in helping understand how games are played and won or lost focuses on the process of communication. What are the important communication processes associated with effective and ineffective group decision-making? In general, research concludes that effective decision making is characterized by four recurring themes of communicative activity.

- **Rigorously evaluating the validity of opinions and assumptions.** When the information and opinions of group members are closely scrutinized, as opposed to receiving only cursory examination, the groups are likely to be much more effective. Not checking facts or allowing people to make grand leaps in logic without asking for some documentation often results in poor decision making because the information has lower quality.

- **Rigorously evaluating suggested courses of action using pre-established criteria.** When groups develop criteria for determining whether an option is good or bad, and each option is evaluated using those criteria, the decision is much more likely to be successful. Playing the College Selection Game is a good example. If no one develops a SWOT analysis for the colleges then they all look alike—there is no way to tell which one is better.

- **Making the final choice based on facts, assumptions, and inferences that are reasonable and accurate.** If an outside observer can normally judge the assumptions and inferences made by the group to be reasonable then the decision is likely to work well. If the group lets members make assumptions on the basis of invalid inferences that are incorrect, then group decision making suffers. An objective third party should be able to tell if this process was effective.

- **Having influential members ask questions, point out important information, challenge unwarranted assumptions, and keep the group from digressing to irrelevant topics.** This is the job description of a leader. When a group does not have that kind of leader, it is more likely to lose its way. Effective task leaders ask questions, they know what important information to continuously bring back to the group, and they keep the group on task.

Chapter 11 will focus on leadership, but from a communication standpoint, these specific activities really define how an effective leader interacts with the group.

Summary

Group decision-making is about making good choices. The more choices the group has for solving its problem, and the more they are committed to implementing the best choice, the better the decision will look in the long term.

Groups are most likely to make better decisions when they pay attention to the process. Members should take the time to establish clear goals, select a coordination strategy for the task they must perform, be clear about what counts as quality performance, promote open communication, develop both task and social leadership roles, foster a clear problem analysis, and be willing and able to have productive conflict. These elements will create a culture to trust, respect, and success.

Groups move through specific phases as they deliberate. They begin by orienting to the task and getting to know one another. As members start to pursue the task a competition for leadership emerges as ideas are tossed around. As members line up with one set of ideas the person who proposed those ideas assumes leadership and a decision starts to emerge. The group then reflects on that decision to decide if the group is effective.

The theories of group decision making focus mostly on how members exchange information. **Structuration Theory** tells us that knowing the constitutive and regulative rules of the discussion are important. **Hidden Profiles Theory** reveals the importance of exchanging both common and unique information. **Communication Process Theory** asks members to reflect on how well they are processing the information necessary to make a good decision.

Lessons Learned

I hope you picked up some recurring themes about how to play effective decision-making talk games in groups. Here are the key lessons that will help you craft more effective talk game strategies:

- **Groups need to enter the decision-making arena with the right focus.** They should enter with an open mind to explore alternatives and be willing to commit to the decisions made by the group.

- **Effective group decision-making requires structure.** Groups need to commit to developing clear goals and clear roles for its members, a team spirit, open communication, a willingness to share private thoughts, and time to build a culture of trust and respect.

- **Groups should not short cut the decision-making process.** Groups should work through the decision-making phases in a deliberate way, taking their time. They should also select a coordination strategy that works for the task they are asked to perform.

- **Group members should define and determine the extent of the problem situation.** Proper analysis and definition of the problem area should help the group determine whether a given alternative will successfully deal with the problem.

- **Alternative options should be considered in light of negative and positive consequences.** That is, group members should determine, for each alternative, the possible benefits, as well as the possible disadvantages. A SWOT analysis of choices is vital to select among options.

- **Avoid glossing over disagreements.** Members should adopt a constructive approach to managing differences. The emphasis should be placed on resolution through critical examination, rather than consensus through superficial appeal.

- **Everyone should be encouraged to participate and communicate.** Members who remain silent almost always have something to say, but, for some reason or another, decline to say it. All members should be asked for input and be assured that the group is interested in hearing what they have to say.

- **Groups ought to be kept relatively small.** As group size increases, the opportunity that group members have to communicate with one another, especially under time constraints, diminishes. Smaller groups are better at soliciting and including member input.

REFERENCE

Kravitz, D. A. & Martin, B. (1986). Ringelmann rediscovered: The original article. *Journal of Personality and Social Psychology, 50,* 936-941.

Chapter 11
Leadership Card Games

Introduction

Do you consider yourself to be a leader? Have you ever performed that role in school, at work, or even in your home? As we learned from the **Chapter 10** focusing on Group Decision-Making, winning those games by making high-quality decisions requires effective leadership. Leaders emerge by proposing ideas on how to define and solve a problem while receiving support from group members. Even appointed leaders must earn their leadership status by helping to define clear goals and developing a process for achieving those goals.

We also learned from the last chapter that leadership is earned through effective card talk play. Another way of framing this idea is that communication is vital to leadership. Leaders who connect well with members, provide good ideas for solving problems, and promote a thoughtful and interesting process stand a good chance of playing successful talk games. To better understand the role of communication in building an effective leadership strategy, consider these leadership talk card games.

Leadership Talk Games

The Vision Game. On May 25, 1961 the President of the United States, John F. Kennedy, addressed a joint session of Congress. In his opinion, and in the opinion of many others, the United States faced a crisis because the Soviet Union (now Russia) had put a man into space before the Americans. To address this crisis, President Kennedy made the following remarks:

"If we are to win the battle that is now going on around the world between freedom and tyranny, the dramatic achievements in space which occurred in recent weeks should have made it clear to us all, as did the Sputnik in 1957, the impact of this adventure on the minds of men everywhere. I believe this nation should commit itself to achieving the goal, before this decade is out, of landing a man on the moon and returning him safely to Earth. No single space project in this period will be more impressive to mankind."

He then asked Congress for a multi-billion dollar increase in funding for space travel, which was granted. His vision not only inspired a nation, but resulted in the United States landing a man on the moon in July 1969, as President Kennedy promised. I saw that landing as it happened and it was certainly a moving experience.

The Defiance Game. On Sunday, March 7, 1965, about 600 people began a 54-mile march from Selma, Alabama, to the state capitol in Montgomery to commemorate the death of **Jimmie Lee Jackson**, shot 3 weeks earlier by a state trooper while trying to protect his mother at a civil rights demonstration. On the outskirts of Selma, after crossing the Edmund Pettus Bridge, the marchers, in plain sight of photographers and journalists, were brutally assaulted by heavily armed state troopers and deputies. I recall watching the brutality on TV and wondered how the nation might hold together.

While this march was led by John Lewis who serves today as a congressman from Georgia, **Dr. Martin Luther King, Jr.**, led a group of marchers 2 days later on the same route to again fight for the civil rights of African Americans. These marches set the stage for the **Voting Rights Act of 1965**, which dramatically increased voter registration by African Americans in the South and around the nation.

Fortunately, Lewis and King realized that oppression is sustained only when the oppressed people give their permission to be oppressed. They knew most importantly that this permission had to be withdrawn, even though the price for challenging the established powers would be high. Their courage helped build a national consensus for civil rights that has expanded to include issues related to women, Hispanics, and others. They played the Defiance Game with great courage and conviction, and we owe them a great debt of gratitude for playing it well.

The Showtime Game. Michigan State has had some great basketball players over the years. Perhaps the most recognizable leader of Spartan basketball is Earvin "Magic" Johnson. When Johnson was in his sophomore year at MSU, the team was not performing well early in the Big Ten season. The coach, Jud Heathcoat, liked to play a slow, half-court game that emphasized running plays and tough defense. After a tough loss, Johnson went to Coach Heathcoate and asked if the team could run more, taking advantage of Johnson's passing and running skills. Exasperated and needing some success, Heathcoate agreed. The next game, the team ran an offense called "**Showtime**" in which the team would run up and down the court with fancy passing and lots of dunks.

If Johnson had not stepped up as team captain and played the Showtime Game, the team might not have gone on to win the national championship in 1979.

Defining Leadership

These talk games illustrate how stepping up and showing a Leadership Card can build a consensus for change. Perhaps the best definition of leadership that captures what's involved in creating and playing this card is from a book called *The Leadership Challenge* by James Kouzes and Barry Posner. They contend that leadership is "**the art of mobilizing others to want to struggle for shared aspirations.**" Another way to think about this is that a **leader** is the person asked by followers to speak for them. After all, they are struggling together to achieve some vision of a better future and they believe that their selected person will provide the right strategy to achieve that better future.

Each of the games played by the leaders in this chapter illustrates this relationship between leaders and followers. The American people asked Kennedy to help solve the problem of Soviet dominance in space. Americans could not conceive of the Soviet empire controlling space so Kennedy needed a bold vision to establish American dominance in space. Lewis and King were also asked by their long-suffering people to lead them into equal citizenship as fully free Americans. And Johnson's teammates sent a clear signal to him as the team captain that something needed to change, prompting Johnson to talk to the coach about playing **showtime basketball** to start winning. Followers were demanding that these people play their Leadership Cards to win these important talk games. Based on Kouzes and Posner's perspective, a Leadership Card should:

Communicate a clear vision of the future. Just like President Kennedy, we want our leaders to present us with **a clear picture of a better future**—one we as followers desperately want. Lewis, King, and Johnson painted a clear and compelling vision with emotion and conviction.

Model appropriate behavior. We want our leaders to practice what they preach. When Lewis and King asked their people to march, these leaders were at the front of the line marching arm-in-arm for freedom.

Inspire us to act. In each situation described in the three talk games, leaders faced life-changing challenges—defending a country, fighting for civil rights, or pursuing a championship. These situations required a strong person to step up to meet the challenge, and in each situation they did. They **inspired** with rhetoric, determination, and powerful deeds. They showed the way and people enthusiastically followed and became better than they thought they could be.

Remain sociable and friendly. Because these leaders stepped up to the challenges they faced they became famous. However, they never lost sight of their need to **connect personally** with followers. They appeared approachable, friendly, part of the group, and always available to listen.

Challenge the process. We also expect a leader to recognize when **the process is not working**, when a crisis is approaching, or when a change is needed. Then we want them to forge a new direction because the old process is broken. **"Fix it!"** the people scream, and the great ones will take it on and succeed.

These are very difficult expectations for leaders to fulfill for followers. The Leadership Card is tough to create and sustain. Sometimes leaders are inspiring, but do not always act appropriately, or are not very friendly. Other times leaders are inspiring, but they don't present a clear vision of the future. When individuals **can pull all of these leadership elements together**, as they did in reaching the moon, rejecting oppression, or being the best college basketball team, we tend to hold them up as examples of exceptional individuals.

The Leaders' Questions. Leadership is earned; it is not given. Even if someone is elected President of the United States, he or she does not become a leader until followers agree to conform to the directions advocated by the leader. The moment in which followers proceed down the path behind an individual is the point at which that person becomes a leader. As more people join this parade, the leadership becomes stronger. Building a Leadership Card begins by asking three critical questions:

What needs to be done to make this place better? The first question is the most important: What needs to be done? The team is here to win, the nation must be free, and man must walk on the moon! How can these goals be achieved? The first job of a leader is to **LISTEN** to others. What are the aspirations of the people? Lewis and King could not have led a march for freedom if people were not ready to fight for freedom. They listened intensely to the stories of oppression and segregation and heard yearnings for a better life and a future that breathed justice. They knew the people were ready and the time was right after many sessions listening to these stories.

What can and should I do to make a difference? After listening and connecting with others, Lewis and King decided that what needed to be done was to stop giving permission to be oppressed and to demand change. They decided they could make a difference by publicly demanding change through speeches, boycotts, and marches. They looked at their own skills and resources and decided they had both the ability to do these things and the courage and motivation to do them. They never would have been successful if they did not look at themselves as individuals and ask what they could do to make a difference.

What should I say to keep the struggle visible and the path to success clear? Leaders are communicators. They must continuously listen to others and also talk to others. They must remain constantly visible to the followers to keep the vision real, maintain enthusiasm for the cause, and most importantly, to inspire. This is the key challenge in playing leadership games in organizations. Leaders have been granted the privilege of leading. As a result, they must constantly be out front in plain view of followers encouraging them to move forward with the vision.

Communication Strategies of Effective Leaders. Besides asking these questions, what else should be on the Leadership Card? Followers expect leaders to use a variety of communication behaviors to mobilize individuals. Here is a list of behaviors that research tells us are common on Leadership Cards. Let's review the list and explore how they promote leadership.

- **Problem identification.** Leaders do a better job of examining the nature of the problem that needs to be solved and keeping people on task to explore it from many different perspectives.

- **Proposing solutions.** They also have good suggestions for how to solve these problems and they are seen as more creative and effective.

- **Seeking information.** Remember that leaders are good at listening. They ask questions and listen to the answers. They do not change the topic to something they want to talk about. They let followers teach them how to lead. Shared aspirations drive leadership behaviors so learning the followers' aspirations from every angle is key.

- **Giving information.** People want leaders to be smart and that usually means providing unique information about the challenges the group faces. Their unique perspectives are valued.

- **Structuring the process of decision making.** Leaders should challenge the process, but more importantly, build a new process for moving forward. If followers want new leadership it is generally because the old leaders were stuck in a dysfunctional process of some kind.

- **Leaders are active, but not pushy.** Leaders communicate and facilitate. They do not force people into compliance. Leaders who push are generally not effective. Leaders who listen are much more effective.

The Leader Card vs The Manager Card

To better understand the Leadership Card and how to play leadership games it is useful to contrast it with the Manager Card. We often think of managers as serving in a leadership capacity, and they certainly do; but their focus is different. Using a nautical metaphor, managers drive the ship, whereas leaders chart the ship's course and destination. Leaders know where the ship is going, whereas managers know how to get the ship into port; it is a team effort. According to Warren Bennis' 2009 book "*On Becoming a Leader*," there are some instructive distinctions between managers and leaders.

Check the behaviors most indicative of **managers**, those most associated with **leaders**, or the behaviors indicative of **BOTH** managers and leaders:

Organizational Responsibilities of Leaders or Managers	Managers	Leaders
1. Maintain basic functions and processes		
2. Develop priorities for growth and change		
3. Rely mostly on control to get things done		
4. Promote change by building trust		
5. Maintain short-range views on priorities		
6. Focus on long-range perspectives		
7. Tend to ask "how" and "when"		
8. Tend to ask "what" and "why"		
9. Concentrate on the bottom line or how things are now		
10. Concentrate on the horizon by looking to the future		
11. Accept the status quo		
12. Challenge the ways things are done now		
13. Are viewed as "good soldiers" doing what is needed now		
14. Take charge of their own destiny		
15. Do things right		
16. Do the right thing		

Answers: **Managers** focus on the odd-numbered behaviors; **leaders** focus on the even numbers. How well did you do? Notice that the managers focus on steering the ship and leaders plot the course. Both should work together ultimately to make the organization successful.

If we review this list in light of the Vision Game at the beginning of the chapter we would certainly claim that President Kennedy was playing his Leadership Card when laying out that moon vision. He developed priorities for growth and he concentrated on the horizon by challenging the idea that putting a man on the moon was not possible. However, President Kennedy was also a manager at times. Not only did he have to guide the ship, but on many occasions, he had to steer it, as well. Presidents work hard to get legislation passed and work through implementing important policies. Thus, Kennedy held and could play both a Manager Card and a Leader Card when he needed to. Many managers are promoted to leadership positions but fail because they have difficulty letting go of their management role. They want to steer the ship instead of charting its course. If all people do is steer, they will soon get lost.

This list also shows how important it is that leaders focus on the vision issue. We expect **leaders** to talk easily and frequently about vision. And, we expect **managers** to speak about keeping the organization running smoothly. In contrast, the first two distinctions indicate that leaders and managers differ in the manner in which they attempt to influence followers to accept their vision. Leaders influence people by communicating a vision that followers support; managers influence people by controlling how resources are allocated to accomplish tasks (**navigating vs. steering**).

Leadership Emergence

A common question about leadership relates to the issue of emergence. Are some people just born to be leaders or are leaders simply made by followers supporting some who best captures and articulates a vision to address their struggle? Put simply, how might one predict who, from among a set of group members, will emerge as the leader?

The Trait Approach. One school of thought is that certain individuals are born with traits that predispose them to become leaders. Traits associated with leadership emergence include intelligence, sociability, and dominance. That is, leaders tend to be more intelligent than the average group member. They tend to be more sociable by being more highly integrated into social networks, and generally possess stronger communication skills. And ,they tend to have stronger needs to dominate than do most group members.

However, these **traits are limited** in their ability to help us understand leadership emergence. Consider the office of President of the United States. Presidents both high and low on intelligence, dominance, sociability, and other traits are quite common. For instance, Jefferson was highly intelligent; Harding was not particularly so. Theodore Roosevelt and Lyndon Johnson were dominant chief executives; Grant was low on this trait. Eisenhower ranks as a very sociable president; Polk was very unfriendly. Yet, each of these men emerged as an important governmental leader in the United States.

The Situational Demands Approach. A second way of viewing leadership is that certain situational demands may favor one type of leader with a specific profile of traits **at one time**, and a leader with a completely different profile at another time. At the beginning of World War II, the United Kingdom needed a war-time leader who could be tough and inspirational. The British people turned to Winston Churchill to serve as Prime Minister from 1940 until July of 1945. After the defeat of Nazi Germany, the British people needed a leader who could turn inward and rebuild the nation. While Churchill was a inspirational leader he had little interest in being a manager and sorting through the details of rebuilding. Instead, the people turned to Clement Attlee of the Labor Party as Prime Minister in July of 1945, a very different type of person who asked "how" and "when" rather than "what" and "why."

The Individual Difference Approach. Aside from analyzing leadership on a case-by-case basis, is there anything of a more general nature that can be said about the manner in which traits and situational characteristics combine to determine leadership emergence? One psychologist, **Fred Fiedler**, argued that people differ in a very important personality trait that might predispose them to emerge in some situations as leaders. He refers to this individual difference as the **assumed similarity of opposites (ASO)**. Persons are high on this dimension to the extent that they see opposites as being alike, or they are low on this dimension to the extent that they perceive opposites to be very different from each other. If you worked in a company and rated your most preferred and least preferred coworker in much the same manner then you would be a high ASO individual. But, someone low in ASO would rate these two people very differently.

Why is this individual personality trait important? Remember from our discussion in **Chapter 10** that some people emerge as task leaders and others as social leaders in groups? The **task leader** focuses on effective completion of the work that the group faces. This type of leader is likely to be seen providing suggestions, opinions, and information to fellow group members, and, perhaps, showing antagonism if they reject them. In contrast, the **socioemotional leader** focuses on the relationships among group members. This type of leader is more likely identified by behavior that displays solidarity.

In his research, Fiedler found that **low ASO** people are likely to become **task leaders**. They focus on and see differences among members of the group that they lead. For example, they have the skills necessary to make personnel and task assignment decisions, skills required of a task leader. On the other hand, those **high in ASO** are likely to become **socio-emotional leaders**. High ASOs focus on and see similarities in people. For instance, when conflict occurs they are able to help manage it by emphasizing to the participants that the ways in which they agree are more pronounced and important than the ways in which they disagree, skills required of a socio-emotional leader.

Leadership as a Combination of Traits and Situational Demands. Rather than relying on either a trait or a situational explanation, it is probably likely that the combination of these two elements provides the best understanding of why some leaders emerge and others do not become leaders. Common sense tells us that many people are presented with situations that demand leadership but few are willing and capable of stepping up. The need for a leader was apparent when MSU's basketball team was dramatically underperforming as in the Showtime Game. The need for leadership to fight for civil rights was apparent when Jimmy Lee Jackson was shot as described in the Defiance Game. And, America needed a leader to fight for a vision when the Soviet Union grabbed leadership in the space race. Only a few stepped up and seized the opportunity. What are the key elements that help us understand when certain people will step up? Fiedler asserts that there are three characteristics of situations that are crucial to leadership.

Leaders and Followers. In many ways, followers anoint leaders. In Chapter 10, we talked about how individuals propose ideas and then others in the group start to support those ideas. Ultimately, a chemistry develops between leaders and followers where the followers just become more confident in one person's vision of how to lead the group. Over time members develop a loyalty to their leader as successes build and members see more traits they like to deal with the situation at hand. I am sure that the character, determination, and courage that King and Lewis showed in marching through Alabama solidified each follower's confidence in their leadership. In fact, these individuals inspired generations of individuals to go on and fight for civil rights not only in the United States, but around the world.

Task Structure. The second element that contributes to some individuals being better able to step up in certain situations more than others is the nature of the task. Some people just have the traits necessary to perform the tasks that members are looking for. They have the skills and the personalities that suit them for the vision that group members prize so highly. One of the key skills that President Kennedy needed was the rhetorical skill to set the vision and then put the pieces in place to carry out the vision. Those were important traits that were needed for that specific task.

The Use of Social Power. In the next section of this chapter, we will describe the various ways in which individuals can build social power with group members. Power is really all about influence. The leader's goal is to use a form of influence that binds group members together and inspires them to work collectively toward accomplishing their shared vision. That influence may be a very **tough** kind of influence that a coach might use when training athletes. Or it may be centered on **respect and admiration**, as in leaders fighting for a social cause. But the combination of the right kind of power in the right situation is a strong predictor of leadership emergence.

Combining these three situational characteristics, Fiedler claims that the situation is **favorable for leadership** when followers support the leader, the task is highly structured, and the leader's power is strong. Conversely, the situation is said to be **unfavorable for leadership** when followers do not support the leader, the task is unstructured, and the leader's power is weak. The key lesson here is that if you are participating in a group and you have been appointed leader but your traits do not mesh with the situational requirements, then your power is likely to be weak and your leadership ineffective. It is best to seek leadership when the group wants a leader and the task is ready-made for you to step up.

Leadership and Power

Power Defined. A leader's **social power** is defined as the extent to which followers perceive that the leader has the ability and willingness to control group outcomes. Let's break down these two perceptions of ability and willingness because often these are two very different judgments. If members believe that the leader has the **ability** to help them achieve their goals, then the question in the minds of followers is whether the leader has the willingness to step up and use that ability. Earvin Johnson certainly had the ability to lead, but stepping up to play the Showtime Game proved he had the willingness, as well.

There are **two forms of social power**: a) forcibly driving change through coercion, and b) encouraging change through persuasion and modeling. Sometimes a coach has to forcibly push a player in a specific direction that the player does not want to go in order to help that player improve. The player certainly does not want to change, but it is the coach's job to find the right kind of power to help the player improve so the team can win. At other times, the coach may use persuasion and modeling to convince the player to change and show the athlete how best to perform.

Power is in Relationships. Power is all about how individuals become interdependent through the roles they play with one another. Professors have no power without students; mothers have no power without children; players have no power without other players and coaches. The key is that **the more interdependent individuals are with one another the more they can influence or have power over one another**. If you had to list the person who has the most power or influence over you right now, your answer would probably be the person that you are closest to relationally, say a parent, sibling, or spousal partner. Sorting out power requires sorting out the nature of the interdependencies that role partners have with one another.

It is important to note that power is a highly subjective judgment based on your perception of how much someone can influence you or you can influence them. Some people use that subjectivity to their advantage by threatening violence, for example, but never following through with the violence. Over time the perception of a leader's power may grow either because the people's dependency on the leader increases or their fear of the leader escalates.

Forms of Social Power. In trying to influence one another individuals can use a combination of strategies. Here are the six strategies that can be used individually or in combination:

1. **Coercive Power:** Forcing individuals through punishments or threatening to withhold rewards.
2. **Reward Power:** Consistently providing something of value to the other person that they find very pleasant or useful in some way.
3. **Legitimate Power:** Compliance based on one's position "Do it because I'm the boss."
4. **Referent Power:** Gaining influence through respect.
5. **Expert Power:** Gaining influence by demonstrating competence in performing skills that the other person values.
6. **Information Power:** Providing data or information that the other values.

Leaders typically combine these strategies as they play their cards. For example, leaders may begin by using coercive power and interrupting the other's talk, changing the topic, using loud and intimidating speech, or directing people about what they should do (a very power-oriented style). Then, they may switch and use referent power by listening attentively, following up on others' topics, and speaking sincerely while giving emotional support (a high affiliation style). These are communicative extremes but leaders who are **situationally competent** can switch their card play depending on what needs to be done to complete the task. Regardless of which strategies the leaders use, the more followers comply with the leader's requests, the more they build their dependency on the leader and submit to the leader's influence.

Leader Longevity

Longevity Varies. In many areas, such as business or sports, the duration of leadership can be very brief. Unless they die in office, are impeached or resign presidents of the United States serve for at least 4 years. Since Franklin D.

Roosevelt, however, no president has served for more than 8 years because the Constitution now prohibits it. The chief executive officer of a major corporation may not last as long. Presidents of major universities in the United States serve, on the average, approximately 7 years.

Throughout human history some kings and queens, czars and chiefs, emperors and emirs, and sundry other monarchs have ruled for lengthy periods. Catherine II reigned as Empress of Russia for 34 years. Henry VIII was King of England for approximately 38 years. Louis XIV was King of France for more than 70 years. Of course, these leaders had the force of the state as a means of preserving their longevity.

But in a different leadership arena Tom Izzo has been the head basketball coach at Michigan State for over 15 seasons as of this writing. Other coaches in the Big Ten have been in place for only a couple of seasons, whereas one, Joe Paterno, has been the head football coach at Penn State for over 30 years. Billy Graham is, and has long been, the leader of his evangelistic organization. Nevertheless, these examples are more the exception than the rule.

In some instances departing the leadership role is a matter of choice; in other cases it is forced upon the occupant of this position. For example, sports coaches are fired all the time for failing to win. Nicholas II, Czar of Russia, was executed. Richard M. Nixon resigned as President of the United States to avoid being impeached. Regardless of the method of departing the role; it is clear that maintaining a position of leadership is as challenging, if not more so, than obtaining the position.

Time Challenges. Specifically, leaders face two important problems relating to time. The first is **time management**. In many contexts in which leadership takes place, the leader's time is the most important commodity for the followers. For example, in modern corporate life employees measure their success by how much time they are allowed to spend with the **Chief Executive Officer**. Thus, obtaining additional time is a major reward, and having one's time reduced or eliminated indicates major career failure. Because time is a finite commodity and there are typically so many time demands, leaders have very little discretionary time. Moreover, what they have of it they tend to guard carefully.

Second, visions have some **time span**. Some visions are premature, or ahead of their time like the group of people who predicted the financial collapse of 2008–2009. Many people raised red flags about the economy and proposed various remedies, but government leaders chose to ignore them or simply didn't believe it could happen. Sometimes visions can also become outdated. For instance, President Franklin D. Roosevelt's **New Deal** gave way to the **Fair Deal**, which yielded to the **New Frontier**, **The Great Society**, and now **Universal Health Care**. Outdated visions that are constantly changing are not unique to American politics. Many companies shift their visions quite often in response to changes in the economic or political environment.

The problem for the leader whose vision has become dated appears to have a straightforward solution—generate a new vision. But, inspiring new ideas do not come to mind easily for most of us. Moreover, it is especially difficult for leaders to generate these new visions because **their followers often prevent it**. The fact that the leader's time is an important reward for the followers, and removal of time with the leader is an important punishment, makes it difficult for leaders either to add people to, or delete them from, the calendar. Leaders may have difficulty being exposed to the sorts of new ideas that would allow them to update, or radically alter, their visions. As a result, a leader's tenure in the job is likely to end when the vision becomes dated.

Focusing Energy. A central problem of leadership maintenance becomes finding methods of avoiding the stale-vision trap. Research shows that successful leaders are careful to **restrict their agenda** so that they pursue only one or two goals at a time. In this way, they avoid micromanaging, spreading their time thinly across a number of issues, many of which are likely to be relatively minor. Moreover, they tend to attack only those problems that they believe are able to be solved.

This focusing tactic is interesting for at least two reasons. First, it implies that these leaders believe that some problems in their organizations are not able to be solved or worth the effort. Restated, even successful leaders are aware that they cannot succeed in eliminating every problem. **Focus** is critical. Second, the idea of focus reinforces the view of leadership as a visionary process aimed at addressing a limited number of critical issues that will move the organization forward. Managers, on the other hand, try to do everything by micromanaging staff. When leaders develop a Leadership Card, it must include topics related to creating and discussing these vision opportunities.

Finally, successful managers take time to sharpen their intellectual skills. Many spend considerable time reading, and their reading is often done in diverse fields. One reason this activity enhances their success is that it improves their ability to form new visions.

Leadership Card Inventory

Now it's time to focus on your own Leadership Card. To what extent do you perceive that you are able to communicate like a leader? Below is a survey of your leadership skills based on the framework offered by Kouzes and Posner. To complete the survey **think of a situation in which you served in a leadership role**. Perhaps it was in a work, sports, or school context. Thinking of that specific context, score yourself on the extent to which you demonstrate these behaviors. Write the number that best represents your answer in the space provided for each item using this scale:

1 = Never   2 = Seldom   3 = Sometimes   4 = Often

In your role as a leader, how often did you:

	1.	Question assumptions underlying how the group worked
	2.	Offer solutions to problems the group faced
	3.	Communicate effectively across different groups in the organization

	4. Have in-depth knowledge of the tak that needed to be performed
	5. Listen to, and incorporate diverse ideas into the decision-making
	6. Seek the commitment of others to common goals
	7. Run meetings and make presentations effectively
	8. Communicate with Customers or clients to learn what they think
	Total

	9. Articulate a clear vision of how individuals might work more closely together.
	10. Generate creative solutions in the midst of chaotic circumstances
	11. Show honestly and forthrightness in dealing with others
	12. Demonstrate a caring attitude toward others
	Total

	13. Work to include all cultural and ethnic groups in the task
	14. Generate new resources to serve organizational goals
	15. Seek input from experts when necessary
	16. Exhibit a sense of humor
	Total

	17. Demonstrate flexibility in responding to tough issues
	18. Consistently build on others' ideas in problem-solving discussions
	19. Step in and redirect destructive conflict
	20. Promote recognition of others' contributions
	Total

Add your scores using the following table:

1 = challenging the process	Total for Items 1-4 =
2 = inspiring a shared vision	Total for Items 5-8 =
3 = enabling others to act	Total for Items 9-12 =
4 = modeling the way	Total for Items 13-16 =
5 = encouraging the heart	Total for Items 17-20 =

If you scored between 60 and 80 points, you have a great deal of confidence in your leadership skills. If you scored between 20 and 40, you probably lack some confidence in your leadership skills. Between 41 and 59 and you are relatively unsure about your skills. Now look at your scores on each dimension. What was your highest and lowest score and what do these differences mean? For example, if you had low scores on **Challenging the Process** and high scores on **Encouraging the Heart** you may think of yourself as more of a social leader than a task facilitator.

Summary

Leadership is earned not given. Members have to decide who will lead them. Leaders must listen first to members' desires for a better future and then be willing to step up to the leadership challenges as their skills and abilities dictate.

Leadership is about vision and communicating effectively to achieve that vision. So often leaders make themselves into managers by not shaping and articulating a clear vision for the group. Leaders can manage, but they should be spending most or more of their time on defining the vision and executing it with effective communication strategies.

Leaders ask important questions. They want to know what needs to be done to make the place better and what they can do to make a difference?

Leadership is about effective communication. Leaders are expected to be effective at identifying problems, proposing solutions, and listening to others while leading the process of decision-making.

Leaders are not born; they are the people who step up when asked. Leaders are not born in the sense that they can lead anywhere or anytime. Leaders have traits that match the situations in which they find themselves. They use these traits by stepping up when called.

Effective leadership is based on respect, not coercion. Think of your most admired leaders. I talked about four at the beginning of this chapter. Each of those individuals lead by respect. They forged a vision and had the courage to see it through. That earned trust and respect from group members.

Leadership is different than being a manager. Leaders look to the future and guide the organization's direction. Managers keep things running smoothly. Both are needed for an organization to be successful, but they require different skills. Many managers who get promoted to leadership positions have difficulty creating a Leadership Card. They want to play their Manager Card when faced with a difficult task.

Leaders who keep the vision alive endure most. Leaders constantly have to build a rationale for their leadership. They must continue to be perceived by group members as the best option for implementing the vision. So, the vision must be constantly updated to keep it fresh and important to group members.

Lessons Learned

- **Assess your own leadership strengths and weaknesses.** Are you willing to step up when needed or are you afraid to assert yourself? Developing a Leadership Card takes time. Each time you play it the card grows and the process is easier.

- **Leadership grows from your own communication skills.** Do not think that leadership is about being glib and slick; that is not the kind of communication needed. What's needed is someone simply willing to ask questions about what's happening and helping others to think about what could happen.

- **Look for leadership opportunities.** One of the great advantages of being a student at a major university is exposure to many leadership opportunities. There are hundreds of groups to join and many work-related groups that students commonly experience. Pick one or two and stretch yourself.

- **Leaders like to learn.** Leaders are constantly reading and listening to others. They want to know what successes and failures others are experiencing. They seek to learn new trends to discover opportunities for their own organization.

- **Start small and think big.** Finally, think BIG. Start with modest opportunities and work your way up to a leadership position. Excellent leaders are rare so start now and pursue it passionately.

REFERENCES

Bennis, W. (2009). *On becoming a leader*. New York: Basic Books

Fiedler, F.E. (1996). Research on leadership selection and training: One view of the future. *Administrative Science Quarterly*, 41.

Kouzes, J. & Posner, B. (2007). *The Leadership Challenge*. New York: John Wiley & Sons.

Chapter 12
Diffusion of Innovation Card Games

Introduction

Most students are obsessed with technology. You see a new cell phone or new computer or reader and you become immediately intrigued about it and want to learn more. The marketing folks at the various tech companies who sell these devices spend a great deal of time trying to get you excited about these electronic tools. The purpose of this chapter is to talk about the process of diffusing innovations or changes through some organization or society. How can we promote change to help people adopt the changes more quickly? It is a question for companies promoting products or any organization that has the challenge of changing what people do or how they think. Let's look at some typical innovation games aimed at promoting change.

Innovation Card Games

The Buzz Game. One of the most experienced companies at promoting technology is Apple. Steve Jobs, the CEO of Apple Computers, is a master of manipulating buzz about the latest and greatest. He certainly got everyone excited about the iPod®, iPhone®, and iTouch® when they came out. Most recently, Apple created lots of buzz about the iPad®, which is a multimedia computing device that can be used for reading newspapers and looking at videos, and more. Their strategy is to first let rumors "leak out" about various "game-changer" technologies that it wants to produce. The goal is to get the techies blogging about what the technologies might be like months in advance of a new product release. Apple then dribbles out product features bit by bit to keep feeding this blogging frenzy. Ultimately, TV and print media pick up on the new Apple device and start running features about what it does. Then a couple of weeks before the items are scheduled to be released Steve Jobs plays his Technology Guru Card and does a multi-media extravaganza about the new device. By the time it is released, everyone wants one because the buzz has been so intense.

The New Policy Communication Game. Diffusion of innovation is really about the broader issue of promoting change in an organization. This is a very difficult challenge for leaders in large organizations. Often the leaders must change policies that directly impact workers. The problem is to figure out how best to **communicate** that change. When playing his or her Boss Card should the boss directly communicate to all employees at once, or talk only to direct supervisors who then tell the employees the message about the change? Research indicates that the second strategy is preferable. This gives the supervisor credibility in looking like an expert and in having a special relationship with the boss. By going around the supervisors to deliver the message the boss undercuts their role and diminishes their credibility with the employees. If supervisors are sharing new information with their employees then they can expand their Supervisor Cards and build their **role competencies**. If rank-and-file staff hears it like everyone else, then the supervisor can only play an Employee Card in asking questions about the new policy.

The Beer Promotion Game. In the late 1950s, diet soda was becoming the rage. Women loved Diet Coke, Diet Pepsi, and Diet Rite (now defunct) cola because they had no calories. So, Miller Beer decided to come out with a product called "Diet Beer." It actually had that name on the can, if you can believe it. It offered one-third fewer calories than regular beer with the same great taste. It failed miserably because mainly women drank diet soda and mostly men drank beer. A man holding a can that says "Diet Beer" was basically saying, "I want to be a woman." After about 5 years, Miller decided to take the exact same product and call it "Lite Beer." They marketed it by showing commercials with manly men fighting about whether the best part of the beer was its taste or that it was less filling. The product became so successful that every beer manufacturer quickly marketed Lite Beer; but it is really 1950s Diet Beer with a different name.

The Cereal City Game. One of Michigan's most famous industries is dried, ready-to-eat breakfast cereal. Prior to the early 1900s, millions of Americans ate breakfasts of meat, eggs, potatoes fried in lard, and homemade bread that was topped with bacon. John Harvey Kellogg from Battle Creek, Michigan noticed that hundreds of patients were suffering from colon cancer, which he believed was caused by an unhealthy diet that was high in fat and low in fiber. In 1894, Dr. Kellogg first produced **toasted cereal flakes as a breakfast food substitute** for his patients. With his older brother, William Kellogg, John established the Battle Creek Toasted Corn Flake Company in 1906, which was an instant hit. By 1912, 107 companies were producing cereal in Battle Creek making it the Cereal City!

To promote corn flakes, Kellogg used mass media advertising to garner public attention, while also offering a free year's supply of Toasted Corn Flakes to housewives who would work to convince their friends to buy Kellogg's cereal. Without knowing it, William Kellogg was using a key diffusion strategy of achieving high source credibility through the use of **homophilous change** agents, or people of similar interests who were able to change the minds of others. Kellogg also gave away tens of thousands of boxes of cereal to convince consumers of the product's advantages. But the message was also key. Kellogg shrewdly associated Toasted Corn Flakes with being the breakfast of industry and modernization in America. In effect, consumers were being told that ready-to-eat cereal was a key ingredient in the lives of progressive and successful Americans. Hot breakfasts were portrayed as a thing of the past.

Defining Diffusion of Innovation

Diffusion is the process by which an innovation is communicated through certain channels over time among the members of a social system, and then ultimately adopted for use by those members. When a new Apple device, a new hairstyle, or a type of cereal becomes popular, that's diffusion at work.

Diffusion consists of four main elements:

1. **The innovation**, an idea, practice, or object that is perceived as new by an individual, company, or society;
2. **Communication channels**, the means by which messages about the innovation are exchanged;
3. **Time**, or the process by which the adoption is promoted; and
4. **A social system**, the structure and function of relations among a set of individuals or other units, such as organizations.

The Innovation. Let's look at each of these elements to understand how they all fit together. First, the innovation is any change that is perceived as new to the target audience. It doesn't necessarily have to be new, but it does have to be perceived that way by the target audience. Lite Beer® was really plain old Diet Beer with a new label. So, it was perceived as new. Is the iPad® really a regular laptop computer without a keyboard? If so, is it really a new product? Apple wants you to think it is so they can sell more keyboardless laptops. I visited the Apple Store in New York City recently and everyone wanted to play with the iPad®. That got my attention! Corn Flakes is a true innovation in the sense that Kellogg invented them and then used very sophisticated strategies to promote them.

Communication Channels. Notice that in all of the talk games listed above there are two basic channels communicators are used to create change: **Mass and interpersonal**. Apple likes to create buzz by "leaking" information to the bloggers so they will start hyping Apple products in the various techie communities. Steve Jobs then likes to have a multi-media extravaganza to ensure that traditional media such as TV and newspapers will cover the event and hype the product. Notice also how Miller Beer promoted their product. They focused extensively on TV advertising once it was determined that the label "Lite" was preferable to "Diet" for their new beer. In whatever way marketers combine their electronic options, the goal is to make people aware of the existence of the new product or idea. Kellogg used mass advertising in newspapers and billboards.

Once people become aware of the products through electronic channels, marketers use **interpersonal** channels to give people hands-on experience with the new ideas. Kellogg's gift of a year's worth of cereal to highly connected housewives was brilliant! They spread the word about the cereal very quickly across America. Today, Apple uses traditional brick and mortar stores to give people a chance to touch their products. The beer manufacturers also like to have taste tests at football tailgates or other events so people can try it. Interpersonal channels are really important for companies who need to explain new policies to employees. Companies who want to do it right empower supervisors to explain new policies to increase trust between employees and supervisors. Interpersonal channels are most important when the innovation is really different, complex, or difficult to understand.

Time. The critical factor that determines whether a new idea or product becomes adopted is taking the time to work through the adoption process. There are actually five stages of the adoption process that are important to work through if the adoption is going to be successful. Rushing the process generally results in failure. The five stages include the following:

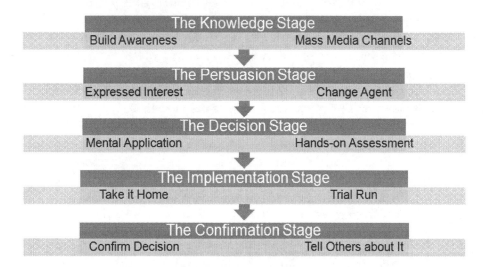

- **The Knowledge Stage.** In this stage, people learn about the idea and begin to get some sense that this is different than other ideas or products and that it's brand new. Apple uses electronic channels to make people aware that each new product is coming. Companies will hint that new policies are coming but will be revealed later. Kellogg used newspaper advertising, which was very effective at the turn of the nineteenth century.

- **The Persuasion Stage.** Once people become aware of the new idea or product, they must be given a chance to express an interest in it and possibly seek additional information. The Internet is a great resource for that persuasion process to begin. People can learn about the new Apple device, or the new company policy if they like. At this stage, a change agent is important for the persuasion to be effective. A "**change agent**" is someone who is invested in the idea and decides to champion it to others. That person could be a friend or someone who has the new iPad® and is willing to let you try it. In a company, it could be the supervisor explaining the new policy. For Kellogg, it was housewives.

- **The Decision Stage.** Once people express an interest in the new idea or policy they begin to make a decision about adopting the innovation. This process involves them making a mental application of it to their lives. They might decide to try out the new iPad® at the Apple Store, taste the new cereal at a trusted friend's home, or try a free sample of new product. This is the hands-on stage, the goal of which is to help people decide how the innovation will fit into their lives.

- **The Implementation Stage.** After people decide to try the new product or idea, then they take it home and see if it is really effective. Most companies have a return policy so if the new product does not work it can be returned easily. For organizations trying to implement a new policy the goal is to give people materials so they can discuss it with their family, coworkers or other peer groups and figure out how to best implement the new policy into their lives. This is the trial run stage in which people try to make the new idea work for them. Once the trial run is over people usually decide to adopt the idea or purchase the product.

- **The Confirmation Stage.** After people have adopted the idea or purchased the product, they seek additional information to confirm their decision. Apple does a good job of constantly making new applications available for their devices. One result of this continuous development is that it creates more value for their products and helps people justify their decision to buy Apple. Kellogg soon added Frosted Flakes®, which are corn flakes with sugar on them, to keep the product fresh. They also introduced several more breakfast cereals to move the market toward children that was very effective. This is the satisfaction stage in which people build their sense of value associated with the new idea.

A Social System. Finally, discussion or adoption of every new product or idea ultimately takes place in a social system or network of some kind in which people have connections and relationships with one another. This is how word of mouth spreads. Someone likes or does not like a new product or idea and those opinions from trusted, credible others like friends, will influence diffusion. The Cereal City Game played masterfully by John and William Kellogg is a good example. They used trusted housewives as credible sources that would talk with other housewives about the cereal. As word of mouth spread, the cereal became more and more popular. The social system was an important part of the diffusion process, just as it is with the Apple technology products, or the acceptance of the policy changes. Understanding the network is key and identifying the **change agents who are the big opinion leaders**, like housewives or techies, is essential in diffusing an innovation successfully.

Diffusion Speed

Innovation Features. Some new ideas, products, or services are adopted more quickly and get diffused throughout a social system more rapidly than others. The first and perhaps most important factor that determines speed are the features of the innovation. Are the **features** of the new thing better than the features of the old thing? If we break this down further we find that there are three issues that drive the perception of whether something is better:

- **Relative Advantage.** The new idea or product must be cheaper and work better than the old one. The new iPad® must be better than other computer readers from competition like Amazon's Kindle®, and do a better job of presenting information. If people are going to compare it to an Apple laptop of some kind, then maybe it is cheaper. But, is it better? Is it lighter, faster, and cooler than the other options? Corn flakes were promoted as being cheaper, more healthy, and better tasting.

- **Compatibility.** The new idea or product must be compatible with or fit into the person's lifestyle. It must be sufficiently familiar that it doesn't freak anyone out, but it also must be perceived as new and have several advantages over the old ideas. The iPad® works like a larger iPhone®, so it is somewhat familiar. Anyone who has worked with one of these Apple products will find the iPad® familiar and that's very intentional. If it is too weird or different, it will not become very popular.

- **Complexity.** It must also be easy to use. If the new idea or product is more complex than the old one, people will be much less motivated to change, unless the relative advantages are really high. If the advantages are stronger, then people might be willing to deal with the complexity. But, most people want it both ways—better and easier. The switch to corn flakes met these two criteria. Pouring a bowl of corn flakes was not only healthier, it was much easier than cooking a large breakfast. This powerful combination helped change people's eating habits, which is no small feat.

The Message. The second factor determining the speed with which new ideas become adopted deals with the informative and persuasive powers of the messages that announce and promote the innovation. Since **innovations are adopted in stages**, the message must change to accommodate changes in audience information that the **audience needs**. In the initial stages, it is important to ensure that the mass media messages get through all the clutter to create some kind of buzz about the new idea. That's the first goal.

Second, once through the clutter, it is important that the message is **informative** while also somehow touching a nerve. It must be relevant and resonate with the audience. Third, once the audience decides to try the new idea the message must change again to talk more specifically about **benefits** and issues like relative advantage, compatibility and complexity. Finally, when interpersonal channels are involved, what persuasive strategies do individuals use to encourage potential adopters to try the new idea?

The Beer Promotion and Cereal City Games are case studies in how important it is to get the message right so that target customers are informed and emotionally engaged. The initial Diet Beer campaign failed because the diet message was all wrong for the male audience to begin with. No guy wanted to hold a manly can of diet beer. Once they changed it to "Lite Beer" and started a very expensive advertising campaign with sports figures arguing whether

Miller Lite® "Tastes Great" or is "Less Filling," then they were able to break through the clutter and engage the target audience emotionally through the competition theme. The Kellogg brothers focused their message on being modern, which was very important to housewives at the dawn of the industrial revolution. People want to be modern and show a significant break from the "old ways."

The Channels. As indicated above, both mass communication and interpersonal channels are needed for the successful diffusion of an innovation. These two talk cards work together to "sell" the innovation. For example, the **New Policy Communication Game** works best if it begins with the boss talking to the supervisors and empowering them to talk directly with the employees. After that interaction has occurred, then the boss can follow-up with an email to everyone or some other mass media message praising the supervisors and reinforcing the message. Over time, it would be useful for the boss to continuously update the supervisors and ask them to update their staff members to further enhance the relationship between supervisors and staff members.

Amount of Time. Time is an important issue in determining the speed with which the innovation is adopted by the target audience. If the time is too short and people try to rush the process, the diffusion can fail. For example, if Steve Jobs just came out with the iPad® one day with no hype or people to try it, the launch would not have been as successful as it was. On the other hand, if **too much time** elapses between introduction of the idea and the target audience's ability to try the product then the product or idea might appear **stale**. The key is that it must appear new and fresh, but there must be plenty of time devoted to setting up the hype about the innovation.

It is also important to understand how audiences react in terms of time when innovations are launched. The audiences do not necessarily adopt an innovation in a linear fashion. They are very slow at first in seeing information or becoming interested in the innovation. Apple speeds that up because they already have a bunch of products out and people are always waiting for the next new electronic toy. For new ideas with no history, audiences are slow at first until the change reaches a **tipping point**. That is, when a certain number of adopters finally pick up on the idea it reaches a **critical mass** making the idea suddenly "popular." At that point, adoption often skyrockets with very fast approval and acceptance. This is what happened with Lite Beer®. It was slow to catch on, then all at once after a certain critical mass accepted it, the product took off.

How Do People React to Innovations?

Uncertainty Reduction. Anytime people are confronted with change, including new products or ideas, they tend to feel personally uncertain about it. **Uncertainty** is the degree to which people can predict how effective or useful the change will be for them personally. If they are highly uncertain, people are reluctant to change if the uncertainty can't be reduced. Kellogg knew that switching from a cooked breakfast to a ready-to-eat breakfast was a big change. After all, cooking was an inherent part of a housewife's identity at the turn of the nineteenth century. To reduce that uncertainty, Kellogg enlisted the help of the housewives to promote his product by giving away the cereal and letting thousands try it at no risk. Combined with the newspaper advertising promoting corn flakes as the choice of modern people, Kellogg was able to reduce the uncertainty, encouraging people to try the product, and make the switch.

Innovations present us with new possibilities and raise new questions for us. Because we do not have experience with them, we are typically uncertain how well they will work. Uncertainty is reduced by carefully considering all the information available about the innovation. "Does the innovation have some key advantages for me, is it compatible with how I live, and is it simple to understand?" are key questions we ask to reduce the uncertainty. More information typically leads to either rejection or adoption, either of which reestablishes a mental state of cognitive consistency by greatly reducing uncertainty.

Card talk plays a significant role in this process. The Kellogg Company encouraged housewives to play their Friend Cards and spread the news about the cereal after they gave away thousands of boxes. Kellogg also played their Advertiser Card informing people about the product in the newspapers and later on radio. By targeting consumers using both strategies, Kellogg helped people reduce uncertainty about the value of the product.

Social Pressure. We have talked extensively in this book about social pressure. It is a key component in **Social Norming Theory** discussed in Chapter 7 focusing on Persuasion. As you may recall from that theory, people are motivated to act normally, or go along with the crowd. People do not want to stick out. This social pressure also drives the diffusion process. If people get the impression that they will meet with peer approval for adopting an innovation or disapproval for not adopting it, they will get on board quickly. When Kellogg got the housewives involved he was putting peer pressure on their friends to try the cereal. If one of your friends strongly advocates that you try something you probably will, particularly if the cost is low. Diffusing innovations successfully installs innovations in key networks to take advantage of that pressure.

The Diffusion Effect. The cumulative result of different people each being subjected to social pressure from their peers is termed the **diffusion effect**, which is a change in the norms of the social system toward the innovation. Social pressure to eat Kellogg Corn Flakes®, felt individually by people in Battle Creek, can cause a diffusion effect in the town as a whole with regard to adopting or rejecting an innovation by people who live there. Eating corn flakes became the "normal" thing to do. I recently gave a seminar to a group of country club managers and told them that promoting their clubs through **Facebook** was becoming a **necessity**. While most resisted the idea, I suspect within a year all of them will have a Fan Page, because a few key opinion leaders in our seminar spoke persuasively about how **Facebook** works well for them. It is free to use and can reach the target audience effectively.

Opinion Leadership. Finally, as you can see from the various card games at the front of the chapter, certain people have more influence in a community than other people. These people usually have the reputation for being the first one to try the change, read about it, and in general understand it. Since they have this reputation they are asked by their friends frequently about these innovations. When you purchased your computer did you ask a friend or someone who was knowledgeable about computers to give you some advice? Most of us who are not techies do that. Thus, **opinion leadership** is the degree to which an individual is informally able to influence other individuals' attitudes or behaviors about a new idea. The power of an opinion leader's influence is that it is informal and based on respect, not on positional or formal authority. That is why we ask friends about the changes we are considering. We know they are trusted and knowledgeable even if they don't hold direct power over us.

Opinion leaders often hold **high positions of authority**, but this is not a necessary condition for them to have influence over other people. A fellow professor is the go-to person for anyone buying a computer because he is very technically savvy. He works frequently with highly technical equipment and talks about all the fun things his computer can do. So, he is an opinion leader both because he is knowledgeable and willing to help.

Many diffusion initiatives fail because a company mistakenly identifies formal authority figures as opinion leaders who are not very personable or able to help. It is important to understand that typically opinion leaders are at the center of communication networks. They communicate a lot, with many different types of people. It is the cumulative decisions of opinion leaders within a social system (like in MSU residence halls) that make the number of adopters for an innovation really take off. Fundamentally, innovations do not diffuse just because they are advantageous, cheaper, or compatible. They diffuse because of the cumulative application of the personal influence of earlier adopters on the decisions of later adopters. **Diffusion is a social process**.

Adopter Types

Innovators. We have talked at length about what drives innovations. Yet, we really have not talked much about the people who are the targets of innovations. What do we know about these target audience members? The key insight from years of research on this topic is that **not all adopters are alike**. It turns out that there are various kinds of adopters, and they are not all positive. If a company runs into the wrong kind of adopter for what they are proposing, it can have disastrous consequences.

Let's look at the group most likely to embrace change. These are the **innovators**. They are adventurous risk takers. They love change. They want to be the first on their block to try the new toy or embrace the new policy or try the new beer. These individuals are typically from more urban environments and are often on the cutting edge of technology. However, this is generally a small group and represents about 2.5 percent of any given society's population. I have a colleague who is constantly reading about the latest innovations in social media applications in marketing. He uses social media like Facebook and Twitter extensively in his courses and attends conferences on social media and marketing. He is well-informed about the latest technologies and many of us consult him about various technology innovations for our teaching and research needs.

Opinion Leaders. This second distinct group of people are called **opinion leaders** and they are much larger than the first group representing about 13.5 percent of the population. They also embrace change and are often among the first to try new ideas, but not necessarily on the cutting edge. However, the key difference between opinion leaders and innovators is that **opinion leaders are pretty vocal** about their interests by telling all their friends about the new products they have tried or ideas they have adopted. As a result, they usually lead or heavily influence the opinions of others who are thinking about adopting the new ideas. Because of their communication skills, these people are heavily involved in social networks as well; they are Kellogg's corn flake housewives. They try new things, they know lots of people, they are highly skilled and they are credible with their friends.

Early Adopters. The third group of individuals is still in front of the adoption curve since they represent about 34 percent of the population. These **early adopters** communicate with the opinion leaders but are slower to accept change. They are open to it, but they are not as **emotionally invested** in change as are the innovators and opinion leaders. They are much more deliberate and thoughtful about what might work and not work for them. As a result, they are not as vocal about their opinions regarding the new ideas they have embraced because they have more of a functional approach to the new ideas. They might like what the new iPad® does, but they cannot necessarily describe the technological features in great detail. They are just deliberate shoppers and good information managers. In playing the New Policy Communication Game, the boss would hope to have some opinion leaders among supervisors who could be really excited about the change and explain it well. But, more realistically, it would be best if the supervisors were at least early adopters and could be thoughtful about how the innovation would actually work and help people.

Late Adopters. Following these three adopter types are two groups of people who are not particularly excited about change. The first group that tends to reject change are the **late adopters**. These individuals represent about 34 percent of the population. They are not out scanning the environment for things that might improve their lives. **They like what they have**, or for other reasons are not interested in change. If the old stuff wears out, these individuals will be at least open to buying something better than the old thing. If they see something better than what they currently use they tend to hold off until the price gets lower. People who often resist change tend to be a bit **older and set in their ways** unlike people in the adopter groups who tend to be younger. These late adopters probably came to embrace the **Kellogg vision of modernity** and corn flakes well after the first wave of adopters. These folks probably waited until everyone else was doing it and the price came down.

Laggards. The final group of people, who represent about 16 percent of the population, are **laggards**. They not only dislike change of any kind, they actively fight it. If their TV broke they would look for one exactly like their old one, whereas a late adopter might actually try and find a better TV. They see change as an intrusion into their lives and an attack on their freedom. They are very traditional in their orientation and are not opinion leaders of any

kind. If you combine these folks with the late adopters you can see that they collectively represent 50 percent of the population. So, about half the population tends to resist change and the other half embraces change.

The significance of these adopter categories for companies trying to sell new products is the need to **attract young people to their brand** who are more likely to **embrace innovation and be open to new ideas**. The Apple commercials on TV show a young, casually dressed male who looks like an average college student representing Apple. The PC guy he is talking to is a pudgy, older-looking guy in a shirt and tie who looks stodgy and out of touch. So, college student, Apple wants you!

On the other hand, advertisers are less interested in older audiences because they have already **fixed their brand preferences**. Over time, people grow to prefer a certain type of car, laundry soap, clothing line, or place to shop. Trying to persuade them to change brands is difficult for advertisers so they tend to concentrate on younger people who are just getting started in life and figuring out what they like. Of course, older people have more money since they have been working longer, but they are also more set in their ways. Thus, despite their economic situation, advertisers all fight to attract younger audiences to their brand.

Assessing Your Adopter Type

What kind of adopter are you? Answer these ten questions to get a feel for the approach you like to use when confronting change. Score each item on a scale of 1-5:

1 = Strongly Disagree, 2 = Disagree, 3 = Unsure, 4 = Agree, 5 = Strongly Agree

Question	Score
1. I like to learn about the latest computer technologies.	
2. If I can afford it, I would buy the latest and greatest cell phone.	
3. I always keep an open mind about trying new things.	
4. I like telling others about the new things I have purchased.	
5. My friends are very technology oriented.	
6. When my friends have something new and different, I like to check it out.	
7. I come from a family of innovators.	
8. Change is easy for me.	
9. I have little patience for people who don't like to try new ideas.	

10. People often come to me for advice about new technologies.	
Total Score:	

If your score is between 45 and 50 you are probably an **innovator**.
If your score is between 35 and 44 you are probably an **opinion leader**.
If your score is between 25 and 34 you are probably an **early adopter**.
If your score is between 20 and 24 you are probably a **late adopter**.
If your score is between 10 and 19 you are probably a **laggard**.

Are you surprised about your score? Most students are probably early adopters or opinion leaders. The fact that you are in college and able to take risks suggests that you are open to change and might even find change interesting and motivating. However, some of you may believe that change is about fashion and fads. Change should have a rationale to justify shifting course in some way. So, reflect on your score.

Forces Controlling Innovation Adoption

We now have a picture about the nature of adoption of innovation, what makes adoption move more quickly or slowly, and something about the audiences that choose to adopt. Now let's put this together in a little larger framework to look more broadly at what it takes for an innovation or change to work successfully. Commercial innovation is really controlled by three main forces:

Market Forces. This is the most important factor in the innovation process because without a market there is no adoption. For example, Thomas Edison invented a machine that instantly counted votes that congressmen made for any given legislative bill. He then presented it to Congress and they immediately rejected it saying, "That's the last thing we need. We don't want to know right away what the vote is." At that point, Edison vowed to never again invent something unless there was a ready market for it. Markets are driven by demographics, income fluxes, prices, cultural orientations, and personalities. A refined understanding of a market is essential for success.

Technology Forces. Science and technology grow rapidly exposing new commercial possibilities every day. If Kellogg had not researched the relationship between diet and colon cancer he never would have invented corn flakes. The invention of computer chips made modern computing possible. It is vital to keep the pace of technology escalating to ensure that technologies are available to stimulate the imagination of innovators who can find creative ways of serving markets.

System Forces. These forces represent the third leg of the innovation stool. Innovations often take shape within large organizations like universities or technology corporations who can support such efforts. After a technology is introduced to the market and people have had a chance to try it out, the new idea will require certain changes to improve user friendliness. If the system is working well then this feedback is quickly received and the innovation is improved. If the system is too bureaucratic and lethargic, then it will ignore consumer input and ultimately fail. The W.K. Kellogg Company has always been effective at identifying changes in the market, and responding to those changes by coming out with new and better cereal options.

Summary

Playing innovation card games must be thoughtful because it's all about change.

Diffusion is about spreading the innovation to large audiences. Diffusing a new idea requires that people must hear about it from multiple communication channels so they become interested in learning more about it. Then, they must perceive that the idea is new and exciting.

Innovations are adopted in stages. People must first become aware of it, then express an interest in it. They must be able to mentally apply it to their lives, get confirmation from a change agent that trying it would be a good idea, and then be able to give it a trial spin before committing to it. This process is often long and tedious for marketers, but skipping steps can often result in poor adoption rates.

The speed by which the innovation diffuses through the target audience depends on many factors. The innovation must be perceived as new and also better than the old idea. It must be compatible with what people already know while also being simple and easy to use. People also must learn about the innovation from mass media channels and also from people they know and trust.

People react differently to innovations. At first everyone is uncertain about the new idea. Eventually that uncertainty is reduced by friends, or opinion leaders, who have tried the new idea and recommend it. Diffusion is a social process.

People also react differently to change. While about half the population is somewhat open to change, the other half is not. Those open to change can be either very excited about it and interested in it, or just open to change when it makes sense. Those who resist change are generally emotionally tied to the status quo and do not want to change. The key in diffusing a new idea is to understand the target audience's orientations toward change.

Lessons Learned

- **Know the Target Market.** Based on what we know about diffusing innovations quickly, the most important requirement is knowing the target audience or market for the innovation. Begin by determining whether most are early adopters or late adopters, for example. If they are early adopters, what messages are likely to resonate with these individuals?

- **Match Innovation Features to the Target Market.** After learning about the market, the next issue is how the innovation meets the needs of the target market. What are the relative advantages, how compatible is the innovation to current practices, and is it simple to use and understand?

- **Focus on the Message.** Kellogg centered on the "modern" message since that theme was important to his target audience for corn flakes. By conducting marketing surveys and focus groups it's possible to determine which messages click and which ones do not. Apple does an excellent job of branding, or creating an image of youthful intelligence and hipness that appeals to their target market.

- **Focus on the Channels.** Whether the innovation is a new kind of beer, policy, computer or cereal, the key message has to get out through channels that the target market values. Electronic channels are particularly effective because they allow getting a message out through a social network created by blogging or posting information on a social media site. But, interpersonal influences are also important. **Opinion leaders do most of the selling while electronic channels do most of the informing**.

- **Focus on the Process.** The actual diffusion process is much messier than the linear stages laid out above. The stages that are typical of how innovations are diffused are meant more as a guideline about how to think about the diffusion process. For example, informing people should come before giving out free samples. Each process is different but there should be a plan about how the diffusion effort should evolve. Make a plan and follow it.

- **Evaluate Campaign Effects.** Every diffusion campaign should be evaluated to both correct and update the messages, but also to update the innovation. When playing the New Policy Communication Game the boss needs to gauge employee reaction to the new policy. If the policy is accepted, that's great, but there's likely to be some pushback. How can the policy be corrected to improve it?

REFERENCE

Rogers, E. M. (1983). *Diffusion of innovations* (3rd ed.). New York: Free Press.

Chapter 13
Media Learning Card Games

Introduction

Do you remember watching a purple dinosaur when you were growing up; do you remember his name? Who was your favorite TV or movie character? If you are a female, maybe it was Princess Jasmine. For males, Spiderman might have been your hero. One of the most important sources of learning comes from the media because it gets us emotionally engaged. We are attracted to the drama—the story, the heroes, and villains. Whether we are watching movies, news, YouTube or network shows, we consume a tremendous amount of media messages.

The amount of media we consume and our normally intense emotional involvement in the action allows the media to have a significant impact in our lives. The two impacts described in Chapters 13 and 14 are learning and entertainment. In other words, what do we learn from all those media messages, and what effects do we experience from the entertainment messages we consume? Let's begin by focusing on the learning issue. What are we learning from all those hours we log while watching TV and movies and playing video games, and how should we respond to the impact these messages are having on us? To begin, consider these Media Learning Card Games.

Media Learning Card Games

The Local News Card Game. If you grew up in a big city and occasionally watched the local news, you may have a feel for the kinds of stories that reporters cover and the style they use to tell their stories. TV reporters are given stories to cover that are visually appealing. There must be exciting pictures that will engage audiences emotionally and give them a story that is similar to a reality TV show. So, in covering a fire or murder, playing the Reporter Card means covering the victims and showing how they suffered emotionally. Then, it is important to find out why this happened and who contributed to the tragedy. As we shall see in Chapter 14, these are the elements of effective drama and reporters are told to cover stories this way to increase their view-ability.

The Teletubby Card Game. Do you remember this show? It's aimed at 1-to-4 year- olds and was produced between 1997 and 2001. You may remember it. The show involved four colorful characters with various antennas sticking out of their heads, and on their tummies was a TV picture tube that showed various episodes of real kids doing fun things. The bright colors, unusual designs, repetitive babbling dialogue, and the occasional physical comedy were very appealing to the young viewers. In airing the show the producers played their Kid Show Producer Card to lure young audiences (and their parents) into a learning experience. However, the show sparked controversy in 1999 when the tele-evangelist Jerry Falwell claimed that Tinky Winky, the purple character with the triangle antenna on his head, was a homosexual role model for children. Falwell played his very unique version of an Evangelist Preacher Card and claimed that the purple color and Tinky Winky's triangular antenna were symbols of the Gay Pride Movement.

The Reality TV Card Game. In contrast to these heavily scripted and edited media presentations is reality TV. This format is very wide-ranging. On the one hand, there are network shows about people losing weight or surviving some game on a deserted island. While these shows use "real people", they are still heavily edited to tell the story the producer wants to tell using a TV format. In Spring 2010, a reality TV crew was filming a police raid on a home in Detroit. In the heat of the raid a police officer accidently shot an innocent victim. In the aftermath of the killing, some were questioning whether the TV crew's presence made the police officers more likely to act aggressively and play a more confrontational Police Card. The point of these unscripted videos is that individuals get to play their normal talk cards so others can see them in action.

The Learning Process

Definition of Learning. To understand how media impact us, let's talk first about what it means to "learn" something. **Learning is the active and passive acquisition of knowledge that has cognitive, emotional, and behavioral effects**. Active acquisition means that we intentionally pursue some knowledge that we need for some purpose. Attending this course is a good example. You need to know something about the communication process so you can perform more effectively in your career. Or you watch the local news to get informed about the day's events.

On the other hand, passive knowledge acquisition is about **incidental learning** that occurs unintentionally while actively pursuing other knowledge. You simply pick up other ideas or feelings as a **secondary reaction** to what you were mainly interested in learning. For example, you might turn on the local news to learn about the latest demonstrations in China or Thailand because you have friends there. That is actively pursuing knowledge. But, you might **passively learn** something about Chinese or Thai culture that you did not expect. You did not turn on the news to specifically learn about Chinese or Thai culture—you just picked that up while pursuing other knowledge. We shall see later that this passive or incidental learning has very significant effects.

How Learning Works. Whether learning is active or passive, it is useful to go into some detail about the process because it will help explain the effects of media messages. In general, learning occurs when we are confronted by some information that creates connections in our heads with what we already know to be true. That is, **learning is the transformation of information into knowledge**. The question is how does this transformation occur?

The transformation of information into knowledge is hierarchical in that the development of these connections is a process that moves from simple awareness all the way to using the knowledge to create something. Consider these steps for how information becomes transformed into knowledge:

- **Awareness.** The transformation begins when we pay attention to some sensory stimuli that are interesting, funny, or colorful. We may decide to focus actively on the stimuli to satisfy some need, or the stimuli might garner passive attention by being interesting or unusual. Kids actively sought out the Teletubby characters because they were fun and energetic. The stimuli are colorful and active, and do a good job of getting kids' attention.

- **Understanding.** The process of understanding happens in three basic steps. **Step 1** is called **Selective Exposure**. Immediately after gaining attention, only some of the stimuli we are exposed to become transformed into information. In other words, we really do not process all stimuli we sense. We are selective about what we process. In general, we only process or seek to understand what we need cognitively or emotionally, and ignore everything else. This process is called **selective exposure**. The idea is that we choose to understand some things and not others based on our needs.

  Step 2 is Categorizing. After selecting a stimulus to focus on, it then becomes "information" when we perceive a sensible pattern to it by categorizing it in relation to what we know to be true. When a stimulus gets categorized into information it becomes "understood" or sensible in some way. When kids turn on the Teletubby show and see characters dancing around, they immediately understand it as a TV show; they have seen it before and it all fits into that "TV Show" category for them. Falwell's claim that Tinky Winky was passively promoting a homosexual lifestyle is only valid if viewers transform the stimuli into information about that lifestyle. Yet, there does not seem to be any evidence that kids were influenced in this way.

Step 3 is Memorizing. The final step of understanding is when the information is placed into memory. We remember only some of the stimuli that are transformed into information. We know from research that we tend to remember the visual information first and the verbal information second. You probably remember someone's face but perhaps not his or her name, for example. I might remember an important person's name because I try harder to memorize it.

- **Teaching.** Once something is understood or categorized and becomes a memory, it really only stays there if the information is applied or used in some way. A good way to intensify the learning process is by asking someone to teach a lesson from what was learned. Teaching involves **helping others see connections** between the new information and what the person already knows to be true. That means the teacher can apply the information by showing how problems can be solved by knowing the information. When you give a speech about some topic, you are teaching others about it and helping them to understand it. You are also expanding your learning by demonstrating how something works. In other words, you "know" the information because you can see it from many different perspectives.

- **Evaluating.** Teaching really cements learning a great deal. Learning can also be expanded by using the newly found knowledge to evaluate the extent to which others have also acquired the knowledge. This evaluation process not only requires that you understand the information, but that you can tell when others are applying it properly or improperly. For example, one of the best ways to learn how to give public speeches is to rate others' speeches. What are they doing well and not so well?

- **Creating.** The final step of learning something is taking the knowledge and creating something new with it. The producers of the Teletubbies show relied on all the knowledge they had about child development and entertainment and pulled together a new show aimed at helping the social development of very young children. This creative process is the ultimate demonstration of whether or not someone knows the information.

Mass Media Elements

The mass media provide a very rich and diverse learning environment because the stimuli are so visceral. We like the fast-paced, colorful, engaging visuals that TV, movies, and video games provide. We have high-definition TV, and even 3D-TV to consume our attention. The potential for learning is great because the stimuli are rich and powerful. There are six elements of the mass communication process.

Professional Communicators. Behind the shows you see are many people who create, produce, direct, and contribute to any kind of mass media presentation. Pulling together a local news broadcast requires a news director, a producer, a director, on-air talent and people to run the equipment. It is a large operation. When playing his or her News Director Card, the person in this role decides which stories to cover and how to cover them. The goal is to get really exciting video that draws a big audience so they can sell more advertising. The Director Card is played by deciding how to stage the broadcast and pull together the various stories to create the maximum effect.

Media Messages. These professional communicators take all the knowledge they have and create messages to inform, persuade, or entertain various audiences within the context of the media channels they are using. For the TV medium, the Local News Card Game seeks to inform and entertain while the commercials on these broadcasts seek to persuade viewers to purchase various products and services. Shows like Teletubbies that target young children are designed to achieve various child development goals related to social skills and intellectual growth. In general, effective media messages must be:

- **Attention getting** by being distinctive, simple, and important to the target viewers
- **Positively reinforcing** to insure that viewers are rewarded for consuming the messages and want to transform them into knowledge
- **Easily interpreted** in the sense that they are consistent with current beliefs and attitudes and are simple to understand
- **Memorable** or able to stick with viewers so they can recall the messages and tell their friends

Media Proliferation. The number of channels for disseminating messages seem to grow by the week. Traditional print media like newspapers and magazines have been around for a few hundred years. Electronic media like radio (which was first used in 1922) and later television are more recent. Now people receive messages through the Internet and their "**smart phones**." These latest developments have really shifted the scope of mass media because the Internet reduces dissemination barriers. Anyone can create a podcast or write a blog and rant about any subject. In fact, the Internet has really **threatened the newspaper business** because most newspaper revenue comes from advertising and classified ads. Since selling stuff is less costly on eBay or Cars.com than in classified ads, people are turning away from newspapers to buy and sell stuff. And, since **targeting messages** is easier online because messages are tailored to individual's search patterns, advertising has shifted to Google, for example, at the expense of newspapers.

Diverse Audiences. Audiences for mass communication are very heterogeneous and large. A total of 93.2 million people watched Super Bowl XLI in 2010. In contrast, about 1 million people watch Jay Leno on the Tonight Show every night. The key to understanding media is that **shows are targeted toward specific groups**. TV dramas, including cop shows, are aimed at women 18-49 because women in this age range are the primary shoppers for consumer goods. Advertisers want to reach these women. If an advertiser wants to sell beer, then that beer company will buy a sports program since mostly men drink beer and watch sporting events.

Audience Learning. As these audiences actively seek out various shows, they inevitably learn a great deal. Let's take a look at the Reality TV Card Game. A viewer might tune into a reality police show because it is exciting to watch police conduct a drug bust, for example. That viewer might be thinking about a career in law enforcement and want to learn what it's like to be in the police force. Indirectly, the viewer might learn something about the police culture or about the drug culture. There might be other learning about the role of violence in society. Nevertheless, we know that people tend to learn a great deal when consuming media.

Media Learning Effects

Now that we understand the elements of mass media the question is how do they combine to impact viewers? What are viewers learning as they consume their various media sources over time? When people watch the evening news what are they learning? When kids watch children's programs what impressions stick with them? This next section details some of the effects of media exposure.

What do People Learn? First, the mass media impact viewers' **attitudes**, or likes and dislikes about people and objects. For example, continuous exposure to violence impacts viewers' attitudes about real-world aggression. Viewers who see a lot of violence come to like, respond more favorably toward, or see as justified actual acts of violence in the real world. Jerry Falwell was apparently concerned that repeated exposure to Tinky Winky as a gay Teletubby would cause children to view homosexuality more positively. Or media might also change our **beliefs**, or what we think is true or false about the world. When we watch a reality TV show about cops we are going to form some beliefs about the police culture, or even about the criminals they confront. Most of us do not have much experience raiding homes with guns so we're vulnerable to forming beliefs about unfamiliar things we see often on TV.

Media impact our **feelings and emotions**. Because entertainment is all about stimulating our emotions, we might learn to be fearful about going out at night after repeatedly watching news programs that highlight gang violence. Or we might watch shows that calm us down when we have had a hard day. My son used to watch Home and Garden TV on cable (HGTV) after a tough day at school. People often feel alienated and despondent about society after watching many negative news stories about violence. Even though crime rates are down significantly across the United States, people still believe the world is less safe today than 20 years ago. Because there are so many news channels producers playing their News Producer Cards, they sensationalize stories to play with viewer emotions.

Finally, the mass media can influence **behavior**. When kids **identify** with characters from TV or movies a few might start to act like them or use language common to these characters. When stories appear frequently in the news, they often drive what people talk about when discussing issues of local or even national importance. This process of driving discussion is called **agenda setting**. Lots of news reporting on the homeless can set the agenda for making homelessness a political campaign issue. Skilled public relations professionals advising political candidates can use agenda-setting to force a debate on these issues when they favor their clients.

Another good example of how media influence our behavior is **advertising**. Research consistently demonstrates that advertising is very effective in persuading us to buy goods and services. The more advertisers spend on consumer products like soap and beer, the more people are likely to buy those products. These ads and commercials are aimed at keeping the products and services foremost in our minds as we shop.

Learning about Violence. We know from research that **violence is pervasive on TV and movies**. The vast majority of movies feature violence because it gets people excited. And, the violence is often glamorized and sanitized. The good guys use violence to solve problems without showing many of the negative consequences of their violent actions. These good guys are slick, drive expensive cars, and appear to enjoy the good life. Since violence is rarely chastised on television, frequent viewers tend to perceive that violence is an acceptable way to solve problems. Unless these perceptions are checked by the person's own thought processes, they are likely to persist.

Research indicates that there are generally three main effects of these pervasive violent portrayals:

- Individuals become increasingly **aggressive** toward others as they see a lot of violence in the media.
- **Emotional desensitization** often occurs when viewers consume a steady diet of violent viewing. They grow increasingly numb or insensitive to aggression in the real world and see it as more "normal."
- Viewers of violent content increase their sense of vulnerability to becoming a **victim of a violent crime**.

However, not all types of violent depictions have the same effect on viewers. Some portrayals increase the risk of harm, whereas others decrease these risks. In essence, **the context or way in which violence is depicted influences how viewers interpret and ultimately respond to televised acts of aggression.** For example, in the Reality TV Card Game, violence is real and the consequences of these acts are seen as devastating to friends and family members. However, violence in movies is generally sanitized, glamorized, and viewed as justified and necessary since it's important for a drama to have the good guys shoot/beat up the bad guys. We like it; it's entertaining!

In addition to context, the **type of viewer** influences the kind of impact that media violence might have on the viewer. Some viewers are more susceptible to the harmful effects of violent media than are others. Studies show that younger children, boys, the characteristically aggressive, those who fantasize about violence, and those who believe television violence is realistic are more at risk for learning aggression. These individuals are already more attracted to risky behavior and selectively attend to violent messages. They will also try to learn them more extensively by teaching the violence to others through re-enacting violent episodes they see.

These effects become even more extensive when kids play violent video games like *World of Warcraft*. Such multiplayer games heighten the violent experience and become addicting over time. If we look at such games as a learning experience it is easy to see why they are so effective. Not only do

players teach one another about how to defeat very powerful enemies, these games require enormous creativity in how to violently destroy enemies, which is the ultimate expression of learning. Kids most heavily impacted are those who play more extensively.

Learning About Sex. Sex is another way that media garner attention. Remember that learning begins by grabbing viewer attention. When scantily clad people appear in all their glory, people are physiologically programmed to focus on these images. Barriers against showing sex on TV or in the movies have quickly disappeared over the years so that now just about anything goes. In fact, research indicates that the prevalence of sex on TV is increasing, with over two-thirds of TV shows featuring, some kind of sexual content. Much of this increase is due to the amount of sexual talk—not behavior—on television.

There is also a significant increase in the amount of sexual intercourse in the media, particularly involving characters in their teenage years. These acts are common in all kinds of TV, cable, and movie programming. Again, **they get attention**. Despite the proliferation of sexual messages, very few programs depict the risks and responsibilities associated with sex. Few shows with any sexual content mention safe sex or the need for thoughtful decision-making associated with sexual practices. Thus, what is most likely to be learned is that sex is fun and carefree, and not necessarily associated with any kind of committed relationship.

While it is clear that exposure to sexual content is extensive, the impact of this exposure is less clear. Some studies show that children can learn sexual terms and phrases from **exposure to educational** as well as dramatic programming. My young son learned to say "Oh Shit" after watching the *Happy Gilmore* movie repeatedly, much to our chagrin! Some research shows that focusing on MTV-like programming can result in more approval of teen premarital sex than were those who are not exposed to such content. It is almost as if approving of such behavior is a requirement of tuning into such programs. It makes it all look more "**normal**" just like reactions to violence.

Massive exposure to sexual content is also much more likely to **desensitize** viewers to sexual indiscretions, just like massive exposure to violence numbs viewers to actual violence. This is particularly the case among male viewers who become **numb** to violence and sexual indiscretion more quickly than female viewers.

There is still one unanswered question about sex in the media, however. That is, does exposure to images of sex contribute to early adolescent sexual activity? Recent research suggests that it might contribute. The study found that adolescents who view more sexual content are more likely to initiate intercourse and progress to more advanced sexual activities during the subsequent year, even controlling for characteristics that might predict these results. Heavy viewers are twice as likely as light viewers to **initiate sex earlier** in their teen years. Parents can address these issues not by just cutting off such content but by initiating conversations about sexual behavior in relationships. Family discussions are the key.

Learning About Stereotyping. Heavy media consumers are also vulnerable to stereotyping simply because of the nature of the medium. A 30-minute TV episode is actually 22 minutes of content and 8 minutes of commercials. In that 22-minute span the show must tell a story with a minimal amount of character development. The program producer must present a **stereotypical character**, like a typical father or criminal, for example, and let the audience "fill in" character traits so the producer can advance the story. Spending too much time on character development leaves less time for the story.

Another hot medium for **perpetuating stereotypes** is **video games**. Again, since character development is far less important than the story or the action, game developers rely on stereotypical images in their games. It should probably come as no surprise that a recent study of video game character images from top-selling American games showed that male characters, as you may have guessed, were much more likely to be portrayed aggressively than female characters. Female characters are likely to be portrayed as scantily clad while also showing a mix of sex and aggression. A survey of teens confirmed that stereotypes of male characters as aggressive and female characters as sexually objectified physical specimens are held even by non-gamers.

The problem is that when individuals have less direct contact with people who are different than themselves, they are more vulnerable to media stereotyping. Research consistently demonstrates that when playing the Local News Card Game, producers and reporters present more crime stories of Blacks and Latinos than of whites. When viewers from any ethnic group have less direct contact of individuals from stereotyped minority groups, these viewers are more likely to have negative appraisals of minority members. Pre-existing prejudices also play into this process.

For example, first-time visitors to the United States often have little direct contact with members of different U.S. minority groups making the recent arrivals more vulnerable to stereotyped media portrayals. A person from Japan who has no direct experience with Hispanics in Japan might be **more vulnerable to stereotyping** than a native U.S. citizen. There are probably other cultural biases at work as well, but the stereotypical media portrayals certainly do not help the problem of racial prejudice.

Failing to overcome learned stereotypes hinders winning card games because communicators make false judgments about people in terms of their orientations, motives, and abilities. On the one hand, we like stereotypes because they make communication easier; since everyone is the same you do not have to exert energy trying to discover differences. On the other hand, stereotyping focuses on **inherently negative attributes** and assumes that everyone who belongs to a specific group has the same flaws or quirks, from our point of view. The best strategy is to be conscious of stereotypes and work to ignore them when communicating with someone from an ethnic group other than your own.

Mass Media Theories

These discussions of violence, sex, and stereotyping are meant to illustrate how attitudes, beliefs, and behaviors are learned from intense media exposure. When producers and reporters show their cards in the context of playing their games, viewers learn all kinds of things, many of which are unintentional. Aside from what we know about how people learn, what theories might explain some of these media effects?

Priming Effects.   One of the more interesting theories explaining how media influence behavior was developed by **Leonard Berkowitz** and his colleagues. The theory was created to explain the short-term, transient impact of media violence on aggressive behavior. Berkowitz argued that the media **prime** or stimulate our memory, which in turn, triggers a reaction. More specifically, he contends that memory is made up of networks of thoughts, emotions, and action tendencies that are interconnected. The pathways linking these networks can be activated or primed by different types of stimuli such as seeing violence on a TV show. These images "prime" or activate previous aggressive thoughts, feelings, and behaviors stored in memory about that specific issue.

For example, my brother and I watched professional wrestling often, because early TV programming options were quite limited. Whenever it came on, we started wrestling ourselves, which often resulted in my older brother torturing me with the holds and slams used by the pros. My mother did not like it much, but these images primed our aggressive tendencies. In other words, the shows stimulated the link between our knowledge of wrestling and our brotherly dislike for one another. By stimulating that pathway we began to "fight" regularly. While this example is about playful boys, the priming effect becomes quite a problem when movie violence primes a teenager to grab a gun and go shoot classmates in school. Again, priming effects are most likely to occur with heavy media exposure, lack of parental supervision, and a history of violent behavior.

Social Cognitive Theory.   This theory, developed by **Albert Bandura** and his colleagues, focuses on the learning process that we discussed at the beginning of the chapter. But it takes a little different tack with respect what happens from the point at which information enters our memory. The theory argues that after categorized information enters our memory, it becomes a model for how to see other things or how to act. For example, if we see a new fashion trend or a new way of speaking, each can become a model that we use when shopping for fashions or talking with friends. Social cognitive theory contends that we will act in a way that is consistent with that model if we are motivated to do so—**if we are reinforced either directly or vicariously** (indirectly) for adopting that new model.

The Teletubby Card Game is meant to encourage young children to model cooperative behavior. The Teletubbies have fun playing together. If kids see this cooperation repeatedly, they are getting rewarded for being cooperative, as well. The real insight about this theory is the idea of **reinforcement**, which is the **social learning** component of the theory. The more frequently a behavior is positively reinforced the more likely people are to model that behavior.

Because violence is so pervasive and good guys get reinforced in the movies for being violent to save the day, it becomes a learned response. Viewers begin to see violence as appropriate and are motivated to use it when necessary because it gets rewarded.

The key difference between **Priming Effects Theory** and **Social Cognitive Theory** is that the priming effect is much more limited in scope. It contends that media images prime memory connections that, in turn, stimulate behavior. The Social Cognitive Theory adds the **motivation** component to the mix. Bandura would argue that violence, or any behavior for that matter, is stimulated only when the individual is motivated to engage in that behavior. That motivation comes from seeing the pro- or anti-social behavior being positively reinforced, and thus, learned.

Cultivation Theory. While these first two theories do a good job of laying out the specific mechanisms that cause us to learn and adopt attitudes, beliefs, and behaviors stimulated by media, a theory developed by **George Gerbner** and his research team sought to explain the long-term cumulative effects of exposure to television. In developing his theory, Gerbner examined the nature of the content that individuals consume on TV. He focused on TV because he contends that it's the medium that is most pervasive in our society—it is the most available and the most viewed.

In general, there are two basic premises to **Cultivation Theory**. First, TV is a cultural "**story teller**." Rather than the family, church, or other societal venues, TV is the major socialization agent of our time. We spend much more time consuming TV and related images (on smart phones or computers) than interacting with family members or school teachers. TV creates a story or narrative about our world—it provides a dramatic model of what life is like consisting of good guys and bad guys and challenges to overcome.

Second, this Cultivation Theory argues that **television delivers largely homogeneous stories or messages**. Independent of genre, time of day, or channel, the "message" of television is relatively uniform. Differences are stripped away to make them simple to understand. Gerbner would certainly support the idea that TV presents stereotyped images of people, ideas, and events to make them easy to understand. All people, ideas, and events start to look alike after a while.

Because TV programming delivers similar or uniform content to large and heterogeneous audiences, heavy viewing "**cultivates**" a shared perspective among otherwise diverse groups. That is, repeated exposure to television cultivates a world outlook that overrides any initial differences due to demographics, personality characteristics or environment. This **enculturation** process is called "**mainstreaming**." Consistent with this theorizing, studies show those heavy viewers of television are more likely than light viewers to perceive the world as a mean and violent place.

Another process in cultivation is **resonance.** In some instances, television offers a "double dose" of reality by mirroring or reflecting viewers' direct experience. The result of resonance is that certain cultivation effects will be more pronounced or amplified when fact and fiction match. The more people watch crime shows, the more they are going to fear being a crime victim. Or the more they are going to look for criminal behavior in order to be a part of the drama just like on TV. Sometimes a show **resonates with viewers** so much that they want to dress like, act like, and be placed in situations just like characters to whom they are really attracted. Some young girls emulate the *Twilight* vampire series.

Cultivation Theory can be applied to other areas besides media violence. For instance, repeated exposure to sexual portrayals that do not feature the risks or responsibilities associated with such mature behavior may cultivate in viewers the belief that safe sex or committed relationships are not important. Or, heavy viewing of **demeaning portrayals of racial minorities may cultivate prejudices** and negative attitudes towards those from different ethnic groups. Perhaps Jerry Falwell had Cultivation Theory in mind when arguing that kids should not be exposed to Tinky Winky because this character cultivated homosexual beliefs.

Media Literacy Theory. A final theory that really brings these others together, in my view, is the idea of media literacy. The basic idea of the theory is that media images present a whole new language to viewers that must be decoded and learned in order for its substance and intent to be understandable. In other words, we must be media literate just like we are linguistically literate. **We must have the ability and the habit of transforming media messages into their appropriate knowledge structures.** We must be able to discriminate between and accurately label a TV cartoon program and a TV cartoon commercial. If we can tell the difference, we're literate. If we can't, then we are illiterate. Let's look at the theory and see how it pulls these others together in a coherent framework.

Media Literacy Theory begins with the idea that messages contain two types of information that we must be able to differentiate:

- **Factual information** that consists of the raw, context free truth about what the source is communicating
- **Social information** that focuses on the intent of the source to inform, persuade, or entertain

In other words, when we are playing the Local News Card Game by watching the news we have to determine first what's factual or true about what we are observing in the story. Does it make sense? Second, we have to decide why we are seeing this message. What is the source trying to do? Is the source simply trying to inform us, or is the source trying to persuade us to take some action? Literacy begins when we can accurately tell **what's factual and what's intentional**.

Based on this kind of discrimination, the theory further contends that the mass media present three general types of messages:

- **News**, which is intended to inform the audience about current events

- **Entertainment** that seeks to evoke a pleasant or rewarding emotional experience of some kinds
- **Advertising**, which is intended to influence purchasing behavior

As you know, the media likes to blend these kinds of messages. Occasionally we will see "**docudramas**" in which an actual event is used as the basic story line for a dramatic story of some kind. These shows are meant to both inform and entertain. Or, we might watch "**informercials**" that seek to inform and advertise. They are often on TV late at night and tell people about juicers or special weight loss drugs. A media literate person knows that docudramas are not real and that the facts might be fudged a bit. And, the media literate person knows that infomercials may not tell the whole story. The new weight-loss formula is probably not the miracle cure it portends to be.

What's important about this theory is that it provides a way forward to use the valuable insights of the other theories mentioned here. It says that we must be able to accurately understand the kinds of violence we see in the media and know that might prime us to act violently ourselves. We should know that watching professional wrestling is not real and not intended to incite us. We should realize that those using violence are getting rewarded because the intent of the person playing the Producer Card is to build the drama and entertain us—not incite us to use that behavior as a model for our own lives. We should be aware that we are vulnerable to **cultivating** an overly simplistic, **stereotypical view** of the world by consuming media that might not be accurate or productive. The bottom line is that we need to create strategies for building media literacy in our lives to see media messages as they are and to understand the cards that are being played when we consume these messages.

Strategies for Increasing Media Literacy

Understand Own Biases. The strategies most likely to be effective for increasing media literacy begin with the need to first understand our own personal biases that might color how we interpret media messages. Are you biased against certain cultural orientations? Do you believe that police are often corrupt, or that women are only sexual objects? Understanding our biases are important because they guide the kind of media that will gain our attention. Remember, the first step in the learning process is gaining our attention. We pay attention to what we are attracted. to Many kids have addiction problems to video games. This attraction is a bias that colors what they consume and how they interpret it—what they see as factual and intentional on the part of the sources.

Gain More Personal Experiences. A second strategy for building media literacy is developing and expanding our personal experiences in the real world. The more diverse these experiences are the better. Have you ever seen real, dramatic poverty with people living in cardboard shacks with dirt floors and talked with these people? If you have you may feel differently about them than if the only poor people you see are on TV. Do you know anyone from an Arab culture? Members of this culture are often featured in the news, yet most Americans know little about how diverse Arab or Muslim culture is. Take risks and get out and talk to people who are different than you!

Understand Media Institutions and Biases. Media institutions are organizations competing for your attention just like any other organization. A large newspaper company like Gannett Corporation owns hundreds of newspapers and many TV and radio stations. What impact does their corporate identity and priorities have on how they report the news? The same conglomerate that owns the tabloid National Enquirer also owns the Wall Street Journal and Fox News. What is their **political orientation**? Does this orientation matter? More importantly can you impact the media? Since media are businesses they want to have an impact and often welcome student input. Be a player and reach out!

Read More. Finally, media institutions are complex and dynamic. They are changing rapidly, yet they are the foundation of our democracy. We are only as strong as we are well informed about what is going on. Read a newspaper every day, write a blog or comment on others' blogs. Staying informed is the best way to stay literate. Everyone is manipulated by the media in some way. Just make sure that the you understand when and how you are being manipulated.

Summary

Learning is both active and passive. When we pursue information it is active learning. When we learn something in the process of these active pursuits, it is called passive or incidental learning.

Learning is a hierarchical process. Learning begins by paying attention to some stimuli, then trying to understand them. After achieving **understanding**, we try to **memorize** these stimuli. We learn even more when we can teach what we have come to understand, evaluate others with respect to this new understanding and then create something that incorporates this understanding.

Media consist of many components. To understand how media work we must focus on the **professional communicators**, the **messages** they produce, the way in which these messages proliferate though many **channels**, and ultimately the **impacts** of these messages on diverse audiences.

Understanding media impact involves answering many questions. What do people **learn** from the media; how do they **stimulate our emotions** and change our behaviors; what **factors** influence the kinds of impact media has on us?

Media effects related to violence, sex, and stereotyping are most important. The media use these three elements frequently to gain attention and promote viewer learning. Only when we understand these effects can we begin to control them.

There are many theories about media impacts. Media impact us by priming, or stimulating our memory and triggering an emotional reaction. Or, media impact us when we see characters that get positively or negatively reinforced for some behavior; we want to model characters that get rewarded and avoid characters that get punished. Media also cultivate a general worldview that reality is an unsafe, dangerous place. Finally, our goal as consumers is to increase our media literacy.

Lessons Learned

- **Media Card Games teach us a lot.** It's really surprising how much we pick up from media messages. If you listed the top ten beliefs you have about people from cultures you have not encountered directly, it's likely that most of these believes came from repeated media exposure. So, the lesson is, reflect aggressively on your beliefs before labeling someone or something you know little about from direct experience.

- **Media messages are complex.** Media messages are highly produced so there is a lot of information contained in them. They are colorful, action packed, and often very subtle. Often they are so entertaining that they suck us in and we're not really able to stand back from them objectively and see what they're doing to us. So, consume these messages with skill and skepticism.

- **Media messages affect us in many ways.** Media messages impact our attitudes, beliefs, and behaviors. Commercials make us want to buy and to believe that we can be popular or more attractive if we do what they want. Make no mistake that these are powerful games and people are playing powerful cards with a lot of money at stake.

- **Media theories provide valuable insights into media effects.** One of the great contributions of these theories is that they provide useful insights into how and why media messages impact us so thoroughly. They tell us how they get into our heads. Armed with this information, you can now better understand these effects and approach your consumption of media messages with more caution.

- **Media literacy is a key part of your social and intellectual development.** The goal of this chapter is to increase your media literacy. Remember, every message asks you to play a card. The advertiser plays his or her Company Card to encourage you to buy their products and services. In return they want to you play your Consumer Card and buy their stuff. Do you really believe that you'll be more popular, more attractive or a better person with more stuff? A media literate person knows the intent of these messages and can form an effective shield against unwanted influence. I hope you have formed just such a shield so you can better play card games with these folks. Good luck!

REFERENCES

Bandura, A. (1994). Social cognitive theory of mass communication. In J. Bryant & D. Zillmann (Eds.), *Media effects* (pp. 61–90). Hillsdale, NJ: Erlbaum.

Berkowitz, L., & Rogers, K. H. (1986). A priming effects analysis of media influence. In J. Bryant & D. Zillmann (Eds.), *Perspectives on media effects* (pp. 57–81). Hillsdale, NJ: Erlbaum.

Gerbner, G. (1997). Gender and age in prime-time television. In S. Kirschner & D. A. Kirschner (Eds.), *Perspectives on psychology and the media* (pp. 69–94). Washington DC; American Psychological Association.

Gerbner, G., Gross, L., Morgan, M., & Signorielli, N. (1994). Growing up with television: The cultivation perspective. In J. Bryant & D. Zillmann (Eds.), *Media Effects* (pp. 17–42). Hillsdale, NJ: Erlbaum.

Chapter 14
Entertainment Card Games

Introduction

Have you ever been completely frightened by a movie, so much so that it prevented you from sleeping? I recall taking my oldest son to see the movie *Twister*, a 1996 release about a professor who chases tornados around the Midwest. Of course, the movie contains several scenes of tornados ripping through farms causing tractors and cows to fly through the air and smash into things. The sounds and sights were truly frightening to my 8-year-old son. I should not have taken him to see that movie because every night afterward if he heard any wind outside before going to bed he would ask if a tornado was coming to get us. He even rigged up a tie-down pole in his room with a belt to keep any tornado from sucking him out of the house. He was probably freaked out for at least 2 months.

The focus of this final installment in our understanding of Card Talk games is on how the media stimulate our emotions by playing Entertainment Card Games. These games are very appealing because they are designed to entertain us by playing with our emotions. They draw us into fascinating tales of various forms and present unbelievable special effects that heighten the experience. Understanding these games and their effects means first understanding emotions and then how media entertainers stimulate them.

Entertainment Card Games

The Scary Movie Card Game. Scary tales have been around for centuries. Movies do a great job of bringing these freighting experiences to life. Most of the movies that fall into this category are aimed at teens and young adults. The genre for these films is called horror movies or maybe slasher films. The formula for films such as *Scream* or *Friday the 13th* is pretty standard: A bunch of young, attractive, single people get away to some remote, spooky location to party. Then all of a sudden, a really horrible-looking bad guy appears and starts killing everyone. Generally only a few good people are left with the hero saving the day by eliminating the slasher (until the next movie, of course). By playing a Scary Movie Producer Card, the producer is asking the audience to play their Scared Bystander Card and act in a frightened way. Audiences comply probably because scary movies are fun to watch and they allow viewers to play other games that I will explain later in the chapter.

The Situation Comedy Card Game. The second card game is played generally on TV in the form of a situation comedy. The formula for this game is also pretty standard. In this game, the main characters are usually young, attractive single people in a big city trying to deal with their friends and careers. Then, they get into all kinds of strange and funny situations. The plots are secondary to the humorous lines and sexual innuendo that permeates the scripts. Notice how these games are aimed at younger viewers showing other young people. Advertisers love these shows because they want to attract young viewers who have not yet established their brand preferences for consumer products like soap and beer. By looking at these shows, you might conclude that the typical urban dweller is witty, thin, sexy, and charming.

The Action Movie Card Game. Blockbuster hits like 2010's *Avatar* and the previous generation's space cowboy adventure *Star Wars* have been a Hollywood staple for many ears. The list of these films is endless from *Batman* to *Spider-Man* to *Iron Man*. The key to this card game formula is that there is an evil villain trying to take over the world and he (generally a he) must be stopped by some unassuming, everyday-looking guy or gal who ends up saving the day. The hero must be ordinary looking and have the same kind of human character flaws that we all have so the audience can identify with the character. The key to the Action Movie and the Scary Movie Card Games is a **gigantic conflict between good and evil** and, as we shall see, our enjoyment level depends upon really building up the evil and then seeing the hero crush it decisively.

Understanding Entertainment

Definition of Entertainment. Consuming media messages for sheer enjoyment, relaxation, and escape without any ulterior motives defines **entertainment communication**. Since we have time on our hands and there are few cultural barriers to pursuing entertainment in the United States, we seek an emotional escape from the daily grind. In other words, we want to stimulate and explore our emotional side to simply feel better. It is fun to get scared, laugh at something amusing, or cry after an intense drama. Early psychologists like Freud felt that our impulses for pleasurable experiences are repressed and that we need entertainment to express these pleasures and relieve our suffering. Later explanations focus on how media entertainment simply satisfies our need for fun and relaxation.

Three Elements of Drama. What makes entertainment like the Action Movie Card Game enjoyable is when it conforms to the three elements of good drama. First, the story must depict an **intense conflict of forces**. Drama dwells on conflict and its resolution by depicting events carried out by protagonists and antagonists who are affected by these events. The good characters are trying their best to achieve important and morally superior goals, or just prevent the bad guys from taking over. Either way, intense conflict is the first requirement of good drama.

Second, viewers must be able to **care about and relate to the characters**; they must really like the good guys. And, they must really despise the bad guys. In the Action Movie Card Game a key element is the need for the good guys to be ordinary people who do extraordinary things. We would like to think of ourselves in the same way making it easy to relate to these folks. When not in his costume, *Spider-Man* is just a regular college student who is smart, but nervous around girls and just blends in socially with the rest of the class. The Marine in *Avatar* is just a regular enlisted man who lost the use of his legs in battle, but ultimately demonstrates a strong moral core that we all aspire to achieve. Conversely, it is important to hate the bad guys and see them as very different from us. That sets up a good conflict. However, it is possible for the good guy to convert the bad guy to achieve redemption, as Luke Skywalker did in *Star Wars* when he converted his dad from the evil Darth Vader back to the good guy Anakin Skywalker.

The third element of successful drama is a **satisfying resolution** of that conflict. We want the good guys to win the large battles to save the world and the small personal battles associated with, say, a marriage or relationship with someone. In the movie *Independence Day*, Will Smith first had to save the world from the ugly alien bad guys, but he also had to repair his relationship with his girlfriend and regain the trust of her son. We want it all wrapped up in a neat package. In fact, as we know from the last chapter, this element of drama causes the expectation that every relational problem ends happily ever after. It happens in every movie, so we often come to expect happy resolutions to problems in real life.

Humor. Comedy is a form of drama. Really, the only difference is that the audience must be given cues that the events they are watching should not be taken very seriously. Of course, bad guys often use hostile humor to punish the good guys, but it only intensifies the audience's dislike for the antagonist. The more common form of humor, typical in the Situation Comedy Card Game, still involves conflict, but it is generally between a character struggling with his or her own issues and getting into weird situations, or a conflict between a couple around some funny family or relationship problem. All *Seinfeld* episodes center around issues related to Jerry and his strange pals. Also, romantic comedies have essentially the same formula. The couple works hard at the beginning to pursue one another, then one person does something stupid that causes them to break up or have a crisis of some type, and then they come back together after resolving the crisis.

Humor is also used extensively in advertising. Research indicates that **humor makes messages more interesting** and attention getting, the **first step** in learning. Since they attend to it they are more likely to process it. Recall from

Chapter 7 that persuasion is much more likely to occur if the audience **thinks deeply** about the message. And, if they are laughing the audience is much less likely to think of reasons not to like the product. Humor also enhances the credibility of the speaker, making this person's message more compelling and believable. The challenge in using humor in advertising is not to make the commercial so funny that no one remembers the product. Humor can easily overwhelm any memory of the product. This does not help when the consumer is thinking about what kind of beer or soap to buy.

Sports. The same elements that make drama entertaining also make sports entertaining. We get a great deal of enjoyment from sports when we really want our team to win. We are the good guys, and the other team represents the bad guys. When the other team is a heated rival, it makes the drama even more compelling. Add to this the suspense, or fear of a negative outcome and the very risky play that is standard fare at big-time games, and it makes us cheer harder for our noble warriors.

Regarding the effects of **sports drama**, research indicates that winning has some personal pay-off for fans. When their favorite team wins consistently, fans' self-esteem and personal confidence improves. **Gender** also impacts sports enjoyment. Women enjoy sports with more moderate levels of suspense, such as volleyball, whereas men want much more suspenseful sports contexts such as American football. Women also prefer the more artistic sports such as figure skating or gymnastics, but these sports do not offer the kind of suspense that men generally prefer.

Suspense. Playing the Scary Movie Game is a lot of fun for many people. I really like suspenseful thrillers, particularly if they involve submarines. The drama inside that claustrophobic boat deep under the water is very intense and riveting for me. I love to submit to this game and play my Audience Card and watch till the good guys prevail.

Because participating in this Scary Movie Game causes audience members so much stress, the question is why do people like it so much? The obvious explanation is that it contains all the elements of drama with good guys and bad guys so that the conflict generated from these portrayals provides the enjoyment. But that explanation is probably not sufficient given the amount of stress that audience members feel when consuming suspenseful content. Research shows that the more the audience suffers along with the leading character, the greater the satisfaction at the end when all is resolved. The most recent explanation of this effect focuses on **emotional empathy**. More specifically, the more emotionally distraught the leading character is the more the audience empathizes with the character and the more eager they are to relieve the character's distress.

Horror. The primary difference between horror and suspense entertainment is the different emotions that are stimulated. Suspense evokes more **anxiety**, whereas horror is designed to stimulate **fear**. Again, the elements of good drama attract people to this card game. There are a bunch of cute, innocent victims and many very evil bad guys. The audience can certainly relate to the innocent victims because they are intentionally cast to look like the target market for the films—young people.

However, audience motivations to watch are quite different for horror than for suspense entertainment. According to research, gender differences are the driving force in making horror attractive. For example, research indicates that men enjoy horror more when they are in the **company of a terrified female**. Men like to show their mastery of fear—they are not afraid of some silly old slasher! Plus, he gets to comfort the terrified female and be a hero to her. Consistent with this finding, women enjoy horror movies when accompanied by a male who exhibits mastery over his fears. She enjoys it less if the guy is screaming too; she wants a hero!

Fear Reactions to Entertainment Content

Because fear is one of the most common emotions stimulated by entertainment content it is useful to understand it a bit more to reveal how this card game is played. People have been telling scary stories for a few thousand years because audience members find it very entertaining, probably because they like the emotional release. In other words, when you play the Scary Movie Game, you know you are going to see many scary scenes. Research indicates that this process is satisfying because you know that ultimately the fear will be relieved when the bad guy is finally eliminated. This **catharsis**, or purging, eliminates your own fears about other problems in your life. For example, you might be afraid to go to a new school, or try a new sport. Research says that being scared in an artificial situation like a movie, and then having that fear eliminated helps relieve some of the other real fears in our lives.

What Scares Us? When attending to scary movies there are generally three situations that produce fear. First, we often become frightened by **dangers and injuries**. Seeing movies about tornados, earthquakes, or violent confrontations between rivals produces fear because we believe we are also vulnerable to these events. Second, **monsters** or distortions of natural forms can be very scary. Huge snakes, gorillas (King Kong), or plants that we normally think of in much smaller forms become very scary when they are distorted and dangerous. Third, we become frightened when we see something **dangerous** happen to a character with whom we empathize. We do not want anything bad to happen to the good guys because we like their motivations and to some extent see ourselves to be just like them. We become attached and we do not want to lose that attachment, so we become frightened.

What Intensifies the Fear? Hollywood producers know well what intensifies the scariness of a particular event. For example, when a scary event appears highly realistic audience members become much more emotional because of **stimulus generalization**. The more we generalize what we are watching on the screen to real life, the more intensely we feel the fear. If it is real life, it could happen to us or our friends. My youngest son refused to watch the movie 2012 in which the world came to an end, because he thought it would be too realistic and he is very uncomfortable with the fact that the world will end some day.

Another cause of intensified fear is **stimulus discrimination**. Younger children often have difficulty **discriminating** fantasy from reality. They might believe monsters are real, or tornados are imminent, or criminals are around every corner. They cannot discriminate fantasy from reality, causing them to become more frightened than a mature adult with a more well-developed cognitive skill set. Of course, if a viewer is watching a documentary that is "real" and sees a frightening event, any distance between reality and fantasy is eliminated, making the content even more imposing on the viewer. There is **no ability to discriminate** because the stimulus is a real event.

Another factor intensifying fear is viewer motivation for attending to the stimulus. If you really like horror films you are more likely to pay attention to what's happening, and more likely to be scared by the content. Or, if viewers are emotionally aroused before seeing a scary event then their fear is intensified. This **excitation transfer** happens as a spillover from a previous event. For example, a movie may begin with a scary event to get audience members emotionally involved. Then, another scary event is introduced and because the viewer is already aroused, the new fear-producing event is intensified. Producers like to play around with music to build a sense of suspense and impending doom. Other techniques involve foreshadowing or forewarning of impending threats. Early in a movie something bad might happen that characters simply dismiss, but the audience knows that it is foreshadowing really bad events later in the movie.

Understanding Emotions

All of these entertainment genres share a focus on stimulating emotions. From a communication standpoint, understanding entertainment effects means understanding emotions, and ultimately, being able to control our emotions. This next section seeks to define emotion and then discuss how you can begin to control your own emotions as you play these entertainment card games.

What is Emotion? Producers and directors playing the Scary Movie or Action Movie Card Games know that their job is to play with our emotions. What are they playing with? **Emotions are defined as feelings that we learn to label or define**. In other words, in reacting to some specific stimuli like a scary horror movie, I might see my palms sweat, my pupils dilate, and my hair stand up on the back of my neck. Seeing all these physiological reactions, I might conclude that "I am scared or frightened." Or, I might observe myself staring into my child's face, and conclude that "I love my son." In other words, emotions are aroused feelings that we make sense out of, or categorize cognitively in some manner. Once we apply words that frame our internally aroused experiences they become **emotions**.

Feelings originate in the **paleocortical circuits** in our brain, located near the brain stem. These circuits were the first part of our brain to develop ("paleo" means ancient). These paleo circuits are responsible for basic mammalian activities such as care and feeding of offspring and basic body maintenance. The purpose of having feelings is that they give the body the resources it needs to **protect itself** from predators and other survival threats. If the body senses threats it must react for self-preservation. However, the labeling or thinking part of emotions comes from the **neocortical circuits** located in the frontal lobe of our brain. It is relatively new ("neo" means new) and distinguishes humans from other mammals. It contains all our speech and abstract thinking circuits.

So, what happens is that when we are aroused in some manner the **paleocortex** sends a signal to the **neocortex** looking for a way to label the aroused feelings. Very quickly our memory tells us if we have felt this way before, and then searches for a label we might have used to describe these feelings previously. Based on that memory we make the call: "I am angry!" When this thought occurs, the label is applied and the feeling becomes an **emotion**.

Sometimes we do not have time to label our feelings. When the slasher jumps out of the shed to vanquish another victim, our body makes us jump and even scream. After the scream you might think to yourself that you are scared. That realization continues to stimulate your paleo circuits and keeps your feelings activated (which is the producer's goal for the movie). Other emotions last for a long time, like "love" for example. In general, when playing their Producer Card, movie-makers know that entertainment means quick affective arousal, accurate labeling of emotion, and then sustaining these audience emotions for the duration of the film.

This scenario illustrates how emotions work. Typically, our paleo circuits become **activated very quickly**, often within milliseconds. Then they typically stay there for a much longer period of time **degenerating fairly slowly**. Generally it is the goal of the movie-makers to keep you emotionally aroused for the duration of the film, but not so activated that you cannot take it and are forced to leave. My son had trouble with the flying cows in *Twister* and left the movie for a few minutes during that part. He was scared to death! In playing the Action Movie Game, *Avatar* director James Cameron, did a great job of directing the characters and action sequences in such a way that we became emotionally involved in the story, but not so freaked out that we wanted to leave.

Emotional Intelligence. Perhaps you have had feelings that you were unable to label. You might believe that you are not very good at controlling your emotions once you experience them. The idea of **emotional intelligence** is being able to both understand and ultimately control your emotions so they contribute to your life rather than detract from it. Being able to understand the effects of entertainment media requires emotional intelligence. There are four steps to achieving **emotional intelligence**:

1. **Self-Awareness:** The ability to accurately label feelings as emotions. This skill is important because we have many different feelings all the time, and being able to discriminate between them ultimately helps control them. Can you discriminate between, say, being scared and being afraid? Can you tell the difference between loving your parents and loving a spouse?

2. **Self-Management:** The ability to control emotions and impulses and adapting to changing circumstances. Is your neocortex able to tell your paleocortex to calm down or rethink an emotional condition? Are you able to judge if you are overreacting?

3. **Social Awareness:** The ability to sense, understand, and react to others' emotions. When the other person plays a card do you understand the emotions that went into that play? Can you put yourself in the other's shoes and feel what that person is likely feeling?

4. **Relationship Management:** The ability to inspire, influence, and develop emotions that will help build relationships constructively. Can you use your emotions strategically to improve your communication so you can develop more productive relationships with others?

Developing Emotional Intelligence. Emotional Intelligence (EI) can be improved through training, programming, and therapy because the biggest challenge to EI is reality testing, problem solving, stress tolerance, and impulse control. To determine if you need to improve your emotional intelligence, take this simple quiz. Mark each response on a scale of 1-5:

1 = Strongly Disagree, 2 = Disagree, 3 = No Opinion, 4 = Agree, 5 = Strongly Agree.

Items	Score 1-5
1. I know which emotions I am feeling and why in most situations.	
2. I realize the link between my feelings and what I think, do, and say.	
3. I understand how my feelings affect my performance in school and work.	
4. I am confident in my ability to manage my impulsive feelings.	
5. I can easily control my fear in most situations.	
6. I know how to stay composed, positive, and cool even in trying moments.	
7. I can think clearly and stay focused under pressure.	
8. I show sensitivity and understanding to others' perspectives.	
9. I show sensitivity and understanding for others' perspectives.	
10. I help out others based on understanding their needs and feelings.	
Total Score	

If you scored 20 or below, you may lack confidence in your ability to understand your own and others' emotions. Your EI is relatively low. However, if you scored 40 or above, you are more likely to be confident in your emotional awareness and have a high EI. If your score is between 21 and 39, you may be unsure about your emotional intelligence. The goal is to increase your score as much as possible so that you can understand your emotions more clearly and effectively and understand how they impact your life.

Selective Exposure

One way to demonstrate **Emotional Intelligence** is to make good decisions about what content you expose yourself to, and understand how it impacts you emotionally. Selective exposure is the idea that people watch what they want to watch. We select programs and content that are consistent with our attitudes, beliefs, interests, and personal needs. For example, my son is a real history buff, so he is always watching *The History Channel*. He particularly likes shows about guns and famous battles in history. Maybe he wants to be in the military!

To understand the selective exposure process, let's focus on TV watching. How do people make decisions about what programs to watch? This may surprise you, but research indicates that people select shows based more on what they **do not** want to see rather than on what they **do** want to see. Maybe you have done this. Most people just turn on TV to watch something, and keep clicking through the channels past content they do not want to see and stopping on something that looks interesting. In other words, the choice of program is secondary to the need to simply watch something on TV.

Exposure and Involvement. Of course, there are exceptions. Sometimes people actively select entertainment programming. One of the most important factors determining the extent to which individuals are impacted by entertainment content is personal involvement or personal connection to the content. If someone is watching a situation comedy that takes place in a hospital setting, and that viewer is a physician, then he or she is personally involved in that content. I know an emergency room physician who watches shows about ER doctors, and he is always commenting on what the doctors are doing to the patients. He's involved! He is constantly flipping through the channels to find reruns of these shows.

One of the most popular programs on TV is *American Idol*. This show allows people to call in and vote for specific contestants. The brilliance of this technique is that it **dramatically increases involvement** in the content. Instead of just mindlessly watching, viewers call in their preferences to determine the outcome of a program. Some shows also ask people to text questions or topics of interest that the show will discuss. Producers of entertainment shows will often develop unique strategies to increase involvement and thus the size of the audience that watches the program.

Exposure and Mood. It is important to realize that most of the time people do not make deliberate choices about the entertainment programs they watch. Most choices are impulsive, spur-of-the-moment decisions depending on their situation, mood or other motives driving the individual's life at that moment. A person with a **boring job** might look for shows that are very **exciting**, such as an action show. Conversely, someone with a very intense job might want shows that are more slow-paced as a change. People in a **bad mood** might select programs that are absorbing as a means of **forgetting** about their mood.

Interestingly, highly agitated, emotional individuals tend to avoid entertainment content all together. They just cannot focus on anything until their level of agitation decreases. Once the agitation has decreased somewhat, these people help calm themselves down further by watching comedy programs. In fact, mood plays a significant role in program selection for children. Young children who feel neglected want to watch shows that present a more nurturing message than shows with no such message. They want to feel attached to someone and will even look to TV for that kind of attachment.

Entertainment and New Technology

Technology has radically changed the entertainment industry over the last 10 to 15 years, which is causing dramatic shifts in the way the industry thinks about audiences and on the kinds of effects entertainment will have on audiences. Let's take a look at these shifts and their implications, beginning with some historical context.

The Old Entertainment Industry. The history of the electronic entertainment industry began in the early twentieth century in New York and later in California. In that world, a handful of large movie studios produced most of the films, had most of the actors and talent under contract to work only for those studios, and they also owned the theatres in which the movies were played. From about 1920 to 1950, most people would go to movies at least two to three times per week, paying about 10 cents for entry. It was the thing to do on evenings because there was no TV, of course, and people loved the movies so much. Studios churned out all kinds of content, much more than they do today, because the demand was so high. The result was that the big stars had a tremendous impact on the audiences. Probably the high point of the movie industry was 1939 in which so many unbelievable films were produced with incredibly big stars such as *The Wizard of Oz*, *Gone With the Wind*, and *Stagecoach*.

This highly controlled industry held a very tight monopoly on entertainment (except for radio, which became big in about 1930). If you wanted entertainment, you went to the movies. A few big studios in Hollywood made fortunes controlling the whole process from writing, to filming to theatre ownership. Then, in the early 1950s congress said that the movie industry had to sell its theatres to break up these monopolies. Plus, about this time, television was starting to be popular. The movie companies began to panic in the face of these two changes. Once TV took hold, and color TV began in the 1960s, movie attendance dropped dramatically. Like the movies, the TV industry was also tightly controlled, being run by a few big networks like NBC, CBS, and ABC.

Then cable TV came along in the late 1970s challenging both the TV and movie industry monopolies over the entertainment industry. Cable TV sends a signal to your home through a cable, and not over the air using an old-fashioned TV antenna on the top of your house. Most of you probably have cable in your homes, and a big cable bill every month, as well. Suddenly, cable brought viewers 100 new channels, with many dedicated to news, and others creating new entertainment networks that went well beyond the traditional three networks that broadcast over the airwaves. This change was the first big break from an entertainment monopoly, and opened up brand new channels focusing on anything and everything.

The New Entertainment Industry. Then, in the mid-1980s, personal computers were popularized shifting from analog to digital technology. The digitalization of content means that all information is translated into computer bits and bytes. This translation represents a fundamental shift in the way information, including entertainment information, is created, stored, presented, and ultimately processed by viewers. Three words describe this shift: **compression, conversion, and convergence**.

- **Compression** means that much more information can be transmitted and stored using digital technology than the old analog format. That creates the opportunity for high-definition TV transmission and the use of many more graphic special effects. It is now possible to expand the quantity of information by a factor of thousands.

- **Conversion** means that this compressed information can be integrated into computer systems, allowing information to be available on any medium that can digitally process it including computers, smart phones, and iPads®.

- **Convergence** reflects the ability to converge all media, thus eliminating any barriers to sharing information. Broadcast communications, movies, wireless devices, and telecommunications are all converging in formats making all information available at all times. We may no longer need separate devices such as landline telephones, televisions, mobile phones, calculators, and computers for information delivery. All these may converge into "the electronic thing."

The effects of this digitization have been enormous both in terms of how society works on a broader level, and how entertainment media are likely to impact people on a more focused level. The introduction of the Internet has completed the transformation of media from being completely controlled by a few big studios, newspaper, or broadcast companies to being completely democratic in that anyone and everyone can create and distribute content now. And, that content is available in every medium. People make movies and upload them to **YouTube** or to their **Facebook** or **Flickr** pages. Independent filmmakers with a little more money can produce films and get them distributed, as well. Cable TV now has hundreds of channels in high definition formats. In terms of passive entertainment, the digital revolution has made virtually all content available to anyone with a broadband connection, whether it is a computer or smart phone, or other device. And, the quality of the experience is much greater and much more involving.

The other, even more profound change that digitization has produced is **interactivity**. My son plays *World of Warcraft*, which is an interactive video game. He participates with his friends online while they play other teams of people around the world. In a sense, they are creating their own action movie. As I listen to them interact, their teammates are cursing and using very profane terms for others playing the game. They become very aggressive while playing and very emotionally agitated. Perhaps you have observed or experienced this yourself. We learned from Chapter 13 that such activity can **prime**, or **stimulate**, emotional reactions. These games are available on phones and other media thereby creating this **hypermedia experience** that is thoroughly integrated into players' lives.

As digitization intensifies this **integration** will also intensify. The effect is that entertainment is not something people do as a separate activity from other parts of their lives. It is not something reserved for after work, or after school. Entertainment is now integrated into our work, our interactions with our friends, and any other experience we have. This integration is particularly profound for folks your age. You grew up with smart phones in your pockets and computers on your desks since you were in middle or high school. You are accustomed to this hypermedia experience. How has it impacted you? When I lecture in class, students who take notes on their computers often devote half the page to my notes and half the page to working their **Facebook** account. However, research indicates that students who integrate entertainment into their note taking perform less competently on exams.

Different Audiences

Another profound change associated with moving to the hypermedia entertainment environment is that audiences are changing dramatically as well. Audiences now are more **interactive, addressable, and engaged**. They have been trained away from the old entertainment industry model where audiences are passive recipients of content aimed at making them escape and enjoy, to the new entertainment industry model of audiences as active players in creating their own experiences. Let's look at these changes to see what implications they have for you.

Interactive Audiences. As indicated above, digitization allows audiences to interact with their entertainment experience. They can change endings on TV shows by voting for different outcomes. They can play video games of all kinds and in essence create their own action movies. The games allow you to replay these experiences so if you missed what you did the first time you can see it again. The net effect of this is that audiences now expect more choices than ever before from entertainment media. They want to pick how programs end, or how characters act, or what kind of emotional experiences they want to have.

Addressable Audiences. Digitization has also shifted from the old model of mass communication in which one message fits all, to what's called the **micromultimedia** environment. In this environment, messages can be addressed directly to individuals. Even cable TV can now customize lists of movies for viewers based on their preferences. Certainly, **Google®** has figured out how to tailor advertising to individuals based on what they are searching for. All searches are recorded and your search history is probably pretty consistent. Consequently, you receive advertisements based on your specific profile. As technology advances so will this customization feature. Satellite radio can be configured to send different programs to each and every car so that you'll only hear the kinds of music you sign up for when you go online to their site.

Engaged Audiences. Not only do audiences interact, but they are also more engaged. We know from the discussion above that more engaged audiences are more vulnerable to media effects because they pay more attention to what they are watching. Audiences now create their own content. They create movies and photo albums and personal profiles online. They write blogs and search for cute videos to entertain others and send out to all their friends. Everyone is both a recipient and a creator of entertainment. There are no more clear lines between who is creating and who is consuming the entertainment. It's all happening together.

The implications of these shifts for industry are profound. First, businesses cannot afford to ignore blogs about their products and services. They must respond to them one-by-one to insure that criticism does not **go viral**, or creates an instant Internet sensation with millions of hits. They must constantly be aware of how their audience's preferences are changing because **everyone has a choice** and wants to exercise it. Second, there is no longer a singular formula for how to entertain people. The industry is much more fluid than ever before and much broader than anyone could have imagined. Third, with more information, companies can better target people for advertising purposes. As people give more information about their needs, advertisers can better tailor messages to meet these needs.

The good news is that this will continue to lead to great experimentation with entertainment media. What you see today is likely to be very different than even tomorrow's forms of entertainment.

Strategies for Managing Entertainment Card Games

The most important strategy for playing any of the card games described here is to first be aware of what impact this game is having on you personally and professionally. If you are sucked into the **hypermedia environment** and you cannot clearly separate your personal and professional lives from your sources of entertainment, can you perform effectively in school, for example? This separation is difficult because your paleocortical connections want to keep you engaged. They are very powerful and tough to fight.

The second strategy is to be aware of your **emotional intelligence**. Are you able to handle the profound emotional impacts of entertainment media? You might think you are becoming numb to the negative effects of media, but repeated exposure to pornography or violence can cause you to look at people and relationships differently. Developing your emotional intelligence will assist in creating a healthier emotional response to any information you are exposed to.

The third strategy that makes sense is to think about entertainment effects for those you care about. It is important to limit the kinds of entertainment that can create more aggressive behaviors, particularly for children. What are they watching, what effect does it have on them, and what should you do or say about it?

Summary

Entertainment is all about emotion. Drama, sports, and humor are produced to get audiences emotionally involved in a story.

Fear plays a significant role in drama. As one of the most important emotional reactions to drama, fear intensifies our attraction to drama, particularly when it looks real or we can relate to the situation in some way.

The key to understanding entertainment effects is understanding how emotion works. Emotions are feelings that we learn to label or define. They come from the paleocortical circuits in our brain. The more we can learn to control them the less negative impact these emotions will have on us.

Developing Emotional Intelligence is an important means of controlling our emotions. When we are aware of our emotions, we can manage them more effectively and even help others manage their emotions.

Selective exposure is driven by our needs. If we lead boring lives we seek stimulating entertainment; if we lead exciting lives we often pick more soothing content.

Media technologies are expanding rapidly. The old-entertainment industry model of passive entertainment has given way to the new model of active entertainment in which people actively participate in the entertainment experience. This shift will have profound impacts across many dimensions of our society.

Lessons Learned

- **Good entertainment is good drama.** The most important element of good entertainment is conflict, whether it's comedy, sports, scary movies, or action TV shows. People are attracted to conflict between good guys and bad guys. And, we really want to care about the good guys and hate the bad guys. We also want the bad guys to pay dearly for their evil nature.

- **Audiences have very different motivations and orientations for watching.** Men and women have different motivations when watching horror movies. Some viewers want a cathartic experience to relive their fears, whereas others simply want to be frightened for fun. Younger audiences are less able to discriminate entertainment shows from real life experiences. People who consume a lot of entertainment programs, or are isolated from real-world experiences, are more vulnerable to believing this entertainment represents real life.

- **Emotions are difficult to control.** While they serve to define our feelings, they originate from the primitive part of our brain and make us vulnerable to impulsive acts. Developing emotional intelligence helps address those challenges.

- **Selective exposure is a key element determining what people watch.** People select entertainment based on gratifying their needs. People who are more involved in some activity in real life and need to know more about it will focus on entertainment consistent with that need. Mood also impacts selective exposure.

- **New technology is dramatically changing audiences.** Audiences are now more interactive, addressable, and engaged than ever before. The digital revolution has changed the way we integrate entertainment into our lives.

Chapter 15
Course Assignments

Below are listed the specific assignments for the course. These point values are listed in the syllabus:

Personal Goals Part 1
Special Occasions Speech
Pro / Con Speech
Personal Goal Part 2
Media Analysis Assignment
Informative Speech
Persuasive Speech

Personal Goals: Part One

Purpose of the Assignment

This assignment is designed to help you both expand your communication skills and to link class content to your personal and professional goals.

Requirements

Write at least **ONE, double-spaced page** assessing your personal goals for the semester as a public speaker. Please include answers to the following questions:

1. What are your **long-term career** goals? Long-term goals relate to major accomplishments that may take some time to achieve. For example, you might want to own your own business some day, or be a veterinarian. You could also say that you want to stay home and raise a family. It is also OK to say you **don't know**; but if you are uncertain about your goals, just list some options you've been considering. Describe at least ONE goal, but no more than THREE. Also, for each long-term goal explain **why it's important to you**.

2. What are your **short-term goals** that will help achieve the long-term goals? Short-term goals are simple steps taken on the journey to accomplishing your long-term goals. Even if you don't know your long-term goals, you can list some ideas about how to discover a career path. Keep in mind that goals should be realistic and attainable. You might include your **educational goals** such as completing your **Bachelor's Degree** and perhaps going to law school, or getting a master's degree. Include goals about getting an **internship**, participating in the **Study Abroad** program, securing a job, or volunteering at a hospital. List at least **THREE** short-term goals that will help you on your way **AND**, for each goal, why you believe they will be helpful.

3. What aspects of public speaking would you like to improve? Perhaps you simply want to be more comfortable in front of an audience, or maybe you want to improve your eye contact or speak at a slower pace. Please identify at least **THREE** elements you would like to improve and why.

4. Better talk cards are needed to accomplish your goals. Describe the personal talk cards in your deck. These are discussed in Chapter 2 of the textbook. Start by describing the **THREE personal cards** you play most such as your Friend, Daughter, Sister, Girlfriend or Roommate Cards. List: a) the name of the card, b) one or two topics you like to talk about when playing this card, c) one or two topics you typically avoid when playing this card, and d) what you would like to improve to play this card more effectively.

5. Describe the **THREE professional cards** in your deck you will need to develop to accomplish your professional goals. For example, everyone needs to develop an Employee Card and a Colleague Card. Others might include a Supervisor Card or a Teammate Card. If you want to be a veterinarian, then you'll need a Veterinarian Card and several others that

must accompany that card. For each card list: a) the name of the card, b) one or two topics that are important to talk about when playing this card, and c) how you plan to develop this card. For example, to develop the Veterinarian Card you might volunteer at a clinic and see how vets talk to their clients.

6. Finally, how will developing your personal and professional cards improve your public speaking? In other words, if you create better personal cards, how might this impact or improve your delivery? If you build strong professional cards, how will they improve your ability to persuade audiences?

This assignment should be typed and double-spaced. Hand-written assignments will not be accepted. Please include on the paper:

- Your name
- Your section number
- Your Section Leader's name

Grading

- Graders will be looking for the following:
- Meets the requirements as listed above
- Answers the questions clearly
- Provides insight relevant to the question
- Assignment is organized and clear
- No spelling or grammatical errors

This assignment is due:

Personal Goals Grading Form

_____ (6) Each question is answered clearly and completely

_____ (2) Answers provide relevant detail and insight

_____ (2) Assignment is organized and easy to follow

_____ Spelling and Grammar—Minus 1 point for every 3 errors

_____ Minus 1 point if assignment is not at least one full page

_____ Minus 1 point if assignment is not double-spaced

_____ (10 points) Total

Special Occasion Speech

Purpose of the Assignment

This assignment is designed to give you experience writing and presenting a short, informal speech that you may be asked to give at some point in your life. Our goal is to help improve your comfort level when presenting these kinds of speeches in these diverse situations.

Requirements

Select ONE type of **Special Occasion** Speech to present in your small recitation section. Speeches that meet the criterion include: toasts, eulogies, introductions, or nominations. Please see next page for speech descriptions. Turn in a complete, typed manuscript of the **Special Occasion Speech**. Note: You MUST bring an **extra copy** if you want to read your speech since the final version is due at the beginning of recitation.

Limit your speech to 1.5 to 2 minutes. One point will be deducted for speaking under or over the time limit.

Answer the following questions to turn in with the assignment:

1. As stated in the textbook, your Talk Card is the package of messages that are communicated in playing a specific role. What Talk Card(s) will you use in your speech and why? For example, if you are delivering a eulogy, are you using a Friend Card, a Minister Card, a Spouse Card? Why do you think this card would be effective for your speech?

2. Describe your Talk Card in terms of its content and style. The **content** is the idea or topic you are communicating. The style refers to how friendly, how formal, and how powerful you want to appear In presenting that topic or idea. Explain the message in terms of **liking, formality, and power.** For example, if you are doing a eulogy using a Friend Card, you might want to talk about what the person meant to you as a friend, and your style might be high friendliness, low formality, and low power.

3. How does the audience influence the cards you choose to play?

This assignment should be typed and double-spaced. Hand-written assignments will not be accepted. Please include on the paper:
*   Your name
*   Your section number
*   Your Section Leader's name

Grading will be based on whether the assignment:

- The speech was interesting and engaging;
- It was clear what Talk Card was used in presenting the speech;
- The word choice was consistent with the Talk Card choice;
- The speaker used effective eye contact, body movement, volume, rate, and use of space;
- The speech was within the time limit.

This assignment is due:

Special Occasion Speech

Toasts. These are used for momentous occasions such as weddings, birth of a baby, reunion of friends, successful business ventures, and anniversaries. The toasts can be personal or generic, are usually accompanied by raising glasses, and are generally short.

Eulogies. This speech is used to deliver a tribute to someone who has died. The speaker should mention the **unique achievements** of the person receiving the tribute and also contain an **expression of loss**. Further, the speaker should turn to the living and encourage them to transcend their sorrow and sense of loss, while also indicating that the audience should feel gratitude that the dead had once been among them.

Note: Eulogies can be about you, a pet, a famous person, or a family member.

Nominations. Nominations involve noting the occasion and significance of the award or office for which the nomination is placed. The speaker should explain clearly why the nominee's skills, talents and past achievements serve as qualifications for the award or position.

Introductions. An introduction is similar to an informative speech. The purpose is to provide the audience with information about the speaker and to ultimately, trigger interest in that person. The main elements include gaining audience attention, building the speaker's credibility and introducing the speaker's subject.

Note: Both nominations and introductions should be about a real person, but they can be a famous person or a person you know personally.

Other Elements:

Special Occasion speeches may be formal or informal so the word choice and language should fit accordingly. For example, some slang may be appropriate in a toast, but not in a nomination. However, the entire audience should be able to follow the speech and not be offended.

Think about the characteristics of the audience when writing this speech. The people in the audience may affect the way you write and present the speech. For example, parents and grandparents would be present at a wedding so stories about drinking or other controversial topics may not be appropriate in a toast.

Special Occasion Speech Grading Form

Written Portion (15)

_____ (3) Questions are answered clearly (One point per question)

_____ (3) Assignment follows one of the given options for speeches and executes the type of speech correctly

_____ (3) Topic and written portion are interesting and engaging

_____ (2) Organized, clear, easy to follow

_____ (2) Assignment is at least one page typed, double-spaced

_____ (2) Spelling/Grammar (Minus 1 point for every 3 errors)

Spoken Portion (15)

_____ (1) Clear distinction of the type of speech

_____ (3) Effective eye contact

_____ (3) Effective body movement and use of space

_____ (3) Effective volume and rate of speech

_____ (2) Appropriate word choice for topic and audience

_____ (2) Engaging for the audience

_____ (1) Meets time limit

_____ Total (30 points)

PRO/CON Speech

Purpose of the Assignment

This assignment is designed to research a current controversial issue, to respond in an argumentative format to a controversial issue, and to practice parts of the Toulmin Model of Argumentation.

Requirements

Work in pairs to formulate a PRO and CON stance on a controversial issue. One student will present the PRO stance and the other student will present the CON stance. Please note: only one student will present each PRO and CON stance on each controversial issue. There will be no duplicate speeches in a small section.

You can work together to discuss the PRO/CON stances to the controversial issue, but the grading for each student will be independent from each other.

Write a <u>speech outline</u> in response to the controversial issue selected.

Follow the **Toulmin Model of Argumentation** presented to you in recitation by your TA.

Limit your speech to 1.5 to 2 minutes. One point will be deducted for speaking over or under the time limit.

This assignment should be typed and should follow the format described below. Hand-written assignments will not be accepted. Please include on the paper:

Your name, section number, and section leader's name.

Cite TWO sources that informed your speech in the actual text of the speech outline and on a References page. See the APA Style Guide or your TA. After each source, write a **Test of Evidence** you think the source/evidence meets and WHY you think it meets this requirement of credibility. Refer to Chapter 16 in your textbook for a list of **Tests of Evidence**.

Format

State the topic and the thesis statement (your Pro/Con stance).

Give an argument why the thesis statement is true:

1. Provide a Claim (the position being argued for)
2. Provide a Grounds for the Claim (a piece of evidence or example to support thesis statement)
3. Provide a Warrant (a reason for why once you know the Grounds, you can logically assume the Claim)
4. Provide Backing (support to the Warrant)
5. Provide a Rebuttal (exceptions to the claim)
6. Provide a Qualification (specifications of limits to the claim, warrant, and backing)

Possible PRO/CON Topics

1. Free parking ought to be available to students.
2. All students should have to complete a senior thesis to graduate.
3. The United States was justified in going to war in Afghanistan.
4. The death penalty should be legalized in all states.
5. Non-medical marijuana use should be legalized.
6. Abortion should be banned.
7. Campus noise violators should be given lighter punishments.

Grading

Graders will be looking for:

- Meets requirements as listed above
- Follows format listed above
- Two sources are cited and includes Tests of Evidence
- Argument is clear and concise
- Word choice and appropriate presentation of a controversial topic
- Effective eye contact, body movement, volume, rate, use of space and within time limits

This assignment is due:

Pro/Con Speech Grading Form

Written Portion (20)

_____ (2) Assignment is presented in the correct outline format

_____ (6) Follows Toulmin's Model

_____ (2) In-text citations with correct APA for at least two references

_____ (3) Reference page with correct APA and at least two references

_____ (2) Reference page includes 2 tests of evidence for 2 different sources

_____ (2) Organized, clear, easy to follow

_____ (3) Spelling/grammar (Minus 1 point for every 3 errors)

Spoken Portion (20)

_____ (4) Arguments are clear and effective

_____ (4) Effective eye contact

_____ (3) Effective body movement and use of space

_____ (3) Effective volume and rate of speech

_____ (2) Appropriate and effective word choice for topic and audience

_____ (2) References are cited orally during the speech

_____ (2) Time limit

_____ Total (40 points)

Personal Goals: Part Two

Purpose of the Assignment

This assignment is designed for students to assess the goals they met over the semester and what goals they may work on in the future.

Requirements

Write at least one page about how you feel your communication skills have improved over the course of the semester. Use your responses in your original **Personal Goals** assignment to answer the following questions:

1. How have you accomplished and/or progressed toward your short- and long-term goals mentioned in your original goals? Have your career goals changed?
2. In your original goals you were asked to list aspects of public speaking that you wanted to improve. Which elements of your public speaking do you feel you improved? Which areas need further improvement?
3. What cards in your Card Deck, both personal and professional, are most important to you? Have these changed since the beginning of the semester? Why or why not?
4. Which cards in your Card Deck were most beneficial in improving your public speaking and accomplishing your goals? How did this class affect your Card Deck? Explain.

This assignment should be typed and double-spaced. Hand-written assignments will not be accepted. Please include on the paper:

Please provide your name, your section number, and your section leader's name

Grading

- Graders will be looking for the following:
- Meets the requirements as listed above
- Answers the questions and provides insight
- Assignment is organized and clear
- No spelling or grammatical errors

This assignment is due:

Personal Goals II Grading Form

_____ (4) Each question is answered clearly completely

_____ (2) Answers provide relevant detail and insight

_____ (2) Answers pull from original goals

_____ (1) Assignment is organized and easy to follow

_____ (1) Original goals are attached

_____ Spelling and Grammar—Minus 1 point for every 3 errors
_____ Minus 1 point if assignment is not at least one full page
_____ Minus 1 point if assignment is not double-spaced

_____ (10 points) Total

Media Analysis Assignment

Purpose of the Assignment

This assignment is designed to challenge you to critically analyze the role of the media in daily life.

Requirements

Please select ONE of the following concepts from lecture and/or the text-book to analyze through the lens of the media:

1. Gender roles;
2. Relationship values;
3. Conflict;
4. Culture;
5. Decision-making;
6. Social identity

Please choose ONE of the following media outlets in which to analyze the chosen concept:

TV, film, magazine, advertising, music, books, Internet, or video games
Turn in at least ONE page written analysis. Please indicate in the analysis what type of media (i.e., TV, film) and what specific content (e.g., Friends, Maxim Magazine, or Pirates of the Caribbean, etc.) you are analyzing. Answer the following questions:

1. What specifically are we learning through the media regarding your chosen concept?

2. Are there benefits for the audience learning this concept through the media? Think critically about this question. Explain why or why not.

3. Are there problems with the audience learning this concept through the media? Why or why not?

Attach a copy of the article, advertisement, web site, book excerpt, etc. used in the analysis, or include a detailed account of examples, lyrics, or parts of a script.

This assignment should be typed and double-spaced. Hand-written assignments will not be accepted. Please include your name, section number, and section leader's name.

Grading will be based on the following:
*   Meets the requirements as listed above
*   Answers the questions and provides insight
*   Assignment is organized and clear
*   No spelling or grammatical errors

Media Analysis Grading Form

_____ (6) Each question is answered clearly with relevant insight

_____ (2) Analysis is communicated effectively

_____ (1) Includes supplemental material

_____ (1) Analyzes one of the given concept AND uses one of the listed media

_____ Spelling and Grammar—Minus 1 point for every 3 errors

_____ Minus 1 point if assignment is not at least one full page

_____ Minus 1 point if assignment is not double-spaced

_____ (10) Total

Informative Speech

Purpose of the Assignment

This assignment is designed to help students inform an audience about something unique to them, which will help build rapport between the speaker and the audience. Also, students will have an opportunity to improve skills in speaking before a small group of people.

Topic

Select a business or organization from your hometown that has impressed you. For example, you could select a tourist attraction, a sports facility, a manufacturing plant or a homeless shelter. You will share information with your audience about the business or organization you have selected. Sometimes students actually visit the owners or managers of the business or get a tour of the organization. This is not required, but it makes the speech much more interesting and sets you up as more of an authority on the topic.

Requirements

Each student will complete a written speech outline and a 4-6 minute speech to be delivered in class.

The speech outline must follow the format shown in the course pack and it must be typed. Hand-written outlines will not be accepted.

There should be at least THREE references cited in the outline and speech. The reference page and in-text citations must follow APA style. See the APA Style guide or your TA.

Note: Students must turn in a copy of the outline to their IAs prior to giving their speech. An additional copy of the outline may be used during the delivery of the speech.

Grading

Please review the grading forms for the requirements.

This assignment is due:

Informative Speech Outline

This is what your outline should look like. Use this format as your template for structuring your outline. The bold sections **are required** for your outline.

Your name and section number:

Title: Be creative!

Topic: The business or organization I want to describe is... (What is the business or organization you have decided to talk about? Make sure you cleared your topic with your section leader.)

Purpose Statement: To inform my audience about ... (What do you want to tell the audience about the business? Is it interesting because of its impact in the community, the unusual nature of what they do, or its historical nature?)

Audience Analysis: You will have about two sentences per sub-point (A., B., C., D.) here. The rest of the speech will have only one complete sentence per point.

In your audience analysis always include **WHY** the fact is relevant to your speech.

A. **Demographics:** Describe the characteristics of your audience. These include sex, age ethnic background, group memberships, etc. How will your speech be affected by the demographics of your audience?

B. **Psychographics:** Describe the biases, knowledge level, mood, attitudes, beliefs, and goals/need/wants of your audience. How will these factors affect your speech?

C. **Verbal Considerations:** Describe the verbal considerations you will need to make, specific to your speech and audience. Why will you implement these strategies?

D. **Nonverbal Considerations:** Describe the nonverbal considerations you will need to make, specific to your speech and audience. Why will you implement these strategies?

Talk Card Used for the Speech:

A. **Talk Card:** What talk card will you use in your speech and why?
B. **Content:** Describe the content of your talk card.
C. **Style:** Describe the style of your talk card in terms of liking, formality and power.
D. **Audience:** How do you expect the audience to respond to your talk card?

I. INTRODUCTION

A. **Attention getter:** Write what you intend to say to get your audience's attention. Examples: story, fact, startling statement.

B. **Thesis Statement:** this should be a clear and specific rewording of your purpose statement.

C. **Preview the main points:** Tell us the three main points you will be making in your speech.
   1. Main Point 1
   2. Main Point 2
   3. Main Point 3

Transition: Insert a statement linking your introduction to the body of the speech.

II. BODY

A. **First main point**-remember only one sentence.
   1. Sub-point. (You can use a definition, an example, or evidence to support your main point.) Be sure to cite your sources in your sub-points.
   2. Sub-point. Don't forget that these need to be complete sentences. The second sub-point could be an example.

Transition: Insert a comment linking your first main point to your second main point.

B. Your **second main point** goes here.
   1. Just like in A (could be a definition).
   2. Could be an example like in A.

Transition: Insert a comment linking your second main point to your third main point.

C. The **last main point.**
   1. Again, complete sentences describing the main point.
   2. Your final sub-point

Transition: Insert a comment linking the body of your speech to the conclusion.

III. CONCLUSION

A. Restatement of Thesis

B. Summary of main points

C. Closing statement: wrap up your speech with a memorable point. You could refer to your attention getter, use a story, fact, or a quote to end your speech.

Be sure to include your reference page, correctly formatted in APA style.

What to Remember for your Speech

- You should have three main points—remember to use a pattern that makes sense when you organize them. (Ex: if you are talking about something chronological, keep events in order.)

- Your speech needs to be 4-6 minutes so plan to speak for 5 minutes. Anything less than four minutes or more than six minutes will be penalized.

- Your outline must be typed or it won't be accepted.

- Remember to bring your grading forms on speech day- all your grading forms are in the textbook. You will lose 10 points from your speech for failure to bring your grading forms on the day of your speech.

- Make sure to practice your speech. You will be more nervous than you think on the day of your speech!

- If you need help be sure to contact your TA or Section Leader before the speech. We are here to help!

Informative Speech Outline

Hand this form in to your Section Leader **STAPLED** with your outline.

_____ (1 pt) Title
_____ (1 pt) Topic
_____ (1 pt) Purpose Statement

AUDIENCE ANALYSIS:
_____ (2 pts) Demographics
_____ (2 pts) Psychographics
_____ (2 pts) Verbal considerations
_____ (2 pts) Nonverbal considerations

TALK CARDS:
_____ (2 pts) Talk Card
_____ (2 pts) Content
_____ (2 pts) Style
_____ (2 pts) Audience

INTRODUCTION:
_____ (2 pts) Attention Grabber
_____ (2 pts) Thesis Statement
_____ (1 pts) Preview of Main Points

BODY:
_____ (6 pts) Three clearly stated main points
_____ (2 pts) Points are well-organized

CONCLUSION:
_____ (1 pts) Restatement of Thesis
_____ (2 pts) Summary of main points
_____ (2 pts) Well thought-out closing statement

MECHANICS OF THE OUTLINE:
_____ (2 pts) Is each line tabbed properly?
_____ (2 pts) Are the sentences complete?
_____ (2 pts) Are the sentences neat?
_____ (2 pts) Are the sentences properly labeled?

OTHER:
_____ (5 pts) Grammar and word choice.
_____ Minus 10 points if the outline is not typed.
_____ Minus 10 points if your sources are not cited BOTH on the reference list AND in the text of the outline. (3 references are required)

_____ **TOTAL OUT OF 50 POSSIBLE PTS.**

Informative Speech Evaluation Form

Hand this form in to your Section Leader STAPLED with your outline.

INTRODUCTION:

_____ (4 pts) Use of effective attention getter
_____ (2 pts) Statement of thesis (thematic statement)
_____ (2 pts) Preview of main points

BODY:

_____ (3 pts) Has 3-5 main points
_____ (4 pts) Use of effective transitions and sign-posts
_____ (3 pts) Use of effective word choice, slang, acronyms, etc.
_____ (2 pts) Main points are well-organized and easy to follow

CONCLUSION:

_____ (3 pts) Restates main points
_____ (3 pts) Closing statement

VERBAL AND VISUAL ELEMENTS:

_____ (5 pts) Makes effective eye contact
_____ (5 pts) Speech was organized and clear
_____ (5 pts) Use of effective vocals, volume, articulation
_____ (5 pts) Use of effective movement, posture, gestures
_____ (4 pts) Sources were cited orally during the speech
_____ Minus any points for time penalties
(Maximum of 5 point deduction)

_____ TOTAL OUT OF 50 POSSIBLE POINTS

LIST 3 ASPECTS THAT THE STUDENT NEEDS TO IMPROVE:

LIST 3 ASPECTS THAT THE STUDENT DID WELL:

Persuasive Speech: Support My New Business

Purpose of Assignment

This speech assignment is designed to help you learn how to create persuasive speeches aimed at convincing a group to support your position on an important issue.

Topic

This speech will focus on persuading your student audience to support a new business venture of some kind. The venture does not have to charge people money. It can be a new website that makes money by selling advertising, like Facebook, which was a college project. Have some fun with the product or service that you would like students to select. Another example would be a valet parking service for students who want to avoid parking tickets. Be imaginative.

Requirements

Each student will complete a speech outline with a reference page, a relevant visual aid and a 5-7 minute speech in front of their small recitation section.

The speech outline must be in the Monroe's Motivated Sequence format as discussed in recitation and in Chapter 16 of the textbook.

The speech outline must be typed and the visual aid must look professional. No hand written outlines will be accepted.

There should be at least FIVE references cited in the outline and speech. The purpose of references is to present research or other relevant information about the need for the product or service. The reference page must follow APA style. See the *APA Style Guide* or your TA.

Grading

Please review the grading forms for the requirements.

The assignment is due:

PERSUASIVE SPEECH GUIDELINE

THIS IS WHAT YOUR OUTLINE SHOULD LOOK LIKE.

(The **bolded items** are what you should actually have on your outline.)

Your name and Section #

Title: Provide a short title for your speech. (e.g., "In a Rush? Valet Today")

Topic: List the name of the business you're going to create and the business venture you're going to provide (e.g., The Valet Kings, Valet Today Parking Service).

Purpose Statement: Your purpose in this speech is to persuade. You need to provide once sentence here that describes the action you want your audience to take. (e.g., Read this brochure about our valet parking service and consider signing up for our valet service.)

Audience Analysis: You will need 2-3 sentences per sub-point (A., B., C., D.) to complete the audience analysis. The rest of the speech will have only one complete sentence per point. In your audience analysis always include WHY the fact is relevant to your speech.

A. **Demographics:** Describe the characteristics of your audience that are relevant to your business venture. For example, what kind of students would be most interested in a valet parking service? Are they students with jobs who have a certain income level? Are they from a certain major or college? Are people interested in the service more likely to be women than men? How will your speech be impacted by the audience demographic profile?

B. **Psychographics:** Describe the attitudes, values and beliefs that students might have that would impact the success of your message. How will these psychological biases impact your speech? For example, students might think that their friends would make fun of them if they used valet parking. Or, they might believe valet parking is bad for the environment since it encourages more driving.

C. **Verbal Considerations:** Describe the verbal considerations you will need to make specific to your speech and audience. Why will you make these changes?

D. **Nonverbal Considerations:** Describe the nonverbal considerations you will need to make that are specific to your speech and audience. Why are these considerations important?

Talk Cards: You will need 2-3 sentences per sub-point (A., B., C., D.) to complete the talk card part of your outline.

    A. Talk Card: What talk card will you use in your speech and why? For example, should you use a Business Founder Card and speak from that perspective? Or, should you speak using a Customer Card? What would be more persuasive and why?

    B. Content: Describe at least five key topics that you will need to have on your talk card to be persuasive. For example, if you are using your Business Founder Card, you would talk about the need for the service, your knowledge of MSU, your financial skills, your management skills, and your entrepreneurial abilities.

    C. Style: Describe the style of your talk card in terms of liking, formality, and power. For example, will you come off as very likeable, but formal in presenting your topics? Will you be formal, but use high power? Describe your style choices and then indicate why you chose them.

    D. Audience: What card do you want the customers to play? If you play your Business Founder Card you are asking the students to play their Customer Card. If you play your Student Card, you will also ask them to play their Student Card. Provide a short rationale for why you want the audience to play that specific card in responding to you.

I. INTRODUCTION

    A. **Attention Getter:** Write something catchy to interest the audience (e.g., a startling statistic, a personal narrative, a joke, etc.)

    B. **Thesis Statement:** This should be a clear and specific rewording of your purpose statement.

    C. **Preview Statement:** (e.g., "Specifically, I am going to discuss...")

        1. You need a sentence describing your need/problem step. (This is the reason students need this product or service.)
        2. You need a sentence describing your satisfaction/solution and action steps (This is the request to participate in the business.)

II. NEED/PROBLEM STEP:

You need one sentence here that summarizes the need for the business. What problem does your product or service solve for the target market? Then, provide two good arguments and/or statements about why solving that problem is important or necessary for the target market. These are important points so make them convincing!

A. **Main Point #1**

    1. Sub-point. You can use a definition, an example, or evidence to support your main point. Be sure to cite your sources in your sub-points.

    2. Sub-point. Don't forget that these need to be complete sentences. The second sub-point could be an example.

Transition Sentence.

B. **Main Point #2**

    1. Just like in A (could be a definition).

    2. Could be an example like in A.

Transition Sentence.

C. **Main Point #3**

    1. Again, complete sentences are necessary in describing the main point.

    2. Your final sub-point.

Transition Sentence.

III. SATISFACTION/SOLUTION: You need one statement summarizing your solution. You will have two general suggestions for audience action: a main suggestion (e.g., try the Valet Today Service risk free for 30 days) and a secondary suggestion (e.g., read the brochure, go to the website, tell a friend). Give an overview of your business that is helping students solve the problems described in the need step. Tell us when the business was founded, by whom, and why they are interested in this problem.

A. Main Suggestion: The main solution for solving the problem (e.g., Try the Valet Today Service risk free for 30 days.)

B. Secondary Suggestion: The secondary solution for solving the problem (e.g. learn more about our service at our website and read reviews from satisfied customers.)

Transition Sentence.

IV. VISUALIZATION STEP: Write one sentence motivating your audience to act on the issue. Usually the sentence describes the key benefits the target audience will receive from the solution you provide.

Transition Sentence.

V. ACTION/CONCLUSION STEP.

A. Action Step: Make a specific request that the audience can do today. (e.g., Review this brochure, go to our website to learn more.)

B. Summary of Main Points: Name the company again and the two main points of the problem/cause.

C. Implication Statement: Explain how the main points prove why the problem is important enough to warrant action.

D. Closing Statement: Finish with a really compelling wrap-up statement that ties into your attention grabber.

WHAT TO REMEMBER FOR YOUR PERSUASIVE SPEECH

- You must use the **Monroe's Motivated Sequence** format (Attention, Need, Satisfaction, Visualization and Action).
- The outline must be **typed** or it will not be accepted.
- Bring **extra outlines** to speak from (if needed).
- The outline must be at least **one page** (not including the reference page).
- There must be at least **FIVE** sources in the outline. They must be cited in your outline correctly. See example handout, APA Style Guide, or ask your TA.
- Be creative and try to use emotional, logical, and credible appeals in the speech. See **Chapter 16** of your textbook for more information.
- The speech must be **5–7 minutes**. There will be penalty going over or under the time limit. The best way to avoid penalty is to **practice**, practice, practice.
- The tabs and indents should look identical to this outline. Suggestion: Turn off auto-formatting on Word.
- PROOFREAD! Points will be deducted for spelling and grammatical errors.

Persuasive Speech Outline

Hand this form in to your Section Leader STAPLED with your outline.

_____ (1 pt) Title
_____ (1 pt) Topic
_____ (2 pts) Purpose statement

AUDIENCE ANALYSIS
_____ (2 pts) Demographics
_____ (2 pts) Psychographics
_____ (2 pts) Verbal considerations
_____ (2 pts) Nonverbal considerations

TALK CARDS
_____ (2 pts) Talk Card
_____ (2 pts) Content
_____ (2 pts) Style
_____ (2 pts) Audience

INTRODUCTION
_____ (1 pts) Attention grabber
_____ (1 pt) Thesis statement
_____ (2 pt) Preview of main points

NEEDS/PROBLEM SECTION
_____ (4 pts) Identify unfulfilled needs—convince your audience that there is a problem.
_____ (4 pts) Have between 2 and 3 good arguments of why there is a problem.

SATISFACTION STEP
_____ (4 pts) Propose a solution that will satisfy those needs—propose a clearly thought out plan; identify an organization whose goal is to solve the needs presented.
_____ (4 pts) Anticipate and refute possible audience objections to the pro posed plan.

VISUALIZATION STEP
_____ (4 pts) Visualize what satisfaction will mean—explain how your proposed plan will rid of the problem.

ACTION/CONCLUSION
_____ (2 pts) Identify specific actions that the audience can take
_____ (2 pts) Summary of main points
_____ (2 pts) Implication statement
_____ (2 pts) Have a memorable closing statement

OTHER:

_____ (4 pts) Arguments were presented logically and connectives were used to maintain the flow of the argument.

_____ (2 pts) Is each line tabbed properly?

_____ (2 pts) Are the sentences complete?

_____ (2 pts) Are all sentences correctly labeled?

_____ (5 pts) Grammar and word choice.

_____ (4 pts) All sources are cited in the text of the outline in correct APA format.

_____ (4 pts) All sources are cited on a reference list in correct APA format.

_____   TOTAL OUT OF 75 POSSIBLE PTS.

Persuasive Speech Form

Hand this form in to your Section Leader STAPLED with your outline. He/she will use it to grade your speech.

MONROE'S MOTIVATED SEQUENCE:

_____ Use of effective attention getter (4 pts)
_____ Identified unfulfilled societal need/problem (4 pts)
_____ Has 2-3 arguments that support the problem (4 pts)
_____ Proposed a solution that satisfies those needs (3 pts)
_____ Visualizes how the proposed plan will satisfy the problem (3 pts)
_____ Action step proposed in conclusion (2 pts)

VISUAL AND AUDITORY ELEMENTS:

_____ Use of effective transitions and sign posts (5 pts)
_____ Makes effective eye contact (5 pts)
_____ Use of effective word choice, slang, acronyms etc. (5 pts)
_____ Speech was organized and clear (5 pts)
_____ Volume was appropriate for the size of the room and audience (2 pts)
_____ Speech rate was rapid enough to be interesting, but not too fast so as to be difficult to understand (3 pts)
_____ Vocal variety was employed to create interest and emphasis (3 pts)
_____ All words were pronounced correctly and articulated well (2 pts)
_____ Use of effective movement, posture, gestures, etc. (5 pts)
_____ Use of persuasive devices in order to move audience (e.g. emotional appeals, statistics etc.) (5 pts)
_____ Sources were cited in the body of the speech (5 pts)
_____ Visual aid was used during the speech (2 pts)
_____ Visual aid was carefully and attractively designed and constructed (4 pts)
_____ Visual aid was used skillfully in conjunction with specific content in the speech (4 pts)
_____ Minus any points for time penalties (Maximum of 5 point deduction)

_____ TOTAL OUT OF 75 POSSIBLE PTS.

Chapter 16
The Art of Public Speaking

Introduction

Most college students have had some public speaking experience, either in a high school class or in a leadership role with some group. Public speaking from a Card Talk perspective is very similar to what you may have learned in a different context. Yet, there are some key differences that are important to point out:

- **Public speakers play talk cards** with their audience just like any other communication activity. You will always show one or more talk cards to an audience while speaking.

- The question is, **which cards are you showing to them?** Are they cards that will help get your point across or distract the audience in some way?

- Also when you play a talk card in a speech **you are also asking the audience to play a complementary card**. Is it the card you want the audience to play in response to your message? When they play it will that help get your point across?

Let's look at the issue of card selection and how it contributes to speech success.

Card Choice in Public Speaking

I Have a Dream. One of the most famous speeches in American History was Dr. Martin Luther King Jr.'s "I Have a Dream" speech from the steps of the Lincoln Memorial in Washington, D.C. on August 28, 1963. Most of you have probably heard of the speech, but if not, you should watch it on YouTube. Dr. King's goal on that day was to set a vision for race relations in America. To achieve his goal, he had to select a card to play that would: a) enhance his credibility, b) allow him to use a powerful, emotional speaking style, c) provide legitimacy to the message, and d) encourage the audience to play a card that would make them more receptive to his message.

Dr. King had many cards to pick from in laying out his message. He was a father, a social activist, an intellectual, an expert on race relations, a husband, and the leader of a movement. He could have played any one of these cards. Yet, the card that made the most sense was his Minister Card, since he had played it thousands of times and he was superb at playing it. Playing this card met all the criteria above. It enhanced his credibility since he was certainly qualified to play it. The Minister Card is very flexible. People would expect to hear powerful, emotional language when playing it. This card legitimized his message because ministers speak from a position of moral authority, which is important in laying out a vision associated with peace and justice.

Finally, playing the Minister Card asks the audience to play their Congregation Card, like they're listening to a sermon at church. Congregations are very receptive to the minister's message, in most cases, so playing a Minister Card opens up the audience to the minister's message.

The Student Speech. One of the first set of choices you'll need to make in presenting your speech is determining what card you want to play, and what card you want your audience to play. For your informative speech, in which you are describing a business, what are your card choices? You could give your speech playing a Student Card in which you also ask the audience members to also play their Student Cards. But, that card might not succeed in engaging the audience effectively. It labels the speech as an academic exercise that is not personally relevant to them.

Another option is that you could play your Tour Director Card and indicate to the audience that you would like them to be a tourist in your town. They might actually want to visit that business if they are in the area. Playing that card would make the information more personally relevant to your audience of fellow students. Another option is to play an Employee Card of the company while asking the audience to play a Customer Card. In essence, you're trying to sell the audience on the business. Again, it makes the experience a little more interesting and might better capture the attention of the audience.

Card Style. The second Card Talk issue that's important to consider is the style you will use in presenting the speech. Generally, you will want to present a style that is: a) friendly so the audience will feel warmly about you and the topic, b) somewhat informal so you can make the audience feel comfortable about your information, and c) low power in which you are not trying to push the audience around in any way.

In most public speaking situations, speeches are either: (a) read from a prepared text, (b) recited from memory (i.e., the speech was written in advance and memorized), (c) delivered impromptu or without any immediate preparation, or (d) delivered **extemporaneously**, where a speech is prepared and practiced in advance, but only brief speaking notes are used during a presentation.

What style messages does each of these kinds of speeches send to the audience? Let's look at each one.

- **Reading a speech** sends the message of low friendliness, high formality, and moderate power because written texts are very formal and unfriendly. This approach is not a choice if you're interested in connecting to your audience.

- **Reciting a speech** is about the same as reading it. People simply run through the script and send the same kind of unfriendly, formal messages.

- **An impromptu speech** can be very friendly and informal, which is useful, but the arguments and evidence might not be very convincing.

- **An extemporaneous speech** is generally best because you have time to prepare, but you are using your own conversational style in which you can be very friendly and engaging. So, **use this style** in your speech.

Language Use. Extemporaneous speech is more structured and more formal than a normal conversation. As a result, it is best to **avoid excessive slang**, **jargon**, **and improper grammar** that you might use in a normal conversation with friends. Again, you're not playing a **Friend Card**. You are playing a card that tries to establish a different kind of relationship with the audience. Public speaking requires a different form of delivery than normal speech. Conversation often contains spacers or interjections like "you know" or "like," and the use of vocalized pauses such as "uh" and "um." Effective public speakers keep things like spacers and vocalized pauses to a minimum while adjusting their voices so they may be heard clearly by all of their audience.

Fear. Fear of public speaking often prevents speakers from selecting an engaging style to connect with the audience. Most speakers feel nervous about speaking in front of a group, even those with considerable experience. **Communication apprehension** comes in many different forms and in different degrees of severity. A little nervousness is a very common and natural. If you are feeling a bit nervous, acknowledge it, and deal with it by preparing carefully for your speech. Then, practice first in the mirror and then later in front of some friends who will give you an honest, but kind, appraisal. **Practice** is the best way to reduce speech anxiety.

It may seem uncomfortable and very silly at first, but practicing a speech in front of the mirror can be very beneficial. Try this first, and then practice in front of friends. Make sure that they will give you **constructive feedback**. Also, consider practicing in the room where you will be giving your speech. Many times classrooms are open early in the morning and in the evenings. Make time to go into the classroom when it is free so that you can close the door and practice your speech undisturbed.

Third, look for **encouraging people** in your audience. You may have some idea before you give your speech that certain people have been good audience members for other speakers. But, if you don't, look around just before you start and try to make eye contact with a couple of people. Doing so will make you more comfortable, and serves as an **invitation** for these individuals to listen to your speech.

To summarize, your card-talk style should be friendly and informal with low power. But, it should not be so informal that it sounds like a **Friend Card** that is too informal. Keep your fear in check by practicing, both in front of friends, and in the classroom where you will give your speech.

Research and Public Speaking

Gathering Research. Once you have a specific topic for your speech, brainstorm a list of vocabulary terms related to your topic. For example, if you were setting up the **Valet Today** service what issues would you need to research to persuade the audience that the service is needed? Consider these terms that I have brainstormed:

- **Traffic and parking regulations at MSU.** Would the MSU Police think it was OK to set up a valet parking service in front of various buildings on campus? Where would the vehicles be parked?

- **Percentage of students late to class.** What percent of students are late to class because they couldn't find parking? Are faculty also affected? Would faculty also like this valet service?

- **Student income levels.** Would students have enough money to purchase this service? What are the average income levels of students? Would the costs be less than paying parking tickets?

- **Pricing the service.** How would pricing be handled? What would students be willing to pay, and how much would be needed to make the business a success?

- **Liability insurance.** Would we need liability insurance and how much would it cost?

- **Student employment regulations.** Since students would be employed as the valets, what are regulations associated with how they would be paid, taxes withheld, unemployment insurance and other issues?

- **Recruiting, paying, and training valets.** How would the valets be recruited, what kind of pay would be needed to attract them, and what kind of training would be needed?

- **Marketing plan.** What goes into a marketing plan for this kind of service? Would social media be best? Or should brochures be distributed to classes? Who would do the marketing?

There are several places to get research information. First, understand that the **Internet** is not the only research resource! For example, there are many places to gather research in the **library**. Start at the Reference Section and ask for help with your speech if necessary. Many libraries have government document sections that may provide a great source of information depending on what topic you are researching. The library also has many electronic databases such as **Proquest, Lexis-Nexis, and Blackwell-Synergy.com**. Sometimes **Google** searches can also be helpful. Use **Scholar.Google.com** for research articles.

Try not to cite information directly from the Internet unless it is from an **established credible source**. Instead, get the original hard copy of the information from the library. If you must cite information from the Internet, and there are topics where this is appropriate, have more than just Internet sources.

Credibility of Evidence. The credibility of the research that you cite in your work reflects upon your personal credibility. Choose evidence from sources that are worthy of being cited in university-level work. Good evidence is relevant to your topic, recent, the source of the **information is identifiable and the source is reputable**. The best cited evidence will meet the requirements of all these tests of evidence. To gain credibility with your evidence, it is sometimes appropriate to mention how your evidence meets the tests of evidence. For example, cite the impressive qualifications of the source to show that your evidence is of good quality.

Citing Research. Citing other people's ideas and work is critical to researching with integrity. Any time you use evidence to supplement or inform work that you wish to present to others you must cite where the information originated from. In the field of Communication, follow the **American Psychological Association** (APA) guidelines for citation rules.

Speech Considerations

All speeches have an **overall goal and purpose**, a specific **topic** discussed to accomplish the overall goal and purpose, a specific **audience** to cater to in order to accomplish the overall goal and purpose, and a **context** in which the speech takes place. A good outline will address these considerations and make it easier to connect with your audience. So, take the time to think about these issues as you are preparing. Let's look at each of these considerations more closely.

Overall Goal and Speech Purpose. Everything you say should have a purpose and accomplish something. **Why are you speaking?** What do you hope to achieve with your speech? What are your goals for the speech? For informative speeches the goal is to have the audience understand or learn something. For persuasive speeches, the goal is to change the audience's mind about something, whether it's shifting positions or feeling stronger about something.

A good purpose statement is **specific, realistic, and results-oriented**. A specific purpose is most often one statement that explains exactly what the speaker hopes to accomplish. It focuses a speech on just one aspect of the topic. For instance, a good purpose statement would not focus on "relationships," but possibly "the initiation of a relationship." A general topic, "skiing," and its purpose may involve any of a number of different subjects, for instance "the cost of skiing," "dangers of skiing," and "skiing fashion," but a specific purpose only focuses on one specific subject or topic.

Topic Selection. Select a topic consistent with the assignment that is important to you. Trying to persuade the audience to buy your **valet service** is important because it is your new business and you want to be successful. The more excited you are about the topic the more excited your audience will be about it, as well. When you select a topic start with something you already know a lot about. People speak best when talking about subjects with which they are familiar. In other words, choose something that interests you so that you will be a motivated and excited speaker. Do not be afraid to put energy and excitement in your speech. If you have chosen a topic that interests you, you are halfway there.

Trying to force a topic at the last minute tends to be counterproductive; instead take time out, read a magazine or watch television, search the internet, talk to other people, search textbooks, listen to talk radio, and **let your ideas coalesce** and put themselves into a hierarchy of interest. The right topic is there, you just need to let it emerge. There are many different ways to choose a good speech topic; just keep in mind that what is important is that you find a topic that will interest both you and your audience.

Audience Analysis. When preparing your speech it is vital to have an idea of who your audience is going to be. Good public speakers are always oriented toward their audience. They ask the questions of "To whom am I speaking?" "What changes am I asking for?" and "What is the best way of presenting my information to get that result?" Good speakers tailor their message to their audience. Here are some considerations that will help that tailoring process:

- **Demographics and psychographics.** Demographics are the external variables that describe people: most often age, sex, ethnicity, religion, amount of education, and amount of income. Psychographics are internal variables such as one's attitudes, beliefs, and needs for inclusion, control, and affection. After a little thought, it becomes readily apparent why demographics and psychographics must be considered. A group of 6th grade Catholic school children will no doubt be different from a group of middle-aged college professors in an Alcoholics Anonymous meeting.

- It is possible to have similar demographic characteristics, **but very different psychographic characteristics**. For instance, consider young Republican or Democrat meetings, or a fraternity house and a group from the women's center. Similar age and education do not necessarily make for similar attitudes and beliefs. Public speakers should be careful not to make too many assumptions based on demographic characteristics. Instead ask questions, do some research, and make careful observations that will reveal how the audience might react to the speaker's topic.

- **Audience Topical Disposition.** Audiences are typically: a) hostile toward the topic, b) uninformed about the topic, or c) supportive of the topic. If the audience is **hostile** toward your position, you can try to just get the audience to listen. If they are willing to listen, then you can work to create doubts in their minds by providing some type of factual evidence. If they are **uninformed**, then your task is to bolster your credibility with some facts, and give information that is most likely to appeal to them. If they are supportive, you can ask for a stronger commitment to the initial position. But, it is imperative to categorize your audience into one of these three dispositions.

- **Speech Context.** Context is an understanding of the events going on surrounding a speech that might impact how the audience is likely to interpret the information presented. For example, presenting a speech to students promoting off-shore oil drilling while a Gulf of Mexico spill is going on would definitely impact the **audience's perceptions** of the speech. On the positive side, if there is a big push for more student conveniences on campus and you are persuading people to use your valet service, then the context might help you. Just be aware of context as you select your topic.

- **Word Choice.** In order to be perceived as a good speaker you need to speak a bit more formally than normal. To effectively communicate, simple clear language is usually the best way to get a message across to an audience. Descriptive, vibrant language can increase audience excitement about your topic. Use words **the audience can understand** and not find offensive. Choose words that will best convey the message, connect with the audience, and set a good tone for your speech.

Informative Speaking. When audiences are interested in learning some kind of new information, it is called informative speaking or even teaching. Every class lecture is essentially informative speaking. The goal of the speaker is simply to meet the audience's information needs. It is not aimed at changing the audiences' attitudes, beliefs, or behaviors. Achieving change is the goal of persuasive speaking, which we will address next. Informative speaking is about helping the audience learn something.

If you recall from Chapter 13, the first step in learning is insuring that the audience is paying attention to the message. If they are interested in acquiring the information, they will pay attention if the message is delivered in an engaging, emotionally stimulating way. So, any informative speech must begin by asking how you can meet the audience's need for information in an engaging, stimulating way so they will learn the information as you intend. If you turn the question around, would you like to hear your own speech; is it good enough for you to listen to? If the answer is **yes** because you are excited about your topic and you think your information is engaging, you are all set.

Persuasive Speaking. In contrast to informative speaking, persuasion is the process of using communication to modify the audience's attitude or behavior toward some topic. This definition implies that there is a discrepancy between the position that the speaker is advocating and the audience's attitude. If the audience is **hostile**, they are aware of the gap and your job is to motivate them to listen to your position. If they are **uninformed**, the gap becomes clear to the audience since you may be asking them to do something different, and change is difficult for everyone. As we have discussed above, the specific goals and purpose of your persuasive speech will largely depend upon the viewpoint of the audience and how much you can reasonably expect to change their minds.

Aristotle identified three different approaches that can be used to persuade an audience: logos, pathos, and ethos. **Logos** refers to appeals to the audience's sense of logic by using evidence. Evidence consists of all examples, statistics, and personal testimony that are used to support the main points. It is vital to select evidence that the audience is likely to find credible. **Pathos** refers to emotional appeals that are designed to generate a specific emotion in the audience such as anger, compassion, fear, joy, reverence, or shame. Audience members will be more motivated to change their beliefs, opinions, and values after experiencing this emotional reaction. **Ethos** is associated with the source's credibility. Do they believe the source is **knowledgeable, trustworthy and dynamic**? Better logical arguments combined with emotional engagement tend to bolster credibility. Thus, if a speaker is perceived as highly credible by using logical and easy-to-follow main points, citing good evidence to support those points, and referring to previous experience with the topic, that person is likely to be very persuasive.

Monroe's Motivated Sequence

Let's see how these persuasion principles are implemented in Monroe's Motivated Sequence. Developed in the 1930s by Alan Monroe, the main idea of this model is that people need to be motivated to change their beliefs, opinions, and values. This is a five-step organizational scheme that works to motivate the audience to comply with the speaker's message. Here are the five steps:

The Attention Step. The first goal of any speech is to gain the interest and attention of the audience. This can be accomplished by making a startling statement, telling a joke, using a visual aid, recounting a dramatic story, asking a series of questions, or telling a story. For the valet service, a good attention getter might be a story about a student late for an exam who failed a course, or a catchy song or YouTube video about the plight of students trying to juggle work and school.

The Need Step. Assuming the attention-getter worked, the audience should now be interested in the topic and ready to hear more about it. At this point, the goal is to make the audience feel that there is a need for a change. They are not going to change their attitudes unless they think there is a good reason to do so. The speaker must provide a **reason** to alter audience members' beliefs, opinions, and values. The reason is a clear explanation of the problem the audience faces that they are motivated to solve. For example, for the valet service, the speaker could cite research about how many students are late to class because of transportation problems. Or, research about the weather patterns in Michigan and how they make it difficult to get to class might be a motivator. Statistics about construction that backs up traffic could also be relevant.

The Satisfaction Step. Now that the audience feels a need for change, they need a solution to the problem. If the audience feels a need for a valet service, they need to know exactly how the solution resolves their need. **Providing details about the solution** will help the audience understand how this solution works. The audience will need to know how much the service will cost, where it will be located, and how valets are insured. The audience will also need evidence that the solution is realistic and will actually solve the problem. They should know how easy it is to use the service and how much it will save in parking tickets. Any research or statistics available to back up the solution will help.

The Visualization Step. It is not enough to tell the audience what they need to do to solve the problem. They must also be able to visualize the solution in action by developing **a clear mental picture** of how the solution will satisfy their needs. You could have a video of the valet service in action and testimonials from satisfied customers. Advertisements for fitness centers often do this by showing extremely athletic models and claiming that you can look just like them in no time. The audience should be able to clearly picture how they will benefit once they adopt the solution.

The Action Step. This final step calls for the audience to take some sort of action. It is important to tell the audience exactly what they must do; the more specific the speaker is the better. Whenever possible, the audience should fulfill this action step right after the speech. For example, people could sign a petition on the spot to create this valet service. Or, if they want to think about it, they could look at a brochure and go to your website looking at all the details. Showing the website and even having a contest on the website might even be better.

Organizing the Speech

These basic strategies for informative and persuasive speeches should give you a sense of what's necessary to be effective with the audience. Here is some additional detail about how to organize a speech to ensure that these ideas are communicated clearly.

The Attention-Getter. The goal of the attention-getting device is to **pull your audience into you and the topic** of the speech. Effective ways to gain an audience's attention include telling a brief story, providing a startling statistic that the audience did not expect, asking a question that would really appeal to the audience, showing a YouTube video illustrating your idea, or using some other visual aid. Try not to tell a joke since most jokes don't succeed.

A Good Thesis. Your thesis statement is the one **central idea** of your speech. A good thesis is a statement, not a question or phrase. Similar to a purpose statement, a thesis should not include slang, figurative language, or vague words. But unlike a purpose statement, a thesis statement is usually delivered to the audience. It is important to note that your thesis is: (a) what your audience will remember when you are finished speaking, and (b) a concise statement of what you intend to say. The thesis reflects the content of the speech and every point and sub-point should be related to it in a logical manner.

The Preview Statement. To keep your audience organized it is important to "say what you are going to say." More specifically, while your purpose and thesis statements provide the audience with clear and concise information regarding the intent of your speech, the preview statement provides a clear list of the specific main points you will discuss. In essence, this list acts as a road map by providing each of your main points, in order, so that the audience has a picture in their mind of what you will talk about. It also provides a smooth transition from your introduction to your first main point.

Transitions. Transitions signal when the speaker is moving from one point to the next, **linking two different ideas** or issues together. It provides a conclusion to the point you are currently discussing, and provides a segue into the next point. Transitions help the audience follow the organization of the speech, and help the speech to flow more smoothly. Think of transitions as the connections between cars on a train. If the entire train is to make it to its destination, the links between cars must be strong.

Transitions should state both the idea you are leaving and the one you are moving to. They do not need to be complex. In fact, the simpler they are the better. Here are a few examples of effective transitions:

Example 1: While downhill skiing is one type of skiing that many people enjoy in the winter, cross-country skiing is another popular type.

Example 2: Now that we have examined why each of us should sign an organ donor card and discuss the decision with our families, let's look at what steps we can take to become organ donors.

Example 3: In addition to organizing a clear, cogent speech, practicing your speech will also help you to become a good public speaker.

Signposts. Signposts are words or phrases that signal the importance of what you are going to say. Signposts signal to your audience that they need **to listen to and remember** what you are going to say next. You can use words to put an emphasis on certain areas of your speech by saying something like:

"If you remember anything that I discussed today, it should be the following... The key to success in public speaking is ..."

Using words that emphasize the importance of what you are saying can be effective, but it is the nonverbal emphasis you put on the words that can make the audience pay attention. Take the last example, "The key to success in public speaking is..." If you emphasize the word "key" you will be telling the audience that what you are saying next is significant. If you put the emphasis on the words "public speaking," you are telling the audience that **what comes next is important**, but only to public speaking situations.

Speech Body. To begin writing your body, you will need to consider how the speech will be organized, and how your supporting evidence will be researched and developed. The first aspect you need to consider is how to organize your main points. Four of the most popular ways of organizing a speech include:

- **Time Patterns:** Arranging a topic chronologically by time or by steps in a process
- **Topic Patterns:** Arranging a speech based on types or categories such as types of valet services, or categories of people interested in the service
- **Problem Solution Patterns:** Arranging the speech by indicating a problem then a solution
- **Cause-Effect Patterns:** Indicating various causes, and then various effects created by the causes or problems

Conclusion. The conclusion to your speech serves two purposes: to review the main points, and to say some pertinent closing remarks. Reviewing your main points is where you "say what you said." Many speakers have a hard time following this form because they feel they are being overly redundant. This is not true. Remember, your audience has never heard your speech before, so it is important to keep stressing to them what point(s) you are attempting to make. Repeating the key points also keeps the listeners organized. Finally, **restating the main points** can serve as a signpost telling the audience you are concluding.

Final Statement. The final statement of your speech is likely to be the most memorable. It is **one sentence** that should not only sum up your speech but leave a lasting impression on your listeners. Many closing statements are remarkably similar to attention getters. Therefore, when you write your final statement, do not use the same technique as you did in the introduction unless absolutely necessary. For example, if you used a statistic as an attention getter, use a story for the close. Yet, try to use the same theme for the conclusion as for the attention getter.

Outlining

The most effective way to organize your speech is to write an outline or skeletal version of your speech. It helps you **focus** on when certain points will be stated, and how much information you have to relay to the audience. You may realize after you write your outline that you have too much information (or too little), or do not have enough pertinent examples. Good advice regarding public speaking is "Say what you are going to say, say it, and then say what you said." The basic speech structure emphasizes this old saying. Thus the standard format for such an outline is:

I. Introduction
    A. Attention-getter
    B. Thesis Statement
    C. Preview Statement

II. Body
    A. Main Point #1
        1. Statement
        2. Evidence or warrant why the statement is true.
        3. Transition to the next main point.
    B. Main Point #2
        1. Statement
        2. Evidence or warrant why the statement is true.
        3. Transition to the next main point.
    C. Main Point #3
        1. Statement
        2. Evidence or warrant why the statement is true.
        3. Transition to the conclusion

III. Conclusion
    A. Review Main Points
    B. Implication Statement that explains how the main points prove your thesis and accomplish your speech goal.
    C. Closing Statement

In a sense, outlining is a language. It has rules and standard formats that must be followed in order for it to be understood. In order to understand this "language" we must know the differences between main points, sub-points, and sub-sub-points.

- **A main point** is a major point that you are attempting to make through your speech.
- **A sub-point** contains relevant and pertinent information to support your main points. They are facts, statistics, and other supporting evidence.
- **Sub-sub-points** help to clarify the sub-points if necessary. Stories and examples can make great sub-sub-points.

Each of these points has a standard format that must be adhered to in an outline. Every formal outline needs to follow this format. This format is provided in **Chapter 15**, as well.

Delivering Speech

This section will give you some tools for delivering your speech more effectively. As you develop these tools or skills you will find that you are less nervous and that your speeches will flow better. The first step in being better prepared is creating effective **note cards** for delivering your speech.

Note Cards. You cannot read your speech in class. **It is best to prepare note cards and deliver your speech using these cards.** A paper outline is permitted, but cards are better because they make it easier to give your speech. If you get nervous in front of your audience and start shaking, then the paper will also shake and your audience will know that you are nervous. Then they will start paying attention to how much your paper is shaking and not to what you are saying.

But how should you write out note cards? Basically, you will want to put your outline on your note cards, but with more detail. It is important when writing out note cards to do the following:

- Put all of the information that you need on the note cards.
- Do not put too much information on each card.
- Include transitions on your note cards.

When creating your note cards you can highlight areas of your speech on which you want to put a special emphasis. You can also draw smiley faces or something that will remind you to smile or look at your audience during your speech. Some people have even written positive thoughts in the margins of the cards to tell themselves that they will survive the speech.

Don't put too much information on the cards since this will cause you to read the cards and not to use them as a guide. **Your speech should not be read to your audience.** That is very boring! Reading also communicates a lack of preparation and interest. Please, **talk to us, don't read to us!**

Nonverbal Communication

Nonverbal communication consists of issues such as body movement, accents and voice styles, space usage, and physical appearance. The key is to use nonverbal behaviors that **support your message** and not distract from it. Body-focused gestures, like flicking your hair or touching your face, tend to distract from your message. Object-focused nonverbals emphasize your message points and are very useful. The key is to control your nonverbals so they add to your speech, not detract from it. Remember the **signal-to-noise ratio**? Let's look at the nonverbal considerations and see how they can maximize the signal and minimize the noise.

Kinesics. How individuals walk or move their arms when they speak is **kinesics**. In your speech, learn to use your natural body movements to your advantage. Begin by identifying your body movement habits that might be distracting to your audience. For example, if you gave your whole speech leaning on your right leg with your left hip thrown out, your audience would focus on your stance and wonder how long you could stand that way without falling over. Or, if you have a habit of twirling your hair or touching your nose, those are body-focused nonverbals that will distract the audience from your message.

Appropriate body movements are those which **make the speaker seem comfortable** and conversational, yet more formal. It is not just a Speaker Card that you are playing, but a bit of a Friend Card as well. This is a difficult mixture to get right. Think about David Letterman. He gives the audience the appearance that he is giving a formal presentation (by standing up straight) but does so in a comfortable, welcoming fashion. He walks around and sometimes even runs (this would not work for your speech, however), but again, not through his entire presentation. Let your personality show because that will be engaging to the audience. Do not pace, but move around comfortably and your audience will respond.

Facial movement, and particularly **eye movement**, is also included in the study of Kinesics. They may be the **most important aspects** of your entire speech. Often speakers complain of an uninterested audience when it was actually the speaker who did not keep the audience involved by failing to make eye contact.

A trick that you can do is to pick out people that you already know before you give your speech. Start your speech by looking at them for encouragement. Sometimes it is even fun to walk toward and look directly at an individual who is not paying attention. When you are making eye contact with an individual, try to maintain it **for at least 3 seconds**. This seems as if it would be an easy thing to do, however, during a presentation 3 seconds can seem like 3 minutes. An easy way to accomplish this is to maintain eye contact through an entire sentence that you speak.

Along with eye contact, smiling can be a key aspect to the presentation of your speech. When beginning a presentation the best way to warm up your audience is to smile at them. This tells your audience that you are a nice person and that you are happy to be there. Studies have also shown that the more people smile, the more attractive they are perceived to be. David Letterman **smiles a lot** as do all successful speakers. Remember, when you play your card, use a style that increases friendliness and some informality. Smiling goes a long way toward this goal.

Vocalics. The auditory component of your speaking voice is called vocalics. Specifically, your rate of speech is important to monitor. It is common for individuals to speak much faster when they give their speech than they did when they practiced it. The best way to control the rate at which you speak is to remind yourself to **SLOW DOWN**! Try to force yourself to speak more slowly than feels natural, and you will not speak as fast. Speaking at a **slower, natural pace** is important because it allows your audience to better understand you. It shows more of your **Speaker Card** than **Friend Card**, which typically displays a much faster rate.

Another aspect of vocalics that can make a speaker difficult to understand is the loudness of an individual's speaking voice. If your audience cannot hear you, they cannot understand you. Try to **speak more loudly** than normal when giving a speech. For many people this is a major hurdle because they naturally do not speak loudly. A great way to learn to speak louder is to go to the recitation room and practice there. Have a friend sit in the back of the room to see if you can be heard there.

For softer speakers it is even more important that you **do not look at your note cards** a lot during your speech. When your audience cannot understand you they will look at your mouth to try to "lip read." If they cannot see you forming the words they will remain confused. Therefore, it may be beneficial to have parts of the speech memorized so that you can maintain good eye contact with your audience.

Proxemics. How individuals use space is called proxemics. During your speech, it is important that you not stand in the back of the room, far away from your audience. Try also to avoid standing too close to one particular individual. Stand toward the middle of the area reserved for speakers, and then stop worrying about proxemics.

Chronemics. Chronemics is the use of time. Timing yourself is important so that you finish within the required amount of time. Often individuals will speak faster when presenting a speech, so when you practice, try to make your speech go as long as the **maximum time limit**. This will ensure that your speech will not go over the maximum time limit, and you can be certain that you will reach the minimum time requirement.

Physical Appearance. Physical appearance refers to your clothing and accessories. When you are preparing to give a presentation, think about how you can **dress to gain respect** from your audience. Dress in comfortable clothing that is nicer than you would usually wear to class. Some individuals dress as if they are going to an interview, which is very impressive. Dressing professionally for your speech is also good practice for those individuals who plan on entering a career that may require that they make formal presentations.

Artifacts. Artifacts are the visual aids that help present information in the speech. These often can make a speech topic "**come to life**" for an audience. For example, one student did a speech on motorcycles and brought in a couple of PowerPoint slides that served as background for his speech. You might do the same for the business you describe, or the business you want to create. Pictures help make your topic come alive to his audience. The two most important issues to remember when using visual aides are that they must be **clear and uncluttered** and you need to **practice** using them. Just like note cards, visual aids can a speech easier or more difficult.

Ethics

Finally, I want to include a word about ethics. **Speakers should speak with integrity**. Whether or not a public speaker actively tries to inform, persuade, or entertain his audience, public speakers should attempt to act in an ethical manner. Ethics in public speaking require that the speaker **respect his or her topic and audience**. Be well informed about your topic, be honest when presenting information, and use reasonable evidence and valid reasoning. Conscientious public speakers ask themselves, "Will my audience receive any benefit from my speech?" and, "does my audience want to know about my topic/information?"

In many cases speakers have to decide whether or not unwanted, but important information should be given. In such cases, speakers try to have plausible, believable, and accessible answers to the questions and concerns that they might raise by their speaking.

Lastly, ethical public speakers, like writers, avoid plagiarism. Public speakers are careful not to take credit for words and ideas that are not their own by telling their audience where they got their information and who inspired their words. Never copy anything word-for-word from a citation unless it is a quote that you specifically identify as a quote and cite appropriately. Remember, ethics is credibility and that's vital for success.

Summary

Here is a summary of the steps to prepare for your final speech product:

- **Decide what card you want to play in the speech.** That will determine what card you want the audience to play as they're listening. Then, from that perspective, craft the speech.

- **First main edit:** Once you have a draft of your speech, be it in outline form or on cards, give the speech aloud to yourself and edit it. Just see how it sounds, out loud.

- **Second main edit:** Get critical feedback from someone else. Try to get as many people as possible to evaluate your speech. Have the person hearing your speech ask cross-examination questions about your speech. Practice defending your speech. Edit the speech based on the feedback you receive.

- **Plan appropriate visual aides.** Visual aides should help the flow of the speech, progress the speech forward, not distract too much from the speech content and supplement the information provided. You should also plan how you will handle the visual aides and practice using them. Make sure that the speech venue has all the necessary equipment for your speech.

- **Plan gestures and where to stand and move strategically in order to emphasize parts of your speech.** An example of strategic moving would be to present the introduction in the center of the front of the room, move to the left side of the front of the room for the first main point, cross to the right side of the room for the second main point, return to the center for the third main point, step forward for the conclusion. Write your nonverbal plan on your speech notes as if you were blocking a drama or play.

- **Practice giving the speech to become familiar with the wording of the speech.** Knowing your speech well will reduce fillers and improve the general flow of the presentation. Circle words your wish to emphasize and the terms your want the audience to focus on. Indicate where you will pause in your speech for effect on your notes.

- **Time each section and the entire speech.** Therefore if you are pressed for time, you will know how long each section takes and be able to edit yourself as you speak. Keep in mind that speakers often speak faster in front of an audience. So **include extra information** or examples in your speech that can be added if your have extra speaking time, yet could also be left out if you did not have the time. Sometimes it helps to have two similar versions of the speech: the short and the long versions to be selected as time permits. Mark "**SLOW DOWN**" on your note cards to remind yourself if you need it.

- **Make sure to bring some speaking "tools" with you to the speech.** Bring several copies of your speech (located in different places of you materials) so if you forget a copy on your desk, you have a backup copy in your backpack, etc. For the COM 100 class, make sure the instructor has timecards to display so you know how much time you have remaining. Bring your visual aides and handouts ("the dog ate it" does not work in the real world). Bring the technology that you need for the venue. Bring water to drink. Carry along a good luck charm if you need it!